Praise for *Essential ASP.NET 2.0*

"No one knows ASP.NET like Fritz Onion. And no one knows .NET security like Keith Brown. Combine the two and what do you get? The most comprehensive and enlightening book on ASP.NET 2.0 industrywide. I'm sure you'll find the book you're holding was worth every penny."

—Aaron Skonnard, member of technical staff and cofounder, Pluralsight

"*Essential ASP.NET 2.0* gets under the hood and dismantles the engine before your eyes. Fritz and Keith understand that we as developers need to understand how it works and this book does exactly that. Their explanation of the ASP.NET 2.0 page event sequence is worth the price of the book alone."

—Shawn Wildermuth, Microsoft MVP (C#), "The ADO Guy"

"*Essential ASP.NET 2.0* is an incredibly useful must-read for any developer. Many books drag you through theory and mindless detail, but this one actually sets up the problems you may encounter with ASP.NET 2.0 and rolls out the alternatives."

—Patrick Hynds, President and Microsoft Regional Director, CriticalSites

"This book is essential for any ASP.NET developer moving from version 1.x to 2.0. Onion and Brown not only cover the new features, but provide a wealth of insight and detail about how to use them effectively."

—Ron Petrusha, author of *Visual Basic 2005: The Complete Reference*

"Drawing on their deep technical knowledge and real-world experience, Fritz and Keith take the reader into some of the less explored and much improved areas of ASP.NET such as diagnostics and state management and performance. Readers will turn to this book over and over again."

—John Timney, Microsoft MVP, Senior Web Services Consultant, British Telecom

"Fritz and Keith, both established developers and writers in our industry, have succeeded again—enlightening us on the latest advancements found in ASP.NET 2.0. If you're new to ASP.NET or a seasoned veteran, you'll benefit tremendously from their overview, analysis, and sample code."

—Joe "MSJoe" Flanigen

"This book seeks not only to explain how to effectively build Web sites with ASP.NET, it also gives the reader an idea of how the process works. This insight is essential to creating applications that work with the infrastructure rather than fighting it."

—Justin Burtch, Vice President, Newbrook Solutions

Essential ASP.NET 2.0

Microsoft .NET Development Series

John Montgomery, *Series Advisor*
Don Box, *Series Advisor*
Martin Heller, *Series Editor*

The Microsoft .NET Development Series is supported and developed by the leaders and experts of Microsoft development technologies including Microsoft architects. The books in this series provide a core resource of information and understanding every developer needs in order to write effective applications and managed code. Learn from the leaders how to maximize your use of the .NET Framework and its programming languages.

Titles in the Series

Brad Abrams, *.NET Framework Standard Library Annotated Reference Volume 1: Base Class Library and Extended Numerics Library*, 0-321-15489-4

Brad Abrams and Tamara Abrams, *.NET Framework Standard Library Annotated Reference, Volume 2: Networking Library, Reflection Library, and XML Library*, 0-321-19445-4

Keith Ballinger, *.NET Web Services: Architecture and Implementation*, 0-321-11359-4

Bob Beauchemin and Dan Sullivan, *A Developer's Guide to SQL Server 2005*, 0-321-38218-8

Don Box with Chris Sells, *Essential .NET, Volume 1: The Common Language Runtime*, 0-201-73411-7

Keith Brown, *The .NET Developer's Guide to Windows Security*, 0-321-22835-9

Eric Carter and Eric Lippert, *Visual Studio Tools for Office: Using C# with Excel, Word, Outlook, and InfoPath*, 0-321-33488-4

Eric Carter and Eric Lippert, *Visual Studio Tools for Office: Using Visual Basic 2005 with Excel, Word, Outlook, and InfoPath*, 0-321-41175-7

Mahesh Chand, *Graphics Programming with GDI+*, 0-321-16077-0

Krzysztof Cwalina and Brad Abrams, *Framework Design Guidelines: Conventions, Idioms, and Patterns for Reusable .NET Libraries*, 0-321-24675-6

Len Fenster, *Effective Use of Microsoft Enterprise Library: Building Blocks for Creating Enterprise Applications and Services*, 0-321-33421-3

Sam Guckenheimer and Juan J. Perez, *Software Engineering with Microsoft Visual Studio Team System*, 0-321-27872-0

Anders Hejlsberg, Scott Wiltamuth, Peter Golde, *The C# Programming Language*, Second Edition, 0-321-33443-4

Alex Homer, Dave Sussman, Mark Fussell, *ADO.NET and System.Xml v. 2.0—The Beta Version*, 0-321-24712-4

Alex Homer and Dave Sussman, *ASP.NET 2.0 Illustrated*, 0-321-41834-4

Joe Kaplan and Ryan Dunn, *The .NET Developer's Guide to Directory Services Programming*, 0-321-35017-0

Mark Michaelis, *Essential C# 2.0*, 0-321-15077-5

James S. Miller and Susann Ragsdale, *The Common Language Infrastructure Annotated Standard*, 0-321-15493-2

Christian Nagel, *Enterprise Services with the .NET Framework: Developing Distributed Business Solutions with .NET Enterprise Services*, 0-321-24673-X

Brian Noyes, *Data Binding with Windows Forms 2.0: Programming Smart Client Data Applications with .NET*, 0-321-26892-X

Fritz Onion, *Essential ASP.NET with Examples in C#*, 0-201-76040-1

Fritz Onion, *Essential ASP.NET with Examples in Visual Basic .NET*, 0-201-76039-8

Ted Pattison and Dr. Joe Hummel, *Building Applications and Components with Visual Basic .NET*, 0-201-73495-8

Dr. Neil Roodyn, *eXtreme .NET: Introducing eXtreme Programming Techniques to .NET Developers*, 0-321-30363-6

Dharma Shukla and Bob Schmidt, *Essential Windows Workflow Foundation*, 0-321-39983-8

Chris Sells and Michael Weinhardt, *Windows Forms 2.0 Programming*, 0-321-26796-6

Guy Smith-Ferrier, *.NET Internationalization: The Developer's Guide to Building Global Windows and Web Applications*, 0-321-34138-4

Paul Vick, *The Visual Basic .NET Programming Language*, 0-321-16951-4

Damien Watkins, Mark Hammond, Brad Abrams, *Programming in the .NET Environment*, 0-201-77018-0

Shawn Wildermuth, *Pragmatic ADO.NET: Data Access for the Internet World*, 0-201-74568-2

Paul Yao and David Durant, *.NET Compact Framework Programming with C#*, 0-321-17403-8

Paul Yao and David Durant, *.NET Compact Framework Programming with Visual Basic .NET*, 0-321-17404-6

For more information go to www.awprofessional.com/msdotnetseries/

Essential
ASP.NET 2.0

■ **Fritz Onion**
with Keith Brown

♦♦ Addison-Wesley

Upper Saddle River, NJ • Boston • Indianapolis • San Francisco
New York • Toronto • Montreal • London • Munich • Paris • Madrid
Capetown • Sydney • Tokyo • Singapore • Mexico City

Many of the designations used by manufacturers and sellers to distinguish their products are claimed as trademarks. Where those designations appear in this book, and the publisher was aware of a trademark claim, the designations have been printed with initial capital letters or in all capitals.

The .NET logo is either a registered trademark or trademark of Microsoft Corporation in the United States and/or other countries and is used under license from Microsoft.

Portions of this material previously appeared in *MSDN Magazine*. © 2004–2006, *MSDN Magazine*. Reprinted with permission.

The authors and publisher have taken care in the preparation of this book, but make no expressed or implied warranty of any kind and assume no responsibility for errors or omissions. No liability is assumed for incidental or consequential damages in connection with or arising out of the use of the information or programs contained herein.

The publisher offers excellent discounts on this book when ordered in quantity for bulk purchases or special sales, which may include electronic versions and/or custom covers and content particular to your business, training goals, marketing focus, and branding interests. For more information, please contact:

U.S. Corporate and Government Sales
(800) 382-3419
corpsales@pearsontechgroup.com

For sales outside the United States please contact:

International Sales
international@pearsoned.com

This Book Is Safari Enabled

The Safari® Enabled icon on the cover of your favorite technology book means the book is available through Safari Bookshelf. When you buy this book, you get free access to the online edition for 45 days.

Safari Bookshelf is an electronic reference library that lets you easily search thousands of technical books, find code samples, download chapters, and access technical information whenever and wherever you need it.

To gain 45-day Safari Enabled access to this book:

• Go to http://www.awprofessional.com/safarienabled
• Complete the brief registration form
• Enter the coupon code MGMY-R8IL-4Z9R-M4MG-EP9X

If you have difficulty registering on Safari Bookshelf or accessing the online edition, please e-mail customer-service@safaribooksonline.com.

Visit us on the Web: www.awprofessional.com

Library of Congress Cataloging-in-Publication Data

Onion, Fritz.
    Essential ASP.NET 2.0 / Fritz Onion, with Keith Brown.
        p. cm.
    Includes index.
    ISBN 0-321-23770-6 (pbk. : alk. paper)
  1. Web site development. 2. Active server pages. 3. Microsoft .NET. I.
Brown, Keith, 1967 Mar. 16– II. Title.

    TK5105.8885.A26O524 2007
    005.2'76—dc22

                                        2006028812

ISBN 0-321-23770-6
Text printed in the United States on recycled paper at Courier in Stoughton, Massachusetts.
First printing, October 2006.

For Susan.
—FO

For Kathy.
—KB

Contents

Figures

Tables

Foreword

ASP.NET IS NOW USED DAILY by more than 2 million professional developers worldwide. It runs some of the most successful Web sites and applications in the world, including the most heavily visited site on the Web today: MySpace.com (which now handles more than 1.5 billion page views each day using ASP.NET 2.0). Every day thousands of new developers begin learning ASP.NET for the first time—supported by an incredible developer community of books, blogs, user groups, forums, and developer Web sites.

Our goal with ASP.NET 2.0 is to enable developers to build rich Web applications faster than ever before. We spent thousands of hours talking with developers and looking at existing applications to identify the common features, patterns, and code that Web developers build over and over today. We then worked to componentize and build these features into ASP.NET.

For example, ASP.NET 2.0 now includes built-in support for Membership (username/password credential storage) and Role Management services out of the box. Master Pages enables flexible page UI inheritance and reuse across sites. The new Profile Personalization service enables quick storage and retrieval of user settings and preferences—facilitating rich customization with minimal code. The Site Navigation system enables developers to quickly build menus and link structures. And the new Web Parts framework enables rich portal-style layout and end-user drag/drop features that would otherwise require writing tens of thousands of lines of code.

Included with all of these great infrastructure features are more than 40 new ASP.NET server controls in V2.0 that enable powerful declarative support for data access, security, wizard navigation, menus, tree-views, portals, and more. In addition to these great features is the new AJAX support we are enabling with ASP.NET 2.0 using the new "Atlas" framework. This enables ASP.NET 2.0 developers to easily add dynamic UI functionality to their applications and build richer and more dynamic user experiences that work with all modern browsers.

Together these rich features enable developers to complete Web projects that used to take days or weeks in a fraction of the time, and deliver outstanding value to customers.

This book provides an excellent guide to learning and mastering all the great functionality that ASP.NET 2.0 provides. Fritz and Keith are ASP.NET experts, and share their experiences and insights throughout the book. They will help teach you how to fully leverage ASP.NET and build robust Web applications faster and better than ever before.

Enjoy!

Scott Guthrie
General Manager
Developer Division
Microsoft Corporation
September 2006

Preface

I REMEMBER SITTING IN A ROOM on the Microsoft campus in August of 2003 listening to Scott Guthrie and others from the ASP.NET team present the wide array of new features coming in ASP.NET 2.0. They astounded us with one demo after another of features that greatly simplified Web development, and in such a pluggable and extensible fashion so that changes could be made at any level as needed during the development process. As with its predecessor, I knew that this release was going to change the way developers built Web applications, and it would be compelling enough to bring many more developers to the ASP.NET platform.

Over the subsequent two years I carefully tracked the Beta releases of ASP.NET 2.0, wrote many articles on the upcoming features, and gave numerous conference talks around the world. In early 2005 I finished writing Pluralsight's Applied ASP.NET 2.0 course, and spent the next year and a half teaching the course, as well as speaking, blogging, and writing about ASP.NET 2.0 in many different forums. This book is the culmination of those activities, and I hope it helps you in your path to understanding ASP.NET 2.0.

Sample Code, Web Site, Feedback

All of the code samples in this book are drawn from working samples available for display and download at http://pluralsight.com/essentialasp.net2/.

The site also contains examples written in VB.NET and a listing of all links and references mentioned in the book. Any errata found after publication will be posted on this site, as well as a supplemental set of more extended examples of the concepts presented in this book for your reference. The authors welcome your comments, errata, and feedback via the forms available on the Web site.

Volume 2, *Not* Second Edition

This book is fundamentally a companion book to my first book on ASP.NET, *Essential ASP.NET with Examples in C#*, and is not a second edition. You will notice little to no overlap between the two books, and, in fact, I strongly encourage you to become comfortable with much of the contents of the first book before jumping into this one. Almost all of the topics presented in the first book are still completely relevant today in the ASP.NET 2.0 release. There are, however, a few topics that can be bypassed in the first book as they have been replaced and/or modified with the ASP.NET 2.0 release. The following is a reader's guide to *Essential ASP.NET with Examples in C#* with the intent of preparing you to read this new book.

Chapter 1—Architecture
The discussion of codebehind should be read only lightly, as it has changed in 2.0, although the ASP.NET 1.1 model of codebehind is still supported.

Chapter 2—WebForms
The discussion of codebehind and server-side control integration can be skipped, as this has changed in ASP.NET 2.0. The last section on building WebForms with Visual Studio can be skipped.

Chapter 3—Configuration
All of this chapter is still completely relevant. Do note that every use of *ConfigurationSettings* should now be *ConfigurationManager* in ASP.NET 2.0.

Chapter 4—HTTP Pipeline

The discussion of asynchronous handlers can be skipped in anticipation of the entire chapter dedicated to asynchrony (Chapter 9) in this new book.

Chapter 5—Diagnostics and Error Handling

All of this chapter is still completely relevant in ASP.NET 2.0.

Chapter 6—Validation

All of this chapter is still completely relevant in ASP.NET 2.0. Be aware that client-side validation now works cross-browser (not just in Internet Explorer as it did in ASP.NET 1.1). Also, there is a new ValidationGroup property you can associate with validation controls and buttons that generate postbacks to selectively fire subsets of validation controls.

Chapter 7—Data Binding

Skip over the discussion of the DataGrid control, as it has been replaced by the GridView control in ASP.NET 2.0. In the template discussion, replace every occurrence of *DataBinder.Eval(Container.DataItem, ...)* with *Eval(...)*, which is the new expression in ASP.NET 2.0.

Chapter 8—Custom Controls

All of this chapter is still completely relevant in ASP.NET 2.0. Whenever you see references to *RegisterClientScriptBlock*, replace it with *ClientScript.RegisterClientScriptBlock* for ASP.NET 2.0. In the discussion of data-bound and composite controls, be aware that there are two new control base classes in ASP.NET 2.0, DataBoundControl and CompositeControl, which should be used as base classes when creating these types of controls. There are also many new designer integration features in ASP.NET 2.0.

Chapter 9—Caching

All of this chapter is still completely relevant in ASP.NET 2.0.

Chapter 10—State Management

All of this chapter is still completely relevant in ASP.NET 2.0.

Chapter 11—Security

All of this chapter is still completely relevant in ASP.NET 2.0. Be aware that many of the features discussed in the forms authentication section are much easier to build in ASP.NET 2.0 because of the membership feature. Understanding the details of how Forms authentication works is still critical to using membership properly, however, and thus this discussion is a good precursor to the discussion about security in Chapter 5 of this new book.

Organization of This Book

Chapter 1, Architecture, covers the changes in the architecture of ASP.NET with this release, including a new codebehind mechanism, new Page events, new specially named compilation directories, a new compiler utility, and Web Application Projects.

Chapter 2, User Interface Elements, looks at the three primary new user interface elements of ASP.NET 2.0: master pages, themes and skins, and navigation controls. This chapter also looks at the new control adapter architecture as a means of altering standard control rendering in a browser-contingent way.

Chapter 3, Data Binding, describes the new declarative data source model introduced with ASP.NET 2.0. It starts with a discussion of the fundamentals of declarative data sources and moves through many different usages, including SQL, stored procedures, and objects.

Chapter 4, State Management, describes three new state-related features of ASP.NET 2.0, including cross-page posting, profile, and the Multi-View, View, and Wizard controls.

Chapter 5, Security, covers the new security features in ASP.NET 2.0 with a special focus on the provider model. It includes lots of practical advice on choosing and configuring Membership and Role providers. It also covers the new login controls and other new features, such as cookie-less forms authentication and configuration file encryption.

Chapter 6, Web Parts, describes the collection of components and controls introduced in ASP.NET 2.0 for constructing customizable portal sites. These components manage the details of storing user customization data, providing the interface for customization, and managing the Web Parts you define as components for users to work with.

Chapter 7, Diagnostics, explores management, instrumentation, and diagnostics in ASP.NET 2.0, focusing on the new health monitoring system. The key abstraction here is the Web event, and this chapter introduces the built-in events and providers as well as helps you build your own. At the end of the chapter is an introduction to ASP.NET 2.0 support for Event Tracing for Windows (ETW), showing how you can diagnose problems in a running ASP.NET application without having to attach a debugger.

Chapter 8, Performance, covers the new performance-related features of ASP.NET 2.0, including many new caching features as well as a client-callback architecture. Among the new caching features covered are data source caching, SQL cache dependencies, post-cache substitution, and configuration file settings for cache control.

Chapter 9, Asynchrony, looks at the new Async="true" attribute on the @Page directive in ASP.NET 2.0, and how it can be used to improve the responsiveness of pages in your site as well as increase the overall scalability of the application. Several ways of introducing asynchrony into your pages are covered, including implicitly using the AsyncOperationManager, explicitly using asynchronous tasks, and at a lower level by using the Page class's AddOnPreRenderCompleteAsync method.

Acknowledgments

I WOULD FIRST LIKE TO THANK my coauthor, Keith Brown, for agreeing to write Chapters 5 and 7 (Security and Diagnostics), and for completing his chapters in such a timely fashion. Thanks go to my family for understanding when I needed time to write. Thanks to Scott Guthrie for agreeing to write the Foreword, as well as taking the time to answer many of the questions Keith and I came up with as we researched topics for the book. Thanks also go to all the members of the ASP.NET team for building such a compelling product, and specifically to Eric Deily and Stefan Schackow for answering questions when we had them. Thanks to *MSDN Magazine* for granting permission to use material in this book that was previously published in articles I wrote. Thanks to my colleagues at Pluralsight for their feedback, including Ian Griffiths, Matt Milner, and Dan Sullivan. Thanks also to my official reviewers, Justin Burtch, Joseph Flanigan, Patrick Hynds, Ron Petrusha, and John Timney, for such careful reading and helpful feedback. Finally, thanks to my editor, Joan Murray, and Addison-Wesley for coordinating all aspects of this project.

Fritz Onion
Mt. Vernon, Maine
August 2006
http://pluralsight.com/fritz/

I've worked with Fritz for the last ten years, and during that time he's become a close friend and business partner. I was honored when he invited me to write a couple of chapters for this book. I refer to his first volume regularly; my copy is rather dog-eared by now! And a warm thanks to the folks at Addison-Wesley for making this all possible.

Keith Brown
Denver, Colorado
August 2006
http://pluralsight.com/keith/

About the Authors

Fritz Onion is a cofounder of Pluralsight, a Microsoft .NET training provider. He is the author of Pluralsight's ASP.NET curriculum, and he teaches course offerings around the world. The author of the highly acclaimed book *Essential ASP.NET with Examples in C#* (Addison-Wesley) and a columnist for *MSDN Magazine*, he is also a regular speaker at industry conferences, including TechEd, VSLive!, and PDC. Fritz received his B.A. from Harvard University and his M.S. from the University of California, Irvine.

Keith Brown is a cofounder of Pluralsight, where he focuses on application security. A contributing editor for *MSDN Magazine*, he writes the Security Briefs column. He is the author of the landmark book *Programming Windows Security* (Addison-Wesley), as well as *The .NET Developer's Guide to Windows Security* (Addison-Wesley), which you can read online at http://pluralsight.com. Keith spends most of his time researching security techniques and technologies, and he has spent close to a decade teaching and developing course material for professional software developers. You can subscribe to Keith's blog at http://pluralsight.com.

■ 1 ■
Architecture

UNLIKE ITS PREDECESSOR, ASP.NET 2.0 is not a fundamentally new way of building Web applications. Instead, ASP.NET 2.0 primarily adds new features on top of an existing architecture with the goal of simplifying many common tasks. This is not to say that this is a small release—quite the contrary. With more than double the number of classes and over 40 new controls, there is more than enough "newness" to keep even the most avid ASP.NET developer busy for quite some time exploring new features.

The core architecture, however, which consists of pages being parsed into class definitions and compiled into assemblies remains essentially unchanged, as does the HTTP pipeline used to process requests. In fact, it is possible to host most sites built for ASP.NET 1.1 directly in 2.0 without modification, as all existing features of the 1.1 runtime are completely supported in this release.

With that in mind, this introductory chapter focuses on the architectural changes that *are* made in 2.0 and how these changes affect the way you build Web applications in ASP.NET. These changes include a new codebehind mechanism, several new Page events, new specially named compilation directories, the new ASP.NET compiler utility that enables static site compilation, and Web Application Projects.

Fundamentals

We'll begin with a brief review of the fundamentals of ASP.NET, leading directly to a discussion of some of the new features in ASP.NET 2.0. This section presents the evolution of generating dynamic content, beginning with traditional classic ASP techniques and culminating in the new declarative data-binding model introduced in ASP.NET 2.0.

Dynamic Content

Writing a page to process a request in ASP.NET 2.0 is very much the same as it has been for the last few years with ASP.NET 1.1, and in fact for simple pages, it's very much the same as its earlier predecessor ASP. The same in-line evaluation syntax is still supported, as are server-side script blocks so that someone with a background only in building classic ASP pages should find this release of ASP.NET very approachable. Listing 1-1 shows a simple page that uses a server-side script block to define a helper method (GetDisplayItem) and then uses interspersed script to dynamically render elements in an unordered list. It also uses the server-side evaluation syntax (<%= %>) to intersperse dynamic content among static content—all common techniques dating back to building pages with ASP. The result of accessing the page through a browser is shown in Figure 1-1.

LISTING 1-1: SimplePage.aspx—A simple .aspx file with dynamic content

```
<%@ Page Language="C#" %>

<!DOCTYPE html PUBLIC "-//W3C//DTD XHTML 1.0 Transitional//EN" "http://
www.w3.org/TR/xhtml1/DTD/xhtml1-transitional.dtd">

<script runat="server">
const int _itemCount = 10;

string GetDisplayItem(int n)
{
    return "Item #" + n.ToString();
}
</script>

<html xmlns="http://www.w3.org/1999/xhtml" >
<head>
    <title>Simple page</title>
</head>
```

```
<body>
    <h1>Test ASP.NET 2.0 Page</h1>
    <ul>
    <% for (int i=0; i<_itemCount; i++) { %>
    <li><%=GetDisplayItem(i)%></li>
    <% } %>
    </ul>
    <%
    Response.Write("<h2>Total number of items = " +
                    _itemCount.ToString() + "</h2>");
    %>
</body>
</html>
```

The difference between this page and a classic ASP page is that in ASP.NET the entire file's contents is parsed into a class definition and then compiled into an assembly. Server-side script blocks are added directly to the class definition. Interspersed script is merged into a Render method of the class, which when called writes all of the static and dynamic content to the response. The class itself inherits from System.Web.UI.Page, which in turn implements the IHttpHandler interface to become an endpoint in the request-processing architecture of ASP.NET. This was the primary shift in the transition from classic ASP to ASP.NET: Instead of using script on your pages to interact with classes, your page becomes a class, and the interaction with other classes is identical to what it would be from any other class. Listing 1-2 shows a slightly simplified version of what the page in Listing 1-1 turns into after ASP.NET parses it into a class definition.

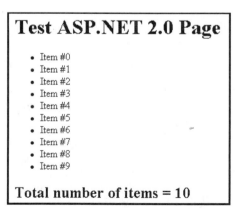

FIGURE 1-1: Rendering of SimplePage.aspx

LISTING 1-2: Parsed class generated by ASP.NET (simplified)[1]

```
namespace ASP
{
  public class simplepage_aspx : Page
  {
    const int _itemCount = 10;

    string GetDisplayItem(int n)
    {
        return "Item #" + n.ToString();
    }

    protected override void Render(HtmlTextWriter writer)
    {
      writer.Write("<!DOCTYPE html PUBLIC \"-//W3C//DTD "   +
                   "XHTML 1.0 Transitional//EN\" \"http://www.w3"  +
                   ".org/TR/xhtml1/DTD/xhtml1-transitional.dtd\">");

      writer.Write("\r\n\r\n<html xmlns=\"http://www.w3.org/" +
                   "1999/xhtml\" >\r\n<head>\r\n<title>Simple page<" +
                   "/title>\r\n</head>\r\n<body>\r\n"                 +
                   "<h1>Test ASP.NET 2.0 Page</h1>\r\n      "       +
                   "<ul>\r\n     ");

      for (int i = 0; i < _itemCount; i++)
      {
        writer.Write("\r\n<li> ");
        writer.Write(GetDisplayItem(i));
        writer.Write("</li>\r\n     ");
      }
      writer.Write("\r\n</ul>\r\n");

      Response.Write("<h2>Total number of items = " +
                     _itemCount.ToString() + "</h2>");

      writer.Write("\r\n</body>\r\n</html>\r\n");

      base.Render(writer);
    }
  }
}
```

---

1. The page shown in this listing is similar to the code that ASP.NET will generate when it parses
   your page. Steps have been taken to simplify some of the details for the purpose of presentation, but conceptually it is identical to the code generated by ASP.NET. If you would like
   to view the actual code that ASP.NET produces for any given page, do the following:

   1. Add Debug="true" to your @Page directive.

   2. Place <%= GetType().Assembly.Location %> somewhere on your page.

   This will print the location of the assembly generated for your page. If you go to that directory, you will also see source code files (*.cs or *.vb) that contain the class definitions.

Server-Side Controls

Of course, most ASP.NET pages do not use interspersed script to inject dynamic content at all. Instead, they rely on the server-side control architecture introduced with ASP.NET. Server-side controls look much like the rest of the HTML elements in an .aspx page, but are marked with the runat="server" attribute and are typically prefixed with the "asp" namespace. When ASP.NET parses the page, these controls are added to the generated class definition not as methods or code, but as member variables representing the specific element (or collection of elements) they are designed to render. As an example, Listing 1-3 shows the same page we've been using rewritten to use server-side controls instead of interspersed script to render the list and H2 elements.

LISTING 1-3: SimplePageWithControls.aspx—A simple .aspx file using server-side controls

```
<%@ Page Language="C#" Debug="true" %>

<!DOCTYPE html PUBLIC "-//W3C//DTD XHTML 1.0 Transitional//EN" "http://
www.w3.org/TR/xhtml1/DTD/xhtml1-transitional.dtd">

<script runat="server">
const int _itemCount = 10;

string GetDisplayItem(int n)
{
  return "Item #" + n.ToString();
}

protected override void OnLoad(EventArgs e)
{
  // Clear out items populated by static declaration
  _displayList.Items.Clear();

  for (int i=0; i<_itemCount; i++)
    _displayList.Items.Add(new ListItem(GetDisplayItem(i)));

  _messageH2.InnerText = "Total number of items = " +
                         _itemCount.ToString();

  base.OnLoad(e);
}
</script>

<html xmlns="http://www.w3.org/1999/xhtml" >
<head>
  <title>Simple page with controls</title>
```

continues

```
</head>
<body>
  <form runat="server" id="_form" >
  <h1>Test ASP.NET 2.0 Page with controls</h1>

  <asp:BulletedList runat="server" ID="_displayList">
      <asp:ListItem>Sample Item 1</asp:ListItem>
      <asp:ListItem>Sample Item 2 ...</asp:ListItem>
  </asp:BulletedList>

  <h2 runat="server" id="_messageH2">Total number of items = xx</h2>
  </form>
</body>
</html>
```

One of the primary advantages of using server-side controls is the complete separation of layout from programmatic logic. Note that instead of adding script elements to generate the dynamic portions of the page, we used the object model of the BulletedList control and the HtmlGenericControl (representing the H2 element) to populate their contents. This example also uses the fairly common technique of populating the static declarations of the server-side controls with sample content so that it is somewhat representative of what it will look like at runtime and will display properly in the designer for layout purposes.

The code generated by ASP.NET is actually a bit cleaner as well. No longer does the runtime have to create a special Render method to interweave interspersed script with static HTML strings. Instead, all static content on the page is represented using LiteralControls, which act like placeholders in the rendering process and return their associated strings when requested to render. Listing 1-4 shows the parsed class definition created by ASP.NET for the page shown in Listing 1-3 (the code has been simplified somewhat for clarity).

LISTING 1-4: Parsed class generated by ASP.NET with server-side controls (simplified)

```
namespace ASP
{
  class SimplePageWithControls_aspx : Page
  {
    const int _itemCount = 10;

    // Control declarations
    protected BulletedList       _displayList;
    protected HtmlGenericControl _messageH2;
    protected HtmlForm           _form;
```

```csharp
string GetDisplayItem(int n)
{
  return "Item #" + n.ToString();
}

protected override void OnLoad(EventArgs e)
{
  // Clear out items populated by control initialization
  _displayList.Items.Clear();

  for (int i = 0; i < _itemCount; i++)
    _displayList.Items.Add(new ListItem(GetDisplayItem(i)));

  _messageH2.InnerText = "Total number of items = " +
                         _itemCount.ToString();

  base.OnLoad(e);
}

protected override void  FrameworkInitialize()
{
  Controls.Add(new LiteralControl("<!DOCTYPE html " +
            "PUBLIC \"-//W3C//DTD " +
            "XHTML 1.0 Transitional//EN\" \"http://www.w3" +
            ".org/TR/xhtml1/DTD/xhtml1-transitional.dtd\"> "));
  Controls.Add(new LiteralControl("<html xmlns=\"http://" +
            "www.w3.org/1999/xhtml\" >" +
            "\r\n<head>\r\n    <title>Simple page " +
            "with controls</title>\r\n</head>\r\n<body>\r\n"));

  _form = new HtmlForm();
  _form.Controls.Add(new LiteralControl("<h1>Test ASP.NET 2.0 " +
                                "Page with controls</h1>\r\n    "));

  _displayList = new BulletedList();
  _displayList.ID = "_displayList";
  _displayList.Items.Add(new ListItem("Sample Item 1"));
  _displayList.Items.Add(new ListItem("Sample Item 2"));
  _displayList.Items.Add(new ListItem("Sample Item 3"));
  _form.Controls.Add(_displayList);

  _messageH2 = new HtmlGenericControl("h2");
  _messageH2.ID = "_messageH2";
  _messageH2.Controls.Add(new LiteralControl("Total number " +
                                "of items = xx"));
  _form.Controls.Add(_messageH2);

  Controls.Add(_form);
```

continues

```
Controls.Add(
        new LiteralControl("\r\n\r\n</body>\r\n</html>\r\n"));

    base.OnPreInit(e);
    }
  }
}
```

Data Binding

Most of the time you won't even have to go through the trouble of pro-grammatically populating the elements of a list control like we did in List-ing 1-3, as all list controls (as well as others) in ASP.NET support data binding. We will cover the details of data binding in Chapter 3, but suffice it to say that you can take any enumerable collection of items and bind it to a server-side control (like the BulletedList control) and it will autocreate the items for you at runtime. Listing 1-5 shows an example of binding an array of strings to the BulletedList control. The process of binding a collec-tion of data to a control consists of setting the DataSource property to an enumerable collection (like the array in our case or, in general, any type that implements the IEnumerable interface). You can also set up data bind-ing completely declaratively, as we will discuss in Chapter 3.

LISTING 1-5: SimplePageWithDataBinding.aspx

```
<%@ Page Language="C#" Debug="true" %>

<!DOCTYPE html PUBLIC "-//W3C//DTD XHTML 1.0 Transitional//EN" "http://
www.w3.org/TR/xhtml1/DTD/xhtml1-transitional.dtd">

<script runat="server">
string[] _displayItemData = {"Item #1", "Item #2", "Item #3", "Item #4",
    "Item #5", "Item #6", "Item #7", "Item #8", "Item #9", "Item #10"};

protected override void OnLoad(EventArgs e)
{
    _messageH2.InnerText = "Total number of items = " +
                        _displayItemData.Length.ToString();

    _displayItems.DataSource = _displayItemData;
    _displayItems.DataBind();

    base.OnLoad(e);
}
</script>
```

```
<html xmlns="http://www.w3.org/1999/xhtml" >
<head>
    <title>Simple page with controls</title>
</head>
<body>
    <form runat="server" id="_form">
        <h1>Test ASP.NET 2.0 Page with data binding</h1>

        <asp:BulletedList runat="server" ID="_displayItems">
            <asp:ListItem>Sample item 1</asp:ListItem>
            <asp:ListItem>Sample item 2 ...</asp:ListItem>
        </asp:BulletedList>

        <h2 runat="server" id="_messageH2">
            Total number of items = xx</h2>
    </form>
</body>
</html>
```

The trio of parsing pages into class declarations, server-side controls, and a generic data-binding architecture are really the three pillars of Web development with ASP.NET. With these three core features and the .NET runtime environment to build on, developers have created many well-designed, scalable Web applications that are in use today. ASP.NET 2.0 builds on these pillars to give developers a more productive set of tools to work from, as we will see over the next several chapters.

Codebehind

One of the big changes in this release of ASP.NET 2.0 is the way you specify a codebehind class for a page. We'll start with a review of how codebehind classes work in ASP.NET 1.x (which is still supported), and then introduce the new codebehind model introduced in ASP.NET 2.0.

Codebehind Basics

ASP.NET 1.0 introduced a new mechanism for separating programmatic logic from static page layout called **codebehind**. This technique involves creating an intermediate base class that sits between the Page base class and the machine-generated class from the .aspx file. The intermediate base class derives directly from Page, and the class generated from the .aspx file derives from the intermediate base class instead of directly from Page.

With this technique, you can add fields, methods, and event handlers in your codebehind class and have these features inherited by the class created from the .aspx file, eliminating the need to sprinkle code throughout the .aspx file.

Listings 1-6 and 1-7 show a sample .aspx file and its corresponding codebehind file using the 1.0 inheritance model. Note the use of the Src attribute in the Page directive that tells ASP.NET which file to compile to create the base class for this page. You can also leave off the Src attribute altogether and compile the codebehind file yourself, placing the resulting assembly in the /bin directory of your application (this is, in fact, the most common deployment model with Visual Studio .NET 2003).

LISTING 1-6: SimplePageWithCodeBehindV1.aspx

```
<%@ Page Language="C#" AutoEventWireup="true"
        Src="SimplePageWithCodeBehind.aspx.cs"
        Inherits="EssentialAspDotNet.SimplePageWithCodeBehindV1" %>

<!DOCTYPE html PUBLIC "-//W3C//DTD XHTML 1.0 Transitional//EN"
    "http://www.w3.org/TR/xhtml1/DTD/xhtml1-transitional.dtd">

<html xmlns="http://www.w3.org/1999/xhtml" >
<head runat="server">
    <title>Simple page with codebehind V1</title>
</head>
<body>
    <form id="form1" runat="server">

    <h1>Test ASP.NET 2.0 Page with codebehind V1</h1>
    <asp:BulletedList runat="server" ID="_displayList">
        <asp:ListItem>Sample Item 1</asp:ListItem>
        <asp:ListItem>Sample Item 2 ...</asp:ListItem>
    </asp:BulletedList>

    <h2 runat="server" id="_messageH2">Total number of items = xx</h2>

    </form>
</body>
</html>
```

LISTING 1-7: SimplePageWithCodeBehindV1.aspx.cs

```
using System;
using System.Web;
using System.Web.UI;
using System.Web.UI.WebControls;
using System.Web.UI.HtmlControls;
```

```
namespace EssentialAspDotNet
{

  public class SimplePageWithCodeBehindV1 : Page
  {
    protected BulletedList       _displayList;
    protected HtmlGenericControl _messageH2;

    string[] _displayItemData =
              {"Item #1", "Item #2", "Item #3", "Item #4",
               "Item #5", "Item #6", "Item #7", "Item #8",
               "Item #9", "Item #10"};

    protected override void OnLoad(EventArgs e)
    {
      _messageH2.InnerText = "Total number of items = " +
                             _displayItemData.Length.ToString();

      _displayList.DataSource = _displayItemData;
      _displayList.DataBind();

      base.OnLoad(e);
    }
  }
}
```

Codebehind 2.0

In this release of ASP.NET, the codebehind mechanism has changed slightly (although the existing 1.0 syntax is still completely supported). The change is so subtle that you may not even notice that it has changed unless you look really closely. Listings 1-8 and 1-9 show the new syntax using the same page as the previous example.

LISTING 1-8: SimplePageWithCodeBehind.aspx using new 2.0 model

```
<%@ Page Language="C#" AutoEventWireup="true"
        CodeFile="SimplePageWithCodeBehind.aspx.cs"
        Inherits="EssentialAspDotNet.SimplePageWithCodeBehind" %>

<!DOCTYPE html PUBLIC "-//W3C//DTD XHTML 1.0 Transitional//EN"
     "http://www.w3.org/TR/xhtml1/DTD/xhtml1-transitional.dtd">

<html xmlns="http://www.w3.org/1999/xhtml" >
<head runat="server">
    <title>Simple page with codebehind</title>
</head>
```

continues

```
<body>
    <form id="form1" runat="server">

    <h1>Test ASP.NET 2.0 Page with codebehind</h1>
    <asp:BulletedList runat="server" ID="_displayList">
        <asp:ListItem>Sample Item 1</asp:ListItem>
        <asp:ListItem>Sample Item 2 ...</asp:ListItem>
    </asp:BulletedList>

    <h2 runat="server" id="_messageH2">Total number of items = xx</h2>

    </form>
</body>
</html>
```

LISTING 1-9: SimplePageWithCodeBehind.aspx.cs using new 2.0 model

```
using System;
using System.Web;
using System.Web.UI;
using System.Web.UI.WebControls;

namespace EssentialAspDotNet
{
  public partial class SimplePageWithCodeBehind : Page
  {
    string[] _displayItemData =
             {"Item #1", "Item #2", "Item #3", "Item #4",
              "Item #5", "Item #6", "Item #7", "Item #8",
              "Item #9", "Item #10"};

    protected override void OnLoad(EventArgs e)
    {
      _messageH2.InnerText = "Total number of items = " +
                          _displayItemData.Length.ToString();

      _displayList.DataSource = _displayItemData;
      _displayList.DataBind();

      base.OnLoad(e);
    }
  }
}
```

There are two significant differences between this model and the standard 1.x model: the introduction of the CodeFile attribute in the @Page directive and the declaration of the codebehind class as a partial class. As you start building the page, you will notice another difference: server-side controls no longer need to be explicitly declared in your codebehind class, but you still have complete access to them programmatically, as shown in Listing 1-9.

The reason this works has to do with the partial keyword applied to your codebehind class. In addition to turning your .aspx file into a class definition with methods for rendering the page, as it has always done, ASP.NET now will also generate a sibling partial class for your codebehind class that contains protected control member variable declarations. Your class is then compiled together with this generated class definition, merged together, and then it becomes the base class for the class generated for the .aspx file. The end result is that you essentially write codebehind classes the way you always have, but you no longer have to declare (or let the designer declare for you) member variable declarations of server-side controls. This was always a somewhat fragile relationship in 1.x, since if you ever accidentally modified one of the control declarations so that it no longer matched the ID of the control declared on the form, things suddenly stopped working. Now the member variables are declared implicitly and will always be correct. Listings 1-10, 1-11, and 1-12 show the relationship between your codebehind class and the ASP.NET-generated classes.

LISTING 1-10: Class for .aspx file generated by ASP.NET

```
namespace ASP
{
  public class samplepagewithcodebehind_aspx :
                    EssentialAspDotNet.SamplePageWithCodeBehind
  {
    . . .
  }
}
```

LISTING 1-11: Sibling partial class generated by ASP.NET

```
namespace EssentialAspDotNet
{
  public partial class SamplePageWithCodeBehind
  {
    protected BulletedList        _displayList;
    protected HtmlGenericControl _messageH2;
    protected HtmlForm            _form1;

    . . .
  }
}
```

LISTING 1-12: Codebehind partial class that you write

```
namespace EssentialAspDotNet
{
  public partial class SamplePageWithCodeBehind : Page
  {
    string[] _displayItemData =
                {"Item #1", "Item #2", "Item #3", "Item #4",
                 "Item #5", "Item #6", "Item #7", "Item #8",
                 "Item #9", "Item #10"};

    protected override void OnLoad(EventArgs e)
    {
      _messageH2.InnerText = "Total number of items = " +
                            _displayItemData.Length.ToString();

      _displayList.DataSource = _displayItemData;
      _displayList.DataBind();

      base.OnLoad(e);
    }
  }
}
```

Note that this partial class model is only used if you use the CodeFile keyword in your @Page directive. If you use the Inherits keyword without CodeFile (or with the Src attribute instead), ASP.NET reverts to the 1.1 codebehind style and simply places your class as the sole base class for the .aspx file. Also, if you have no codebehind at all, the class generation acts very much the same as it does in 1.1. Since ASP.NET 2.0 is backward compatible with 1.1, we now have a range of codebehind options at our disposal as Web developers. Visual Studio 2005 uses the new partial class codebehind model for any WebForms, and it will also happily convert Visual Studio .NET 2003 projects to using the new model as well if you use the Conversion wizard. It is best, if possible, to convert all files to the new codebehind model, since some of the new features of ASP.NET 2.0 depend on it.[2]

---

2. As an example, strongly typed access to the Profile property bag is added to the sibling partial class for codebehind classes in 2.0, but if you use the 1.1 codebehind model, that strongly typed accessor is added directly to the .aspx-generated class definition, and it will be unavailable to your codebehind class. This is also true for strongly typed master page and previous page access.

Page Lifecycle

One of the most important things to understand when building Web applications with ASP.NET is the sequence of events during the processing of a page. If you're not careful, you can make changes to a control that are then overwritten, which can result in unexpected behavior. As you build a page, you must take care that the code you write is called at the right time during the request processing to have the impact you expect. Fortunately, there are many events at your disposal in the Page base class. You can usually find the correct point in time to populate controls with default values, dynamically alter the control hierarchy, harvest POST data from the client, or whatever else you are trying to accomplish.

Common Events

The most common events to handle in ASP.NET are the Init and Load events. The **Load event** is issued prior to the rendering of a page, and it is the ideal location to initialize control state. It is also called after the state in a POST request has been processed and used to populate the control hierarchy, and so it can be used to inspect the contents of data sent by the client. The **Init event**, on the other hand, is called before any state restoration occurs and is commonly used to prepare the Page for processing a request. You can even do things like modify the control hierarchy in the Init event if there are dynamic changes you would like to make to a page. Most ASP.NET applications use a fairly standard event scheme in their interactive pages.

1. They initialize the state of controls for the first time in the Load event if it is the initial GET request to a page (the IsPostBack property of the page is set to false).
2. Next, they process user responses inside the server-side event of the control that generates the subsequent POST request.

Listings 1-13 and 1-14 show an example of this common practice with a page and its codebehind class.

LISTING 1-13: CommonEvents.aspx

```
<%@ Page Language="C#" AutoEventWireup="true"
               CodeFile="CommonEvents.aspx.cs"
               Inherits="EssentialAspDotNet.CommonEvents" %>

<html xmlns="http://www.w3.org/1999/xhtml" >
<head runat="server">
    <title>Common Events Page</title>
</head>
<body>
    <form id="form1" runat="server">
    <div>
    <h3>Enter name: </h3>
    <asp:TextBox id="_nameTextBox" runat="server"/>
    <h3>Personality: </h3>
    <asp:DropDownList id="_personalityDropDownList" runat="server" />
    <asp:Button id="_enterButton" Text="Enter" runat="server"
                OnClick="_enterButton_Click" /><br />
    <asp:Label runat="server" id="_messageLabel" />
    </div>
    </form>
</body>
</html>
```

LISTING 1-14: CommonEvents.aspx.cs

```
namespace EssentialAspDotNet
{
  public partial class CommonEvents : System.Web.UI.Page
  {
    protected void Page_Load(object sender, EventArgs e)
    {
      if (!IsPostBack)
      {
        _personalityDropDownList.Items.Add(new ListItem("extraverted"));
        _personalityDropDownList.Items.Add(new ListItem("introverted"));
        _personalityDropDownList.Items.Add(new ListItem("in-between"));
      }
    }

    protected void _enterButton_Click(object sender, EventArgs e)
    {
      _messageLabel.Text = "Hi " + _nameTextBox.Text +
                          ", you selected " +
                          _personalityDropDownList.SelectedItem.Text;
    }
  }
}
```

New Events

This release of ASP.NET introduces even more events in the Page class, increasing the number of options you have for how to interact with the request processing of the Page. For the most part, the new events are "pre" and "complete" events that wrap one of the existing events. For example, there is now both a PreLoad event as well as a LoadComplete event in addition to the standard Load event. Figure 1-2 shows the updated sequence of events as well as the activities that occur during the processing of the page between the events.

Most notable among these new events are the PreInit and LoadComplete events. **PreInit** is important because, as you will see in Chapter 2, themes and master pages are applied between PreInit and Init. This means that PreInit is your only opportunity to make programmatic modifications to the selected theme or associated master page of a page. The **LoadComplete**

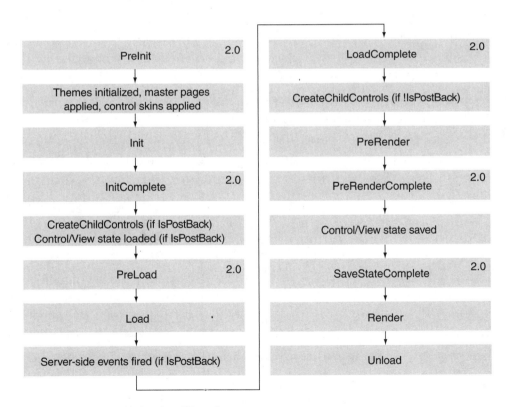

FIGURE 1-2: Events in the page lifecycle

event is also potentially quite useful as it is fired after the server-side events have fired but before the PreRender event takes place. Many applications written in ASP.NET today resort to using the PreRender event to make last-minute changes to control contents after server-side events fire. LoadComplete is now the proper place to make post-event modifications to a control, leaving PreRender as a hook for other activities.

Note that the PreInit, InitComplete, PreLoad, LoadComplete, PreRender-Complete, and SaveStateComplete are brand new events, and that they are only available in the Page class but not in individual controls as the other events are.

Implicit Event Subscription

One of the first things you will notice that is different in ASP.NET 2.0 is that Visual Studio 2005 creates event handlers for page events by enabling AutoEventWireUp and using specially named methods that are implicitly registered as event handlers—instead of explicitly registering delegates as the previous release did.[3] For example, to add a handler for the Load event of the Page class, Visual Studio 2005 adds a method to your codebehind class (or inline in a server-side script block) named Page_Load. Table 1-1 shows the complete list of method names that will be implicitly subscribed to events if they are added to your Page class.

Implicit delegate wireup occurs when a page has the Auto-EventWireUp attribute set to true (which is the default), and one or more of the page's methods matches one of the names shown in Table 1-1. The method must also have the correct signature expected by the delegate defining the event (typically just EventHandler). At the beginning of the request cycle, the Page class invokes its SetIntrinsics method, which in addition to setting the intrinsics (meaning the Response, Request, Session, Application, and so on) calls the TemplateControl base class' HookUp-AutomaticHandlers method. This method walks through the list of method names shown in Table 1-1 and uses reflection to identify methods with the same name and proper signature defined in your class. If it finds a match, it creates a new delegate of the appropriate type, initializes it with your method, and adds it to the list of delegates to fire when that event occurs.

---

3. This is only true for Web applications written in C#, as VB.NET still uses its "Handles" syntax to wire up control events.

TABLE 1-1:   Method names and the events they bind to in ASP.NET 2.0

Method Name	Event
Page_PreInit	Page.PreInit
Page_Init	Control.Init
Page_InitComplete	Page.InitComplete
Page_PreLoad	Page.PreLoad
Page_Load	Control.Load
Page_LoadComplete	Page.LoadComplete
Page_PreRender	Control.PreRender
Page_DataBind	Control.DataBinding
Page_PreRenderComplete	Page.PreRenderComplete
Page_SaveStateComplete	Page.SaveStateComplete
Page_Unload	Control.Unload
Page_Error	TemplateControl.Error
Page_AbortTransaction	TemplateControl.AbortTransaction
OnTransactionAbort	TemplateControl.AbortTransaction
Page_CommitTransaction	TemplateControl.CommitTransaction
OnTransactionCommit	TemplateControl.CommitTransaction

Each of these events is fired by a virtual method defined in the Page base class (or a virtual method in the Control base class and inherited by Page). This means that it is technically possible to register for any of these events in three different ways. For example, to handle the Load event, you can do any of the following:

- Wire up a delegate explicitly to the event yourself (typically in your Page's Init handler).

- Write a method named Page_Load with the event signature.
- Override the virtual OnLoad method.

Each of these techniques essentially accomplishes the same task, and in the end it doesn't matter which way you do it. The virtual method override is going to be marginally faster than the explicitly or implicitly wired delegate approaches, but in general the difference in overhead will typically be dwarfed by other activities in your page (like data access). If you are using Visual Studio 2005, the technique it uses for you by default is the implicit delegate wireup based on the method's name.

Compilation

The number of ways you can compile your code increases many times over with the release of ASP.NET 2.0. In addition to the precompiled bin directory and the delay-compiled Src attribute deployment options in ASP.NET 1.x, you can now deploy raw source files to specially named directories (like /App_Code). There is a new utility, aspnet_compiler.exe, which will precompile an entire virtual directory to create a zero-source deployment (including .aspx file content). Web Deployment Projects also has a supplemental addition to Visual Studio 2005, which provides even more alternatives for compilation and deployment. We will cover each of these new compilation features in this section.

Compilation Directories

In ASP.NET 1.0, the only way to deploy supplemental classes with your Web application locally is to compile them into an assembly and place them in the /bin directory under the virtual application root. Any assembly placed in the /bin directory of an application is shadow copied to a private directory during site compilation, and every compile that ASP.NET issues for that site includes a reference to the shadow-copied assembly. This ensures that you can replace the assembly in the /bin directory with an updated one without having to shut down the Web server. When the timestamp on a particular assembly in the /bin directory is updated (typically by replacing it with a new version), the contents of the site is recompiled with references to the new assembly (which is again shadow copied prior to reference).

This technique of deploying precompiled assemblies is still supported in ASP.NET 2.0, and depending on how you structure your site and your build process, this may still be your best option going forward. There is another option in this release, however, which is to place any source code files that you would like to have compiled and referenced by your site's other elements in the new top-level App_Code directory. In fact, there are seven new top-level folders that have special meaning in ASP.NET 2.0, as shown in Table 1-2.

TABLE 1-2: Special compilation folders in ASP.NET 2.0

Directory Name	Contents	Compilation
App_Browsers	.browser files (XML format files used to describe browser capabilities)	Each .browser file is compiled into a method in the local ApplicationBrowserCapabilitiesFactory class that is used to populate an instance of HttpBrowserCapabilities when needed.
App_Code	Source code files (.cs, .vb, etc.), .wsdl files, .xsd files (extensible)	Source code files are compiled into an assembly for use in your application. .wsdl files are parsed into Web service proxies and then compiled. .xsd files are parsed into strongly typed DataSet classes and then compiled.
App_Data	Database files, xml data sources, other data source files	No compilation takes place.
App_GlobalResources	Resource files (.resx and .resources)	Compiled into a resource-only assembly with global scope.
App_LocalResources	Resource files (.resx and .resources) that are associated with a particular page or user control	Compiled into a resource-only assembly for access by the associated page or user control.

continues

TABLE 1-2:   Special compilation folders in ASP.NET 2.0 (*continued*)

Directory Name	Contents	Compilation
App_Themes	.skin, .css, images, and other resources	Compiled into a separate assembly containing resources for a particular theme.
App_WebReferences	.wsdl, .xsd, .disco, .discomap	Generates a Web service proxy for each endpoint described.
Bin	.dll assembly files	No compilation takes place. Assemblies placed in this directory are shadow copied and referenced during all other compilations associated with the site.

Any source files placed in the App_Code folder will be compiled along with all of your pages and their codebehind files when ASP.NET processes requests for your site (or during site precompilation). This means that you now have a complete range of deployment options, ranging from placing all of your source code on the server (including utility classes, business layers, data access layers, etc.) to precompiling any subset and placing the resulting assemblies in the /bin directory (or even deploying machine-wide in the global assembly cache (GAC)). Note that the decision of where to place your code files is purely a matter of convenience and organization. There is no difference in performance between a precompiled assembly and code that is placed in the App_Code folder and compiled at request time once the compilation has taken place.[4]

As an example of using the App_Code folder, consider the class in Listing 1-15 that we intend to use as a data source for various pages in our site.

---

4. There can be additional overhead the first time a request is made to a site using the App_Code folder, but even this can be eliminated by precompiling the site (which we will discuss shortly).

LISTING 1-15: Custom data source class for deployment in the App_Code directory

```csharp
// File: MyDataSource.cs
namespace EssentialAspDotNet.Architecture
{
  public static class MyDataSource
  {
    static string[] _items =
      {"Item #1", "Item #2", "Item #3", "Item #4",
       "Item #5", "Item #6", "Item #7", "Item #8",
       "Item #9", "Item #10"};

    public static string[] GetItems()
    {
      return _items;
    }
  }
}
```

To deploy this file, you would manually create a directory at the root of your Web application named App_Code and place MyDataSource.cs in it. All pages (and other generated types) in your site would then have access to the compiled class implicitly. The class will be compiled as part of the request sequence in much the same way .aspx files and their codebehind files are compiled. For example, we could now rewrite our earlier data-binding example using the ObjectDataSource control to declaratively associate the GetItems method as the data source for our BulletedList as shown in Listing 1-16. Chapter 3 covers the details of the ObjectDataSource; for now, note that it can be initialized with a type name and a method name, and when associated with the DataSourceID of a data-bound control, it will bind the results of invoking the method on the object to the control prior to rendering.

LISTING 1-16: Simple page with declarative data binding using custom data source class

```
<%@ Page Language="C#" %>

<!DOCTYPE html PUBLIC "-//W3C//DTD XHTML 1.0 Transitional//EN"
    "http://www.w3.org/TR/xhtml1/DTD/xhtml1-transitional.dtd">

<html xmlns="http://www.w3.org/1999/xhtml" >
<head runat="server">
    <title>Simple page with declarative data binding</title>
</head>
<body>
    <form id="form1" runat="server">
```

continues

```
<h1>Test ASP.NET 2.0 Page with declarative data binding</h1>
<asp:BulletedList runat="server" ID="_displayList"
                  DataSourceID="_itemsDataSource" >
    <asp:ListItem>Sample Item 1</asp:ListItem>
    <asp:ListItem>Sample Item 2 ...</asp:ListItem>
</asp:BulletedList>

<h2 runat="server" id="_messageH2">Total number of items = xx</h2>

<asp:ObjectDataSource runat="server" ID="_itemsDataSource"
        TypeName="EssentialAspDotNet.Architecture.MyDataSource"
        SelectMethod="GetItems" />
</form>
</body>
</html>
```

Site Compilation

Perhaps the most significant addition to the process of compilation in this release is the introduction of the ASP.NET compiler. The **ASP.NET compiler** (aspnet_compiler.exe) gives you the ability to completely precompile an entire site, making it possible to deploy nothing but binary assemblies (even .aspx and .ascx files are precompiled). This is compelling because it eliminates any on-demand compilation when requests are made, eliminating the first post-deployment hit seen in some sites using ASP.NET 1.0. It also makes it more difficult for modifications to be made to the deployed site (since you can't just open .aspx files and change things), which can be appealing when deploying applications that you want to be changed only through a standard deployment process.

Figure 1-3 shows an invocation of the aspnet_compiler.exe utility using the binary deployment option and the resulting output to a deployment directory. Note that the .aspx files present in the deployment directory are just marker files with no content. They are there to ensure that a file with the endpoint name is present if the "Check that file exists" option for the .aspx extension in an IIS application is set. The PrecompiledApp.config file is used to keep track of how the application was deployed and whether ASP.NET needs to compile any files at request time. Note that this utility is also accessible graphically through the Build | Publish Web Site menu item of Visual Studio shown in Figure 1-4.

In addition to the binary-only deployment model, the aspnet_compiler also supports an "updatable" deployment model, where all source code in

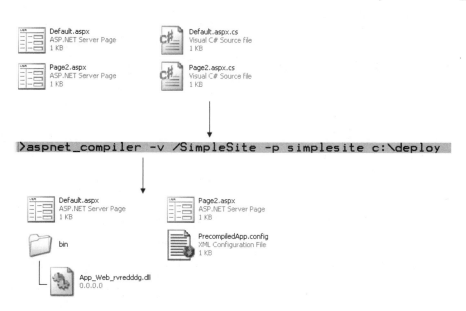

FIGURE 1-3: Binary deployment with aspnet_compiler.exe

a site is precompiled into binary assemblies, but all .aspx, .ascx, .master, .ashx, and .asax files are left intact so that changes can be made on the server. This model is possible because of the inheritance in the codebehind model so that the sibling partial classes containing control declarations can

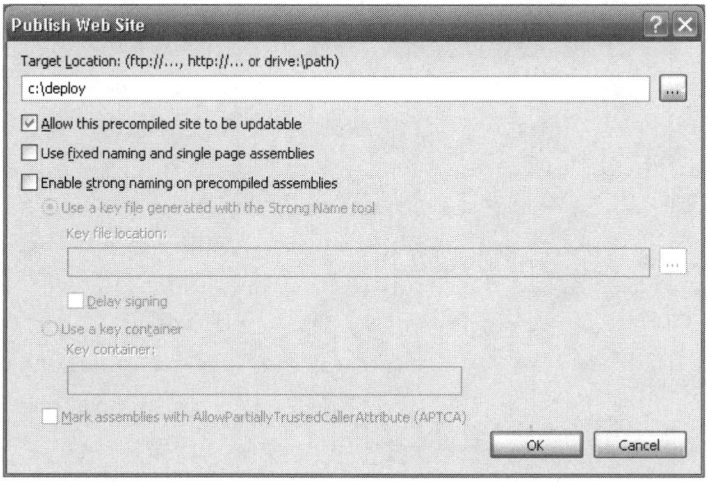

FIGURE 1-4: Build | Publish Web Site tool in Visual Studio 2005

be generated and compiled independently of the actual .aspx file class definitions. To generate the "updatable" site you would use -u with the command line utility, and the resulting .aspx files would contain their original content (and not be empty marker files).

With the aspnet_compiler utility in hand, you can work on your applications without worrying about how your application will be deployed, for the most part, since any site can now be deployed in any of three ways: all source, all binary, or updatable (source code in binary and .aspx files in source), without any modification to page attributes or code files used in development. This was not possible in previous releases of ASP.NET, since you had to decide at development time whether to use the Src attribute to reference codebehind files or to precompile them and deploy the assemblies to the /bin directory. Complete binary deployment was not even an option.

Assembly Generation

Now that compilation into assemblies can happen in one of three places (explicitly by the developer, using aspnet_compiler.exe, or during request processing), understanding the mapping of files into assemblies becomes even more important. In fact, depending on how you write your pages, you can actually end up with an application that works fine when deployed as all source or all binary, but which fails to compile when deployed using the updatable switch.

The general model ASP.NET uses is to create separate assemblies for the contents of the App_Code directory as well as the global.asax file (if present), and then to compile all of the .aspx pages in each directory into a separate assembly. User controls and master pages are also compiled independently from .aspx pages. It is also possible to configure the App_Code directory to create multiple assemblies if, for example, you wanted to include both VB.NET and C# source code in a project, as you will see shortly. Table 1-3 describes which of your Web site components compile into separate assemblies based on the deployment mode you are using (note that we are ignoring the resource, theme, and browser directories since they don't contain code, although they are compiled into separate assemblies as well).

There is one other twist in the assembly generation picture: You can use the -fixednames option in the aspnet_compiler to request that each .aspx

TABLE 1-3: Assembly generation

	Deployment Mode		
	All Source	**All Binary**	**Updatable (Mixed)**
What Compiles into a Unique Assembly	App_Code directory	App_Code directory	App_Code directory (D)
	global.asax	global.asax	global.asax (R)
	.ascx and associated codebehind file (separate assembly for each user control)	.ascx and .master files and their associated codebehind files	.ascx and .master files (R)
	.master and associated codebehind file (separate assembly for each master page)	All .aspx files and their codebehind files in a given directory (separate assembly per directory)	Codebehind files for .ascx and .master files (D)
	All .aspx files and their codebehind files in a given directory (separate assembly per directory)		All .aspx files in a given directory (separate assembly per directory) (R)
			All codebehind files associated with .aspx files in a given directory (separate assembly per directory) (D)
When It's Compiled	Request time	Deployment time	(R) = Compiled at request time
			(D) = Compiled at deployment time

file be compiled into a separate assembly whose name remains the same across different invocations of the compiler. This can be useful if you want to be able to update individual pages without modifying other assemblies on the deployment site. It can also generate a large number of assemblies for any site of significant size, so be sure to test this option before depending on it.

If this is sounding complicated, the good news is that most of the time you shouldn't have to think about which files map to separate assemblies. Your .aspx files are always compiled last, and always include references to all other assemblies generated, so typically things will just work no matter which deployment model you choose.

Customizing Assembly Generation

You have additional control in how assemblies are generated in the App_Code directory. You can use the codeSubDirectories element to further specify that subdirectories should be compiled into individual assemblies. This can be useful if you find the need to house C# and VB.NET source code in the same project, as usually they could not be placed in the same App_Code directory. Figure 1-5 shows a sample layout that maps four distinct directories to different assemblies during compilation.

Web Application Projects

In May of 2006, Microsoft released an addition to Visual Studio 2005 called **Web Application Projects,**[5] which gives you a completely different model for building Web applications with ASP.NET 2.0, one much more similar to the model developers are familiar with using Visual Studio .NET 2003. As with Web projects in Visual Studio .NET 2003, all code files in the project are built into a single assembly, which is deployed to the local /bin

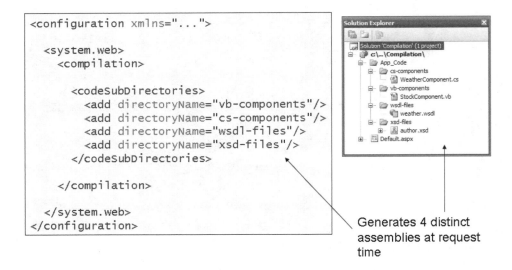

```
<configuration xmlns="...">

  <system.web>
    <compilation>

      <codeSubDirectories>
        <add directoryName="vb-components"/>
        <add directoryName="cs-components"/>
        <add directoryName="wsdl-files"/>
        <add directoryName="xsd-files"/>
      </codeSubDirectories>

    </compilation>

  </system.web>
</configuration>
```

Generates 4 distinct assemblies at request time

FIGURE 1-5: Creating multiple assemblies from the App_Code directory

---

5. You can download the Web Application Projects installation from http://msdn.microsoft.com/ asp.net/reference/infrastructure/wap/default.aspx. Note that this project model does not install with the Express versions of the product.

directory. Because Web Application Projects have a project file and are compiled like any class library project, they have complete support for all class library project settings. Figure 1-6 shows a sample Solution Explorer window from a Web Application Project.

Unlike Web projects in Visual Studio .NET 2003, Web Application Projects do not require a virtual directory to be set up properly before the project can be opened. By default, they use the same ASP.NET Development Server listening on an open port for hosting pages, just as the Web site model does. They of course support the ability to work directly against a virtual directory hosted in IIS just as you can with Web sites.

The new partial class codebehind model is used by default with this model just like the Web site model does; however, it also supports the 1.1 style of codebehind with no issues, which means that migrating a site from Visual Studio .NET 2003 to Visual Studio 2005 is trivial using the Web Application Projects model. This makes it very appealing for larger sites that need to migrate to 2.0 without reworking all of their project settings and codebehind files. When the partial codebehind class model is used, there is a new source code file that is added called "*xxx*.aspx.designer.cs," where *xxx* is the name of the Web form. This file contains the control declarations that are added implicitly by ASP.NET in the Web site model. Many developers find this approach more compelling because all of the code for your codebehind classes is in one place and easy to view. It is no longer necessary to use the App_Code directory, because all source code files are compiled as part of the project (if they are included).

FIGURE 1-6: Web Application Projects' Solution Explorer window

The following are some other advantages to using the Web Application Projects model:

- Faster compile times. Since only the source code for the project is compiled when a build is performed, build times are faster—sometimes much faster. The drawback is that syntax errors on .as*x files will not be detected until runtime.
- All code files are compiled into a single assembly deployed in the local /bin directory, so it is easy to understand the dependencies in your project.
- The project file lets you easily exclude files (and directories) from the build process, whereas in the Web site model you must rename a file with the .exclude extension to exclude it.
- It uses the standard MSBuild compilation process, which can be extended using the MSBuild extensibility rules.
- All debugging features available for projects are available, including features like Edit and Continue and pre- and post-processing steps.

Which model you end up using for building ASP.NET 2.0 applications depends on what environment you are working in and what you are used to. Web Application Projects were introduced to give enterprise developers used to working with project files and performing builds a way to incorporate their Web applications into their standard working environments. Future releases of Visual Studio will include Web Application Projects as one of the built-in options for creating Web applications with ASP.NET.

SUMMARY

This release of ASP.NET builds upon the substrate for building Web applications introduced in version 1.0. All of the architectural features of the ASP.NET 1.x runtime are still present in 2.0, but elements were added to make development of Web applications more intuitive and efficient. One of the most significant additions is the partial class codebehind model, in which instead of manually declaring control variables in your codebehind file, ASP.NET generates a sibling class that is merged with your class definition to provide control variable declarations. The events in the lifetime of a Page were augmented as well, to include many pre- and post-events to give more granular access to points in time during a Page's lifecycle. The other major change architecturally is the compilation model. It is now possible to deploy Web sites as nothing but binary assemblies, as well as all source, and many gradients in between. Developers now have many more options for both development and deployment of Web applications with ASP.NET.

2

User Interface Elements

A SP.NET 2.0 INTRODUCES SEVERAL FEATURES that make it easier to build compelling, unified user interfaces. In this chapter we look at the three primary new user interface elements of ASP.NET 2.0: master pages, themes and skins, and navigation controls. **Master pages** introduce a standard way of sharing a common look and feel across many pages of your site in a model that is intuitive and flexible to use. **Themes** and **skins** provide a way of centralizing all of the style-related elements of your site, including stylesheets, server-side control attributes, and resources like images or JavaScript files. Once these elements are localized, it is straightforward to replace them with a new set of elements, either statically for the entire site or dynamically on a per-client basis. Finally, **navigation controls** include standard implementations of menus, tree views, and "bread crumbs" to quickly add navigational elements to your site. This chapter covers the details of using each of these features, as well as a look at the new control adapter architecture for altering control rendering based on browser type.

Page Templates

It is very common in Web site design to define a standard "look and feel" for all pages. This may include common headers, footers, menus, and so on that provide a core set of features and appearance throughout the site. For dynamic sites, built with technologies like ASP or ASP.NET, it is extremely useful if these common features of all pages are factored into some type of page template, allowing each page to consist only of its own unique content and providing a central location for making site-wide changes in appearance and behavior. As a simple, concrete example of a site that would benefit from some type of page template technique, consider the page displayed in Figure 2-1.

This particular page has a header at the top, a footer at the bottom, a navigation bar on the left, and an area for page-specific content filling out the remainder. Ideally, the header, footer, and navigation bar should be defined only once and somehow propagated to all pages in the site.

This is precisely the problem that master pages in ASP.NET 2.0 solve simply and cleanly. By defining one master page and then creating many content pages based on that one master page, you can very easily create sites with a common look and feel driven by a single template (the master page).

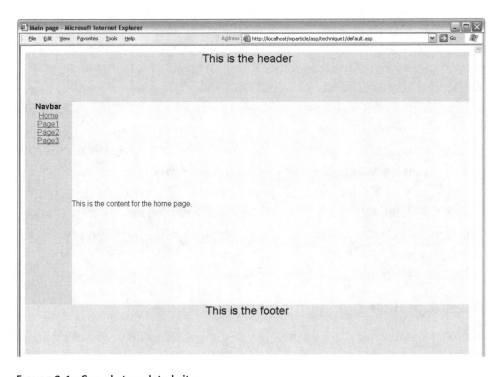

FIGURE 2-1: Sample templated site

Master Pages

Master pages in ASP.NET 2.0 are a general solution to site templating. They provide site-level page templates, a mechanism for fine-grained content replacement, programmatic and declarative control over which template a page should use, and perhaps most compelling of all, integrated designer support. Figure 2-2 shows the conceptual relationship between a master page and content pages that are tied to the master page.

The implementation of master pages in ASP.NET 2.0 consists of two conceptual elements: master pages and content pages. **Master pages** act as the templates for content pages, and **content pages** provide content to populate pieces of master pages that require "filling out." A master page is essentially a standard ASP.NET page except that it uses the extension of .master and a directive of <%@ Master %> instead of <%@ Page %>. This master page file serves as the template for other pages, so typically it will contain the top-level HTML elements, the main form, headers, footers, and such. Within the master page you add instances of the ContentPlaceHolder control at locations where you want content pages to supply page-specific content, as shown in Listing 2-1.

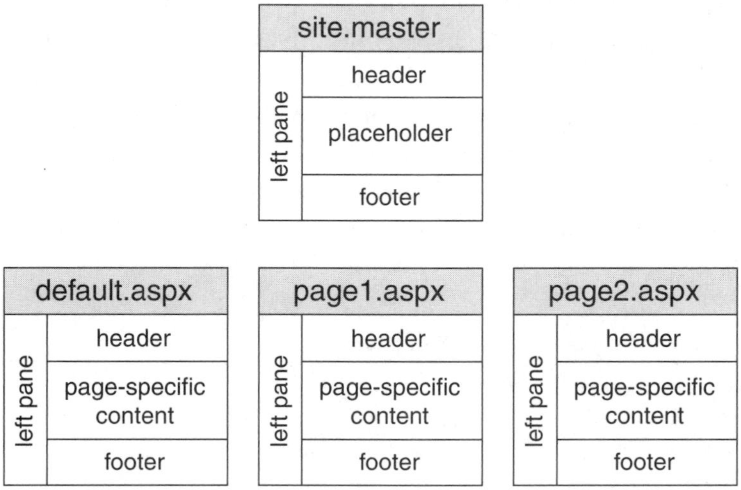

site.master		
left pane	header	
	placeholder	
	footer	

default.aspx			page1.aspx			page2.aspx		
left pane	header		left pane	header		left pane	header	
	page-specific content			page-specific content			page-specific content	
	footer			footer			footer	

FIGURE 2-2: Master page concept

LISTING 2-1: Sample master page—SiteTemplate.master

```
<!-- File: SiteTemplate.master -->
<%@ Master Language="C#" %>

<html xmlns="http://www.w3.org/1999/xhtml" >
  <head runat="server">
    <title>Default title</title>
  </head>
  <body>
   <form runat="server">
    <h2>Common header</h2>

    <asp:ContentPlaceHolder  runat="server"
                        ID="_mainContentPlaceHolder" />

    <h2>Common footer</h2>

     <asp:ContentPlaceHolder ID="_footerContentPlaceHolder"
                        runat="server">
      Copyright © 2006, My Company, Inc.
     </asp:ContentPlaceHolder>
   </form>
  </body>
</html>
```

Content pages, in contrast, are just ordinary .aspx files that specify an associated master page in their page directive using the MasterPageFile attribute. These pages must contain only instances of the Content control, as their sole purpose is to supply content for the inherited master page template. Each Content control must map to a specific ContentPlaceHolder control defined in the referenced master page, the contents of which will be inserted into the master page's placeholder at rendering time. The content page in Listing 2-2 provides content for the SiteTemplate.master master page shown earlier.

LISTING 2-2: Sample content page—Default.aspx

```
<%-- file: default.aspx--%>
<%@ Page Language="C#"
    MasterPageFile="SiteTemplate.master" Title="Home Page" %>

<asp:Content ContentPlaceHolderID="_mainContentPlaceHolder"
            ID="_mainContent" runat="server">
  This is the content for the default page.
</asp:Content>
```

Note that with this mechanism we are able to specify content to be placed at very specific locations in the master page template. The example in Listing 2-2 shows how the subtle problem of generating unique page titles with templates is solved easily by using the new Title attribute of the @Page directive. This Title attribute works with any page (even one that is not using a master page) as long as the <head> element is marked with runat="server", but it is particularly useful when using master pages since content pages inherit their title from master pages by default. Listing 2-2 also illustrates how master pages can supply default content for placeholders, so if the content page decides not to provide a Content control for a particular placeholder, it will have a default rendering.

With the fundamental mechanics of master pages in place, we can now revisit the templated example shown in Figure 2-1. This example defines a master page containing replaceable-content placeholder controls for the header, navigation bar, and footer. The master page template lays out the page using these elements, and the content page supplies the inner content for the page. Figure 2-3 shows the rendering of this example using master and content pages.

Even more compelling is the fact that master pages are understood by the designer in Visual Studio 2005. When you are visually editing a content page, it displays the content of the inherited master page in a grayed out region, so it is obvious what the ultimate rendering of the page will look like. Figure 2-4 shows our continuing example of using master pages as it would appear when editing a content page affiliated with our master page.

Implementation Details

The implementation of master and content pages is quite similar to the approach taken by many developers building their own custom templating mechanism in ASP.NET 1.x. In particular, the MasterPage class derives from UserControl and thus inherits the same generic container functionality that user controls provide. The templates defined by master pages are injected into the generated control hierarchy for the requested page. This injection happens just before the Page class' Init event; this way, all of the controls will be in place prior to Init, when it is common to perform programmatic manipulation of controls. The actual merging of the master page's control hierarchy and the page's control hierarchy is performed as follows:

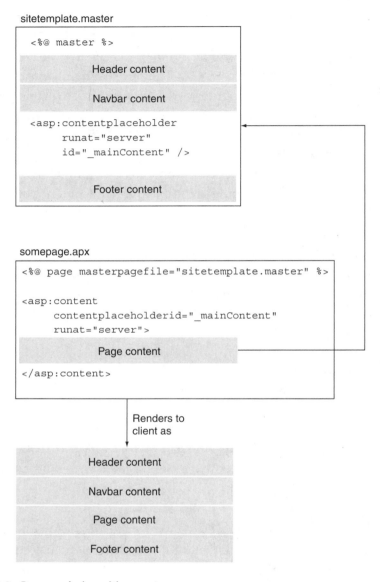

FIGURE 2-3: Page rendering with a master page

1. The top-level control of the master page (which will be named the same as the file containing the master page) will be inserted as the root control in the new page hierarchy.

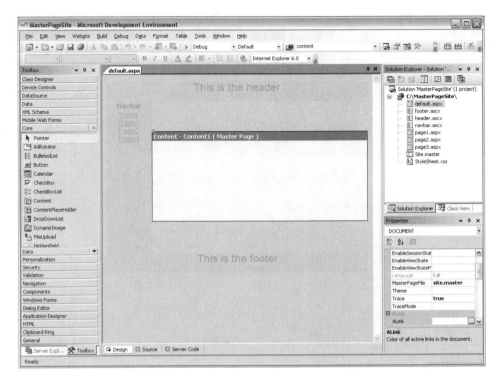

FIGURE 2-4: Designer support for master pages in Visual Studio 2005

2. The contents of each Content control in the page is then injected as a collection of child controls underneath the corresponding Content-PlaceHolder control.

Figure 2-5 shows a sample content page with an associated master page and the resulting merged control hierarchy that is created just prior to the Init event during the page processing.

One of the implications of this implementation is that the master page itself is just another control in your Page class' hierarchy, and you can perform any of the tasks you are used to performing on controls with the master page directly. The current master page associated with any given page is always available via the Master property accessor. As an example of interacting with the master page, in the default.aspx page shown in Figure 2-5 you could add code to programmatically access the HtmlForm that was implicitly added by the master page, as shown in Listing 2-3.

sitetemplate.master

```
<%@ master language="C#" %>

<html>
  <head>
    <title>
      <asp:contentplaceholder runat="server" id="_titleContent">
        Standard title
      </asp:contentplaceholder>
    </title>
  </head>
  <body>
        <form id="_theForm" runat="server">
          <h2>Common header</h2>

          <asp:contentplaceholder runat="server" id="_mainContent" />

          <h2>Common footer</h2>
        </form>
  </body>
</html>
```

default.aspx

```
<%@ page language="C#" masterpagefile="sitetemplate.master" %>

<asp:content contentplaceholderid="_titleContent" runat="server">
Main page
</asp:content>
<asp:content contentplaceholderid="_mainContent" runat="server">
                This is the content for the default page.
</asp:content>
```

Merge to generate

Resulting page hierarchy

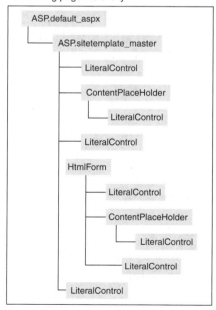

FIGURE 2-5: Master page/content page merged hierarchy

LISTING 2-3: Programmatic access to master page controls

```
void Page_Load(object sender, EventArgs e)
{
  HtmlForm f = (HtmlForm)Master.FindControl("_theForm");
  if (f != null)
  {
    // use f here...
  }
}
```

Working with Master Pages

It is a fairly common requirement to change some aspects of a master page depending on when and where it is being applied. For example, you may want to selectively enable or disable a collection of links in a master page based on which page is currently being accessed. While something like this is possible using the programmatic access to controls on the master page described earlier, it is generally better to build logic into your master page to manipulate the controls and to expose that logic as methods or properties on the master page. For example, Listing 2-4 shows a master page with a panel control containing a set of hyperlink controls, along with a corresponding property, ShowNavigationLinks, that controls the visibility of these links.

LISTING 2-4: Master page exposing a property

```
<%-- File: SiteTemplate.master --%>
<%@ Master Language="C#" %>

<script runat="server">
  public bool ShowNavigationLinks
  {
    get { return _navigationLinksPanel.Visible; }
    set { _navigationLinksPanel.Visible = value; }
  }
</script>

<html xmlns="http://www.w3.org/1999/xhtml" >
<head runat="server">
    <title>Default title</title>
</head>
<body>
    <form id="form1" runat="server">
    <!-- ... -->
```

continues

```
        <asp:Panel runat="server" id="_navigationLinksPanel">
          <asp:HyperLink ID="homeHyperLink" runat="server"
              NavigateUrl="~/Default.aspx">Home</asp:HyperLink><br />
          <asp:HyperLink ID="page1HyperLink" runat="server"
              NavigateUrl="~/Page1.aspx">Page 1</asp:HyperLink><br />
          <asp:HyperLink ID="page2HyperLink" runat="server"
              NavigateUrl="~/Page2.aspx">Page 2</asp:HyperLink>
        </asp:Panel>
        <!-- ... -->
        </form>
      </body>
</html>
```

A particular page could then access the master page via the Master property of the Page class, cast the result to the master page type, and set the ShowNavigationLinks property of the master page to true or false. Listing 2-5 shows a sample content page that disables the links via the exposed property.

LISTING 2-5: Content page accessing master page property

```
<%@ Page Language="C#" MasterPageFile="~/SiteTemplate.master" %>

<script runat="server">
  protected void Page_Load(object sender, EventArgs e)
  {
    ((ASP.sitetemplate_master)Master).ShowNavigationLinks = false;
  }
</script>
<!-- ... -->
```

You can take this one step further and eliminate the cast by using the MasterType directive in the content page. Adding a MasterType directive causes ASP.NET to generate a typesafe version of the Page class' Master property that is strongly typed to the master page referenced in the Virtual-Path attribute. It essentially takes care of doing the cast for you, with the added advantage of IntelliSense in Visual Studio 2005 showing you all of the properties defined in your master page. Listing 2-6 shows an example of using the MasterType directive to create this strongly typed accessor and the simplified code for modifying the same property we modified before.

LISTING 2-6: Strongly typed access using the MasterType directive

```
<%@ Page Language="C#" MasterPageFile="~/SiteTemplate.master" %>
<%@ MasterType VirtualPath="~/SiteTemplate.master" %>
```

```
<script runat="server">
  protected void Page_Load(object sender, EventArgs e)
  {
    Master.ShowNavigationLinks = false;
  }
</script>
<!-- ... -->
```

The MasterType directive also supports a TypeName attribute that you can use instead of the VirtualPath attribute if, for example, you don't want to create a hard-coded affiliation between your content page and its master page. You might find it useful to create multiple master pages that could be applied to a page based on some criterion (like a user preference stored in profile or the request's time of day). In this case you couldn't use the Virtual-Path attribute, as the cast would fail if the master page changed. Instead, you could create a base class that inherits from MasterPage, add the necessary properties and methods to that base class, and then have all of your master pages inherit from that common master page base class. Your pages would then use the TypeName attribute in their MasterType directive to gain strongly typed access to the common base class.

Listings 2-7, 2-8, and 2-9 show a sample common base class, a master page that inherits from that base class, and a content page that uses the TypeName attribute to strongly type the Master property to the shared base class, respectively.

LISTING 2-7: Common master page base class

```
// File: CommonMasterPage.cs
namespace EssentialAspDotNet
{
  public abstract class CommonMasterPage : MasterPage
  {
    public abstract bool ShowNavigationLinks {get; set; }
  }
}
```

LISTING 2-8: Master page inheriting from a common master page base class

```
<%--File: SiteTemplate.master--%>
<%@ Master Language="C#" Inherits="EssentialAspDotNet.CommonMasterPage"
%>

<script runat="server">
  public override bool ShowNavigationLinks
```

continues

```
  {
    get { return _navigationLinksPanel.Visible; }
    set { _navigationLinksPanel.Visible = value; }
  }
</script>
<!-- ... -->
```

LISTING 2-9: Strongly typed access to a common master page base class in a content page

```
<%@ Page Language="C#" MasterPageFile="~/SiteTemplate.master" %>
<%@ MasterType TypeName="EssentialAspDotNet.CommonMasterPage" %>

<script runat="server">
  protected void Page_Load(object sender, EventArgs e)
  {
    Master.ShowNavigationLinks = false;
  }
</script>
<!-- ... -->
```

Using a common base class for a master page makes the most sense if you plan on having multiple master pages that could be affiliated with a page and then adding the ability to change the affiliation at runtime. To change the master page affiliation, you can use the MasterPageFile property, which is exposed as a public property on the Page class and can be modified in the code for any page. Any modifications to this property must be made in a handler for the PreInit event of the Page class for it to take effect, since the creation of and merging with the master page happens just prior to the Init event firing. Keep in mind that if you do change the master page programmatically, the new master page must have the same set of ContentPlaceHolder controls with matching identifiers as the original master page; otherwise, the mapping between Content controls and their corresponding placeholders will break.

The override of the OnPreInit method in Listing 2-10 could be added to any Page class using a master page to programmatically change the master page affiliation.

LISTING 2-10: Changing the master page at runtime

```
protected override void OnPreInit(EventArgs e)
{
  this.MasterPageFile = "AlternateSiteTemplate.master";

  base.OnPreInit(e);
}
```

Details of Usage

As you begin to use master pages in your site design, you will run into some issues that may not have occurred before if you have never used a site-level templating mechanism. The first issue is that of relative paths in referenced resources like images or stylesheets. When you are creating a master page, you must keep in mind that the directory from which relative paths are going to be evaluated may very well change based on the page being accessed. Consider the directory structure of the site shown in Figure 2-6.

If you were to add a reference to the Check.gif image in the images directory from the Site.master in the masterpages directory, you might be tempted to add a simple image element like this:

```
<img src="../images/check.gif" />
```

Unfortunately, this would only work for pages that were in a similar relative directory location to the image as the master page was (like

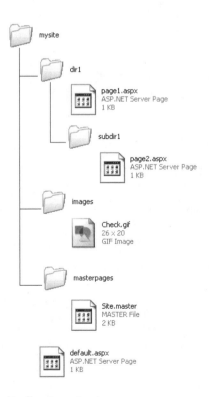

FIGURE 2-6: Sample Web site directory structure

page1.aspx). Any other page (like default.aspx) would not correctly resolve the relative path. One solution to this problem is to use the root path reference syntax in ASP.NET and ensure that all relative references are made from server-side controls (which is the only place this syntax works). So the preceding image reference would become:

```
<img src="~/images/check.gif" runat="server" />
```

Another option is to rely on the fact that relative path references in server-side controls are evaluated relative to the master page in which they are placed. This means that it would also be sufficient to change the image reference to:

```
<img src="../images/check.gif" runat="server" />
```

Server-side path references in pages that reference master pages are still relative to the page itself, so you should not have to change any techniques you may already have in place to deal with relative references in pages.

Another common request when ASP.NET developers first encounter master pages is to somehow enforce that all pages in an application be required to be content pages referencing a specific master page. While there is no "must use" attribute, you can designate a master page to be used by default for all pages in an application by adding a pages element to your web.config file specifying a common master page:

```
<configuration>
  <pages masterPageFile="~/sitetemplate.master" />
</configuration>
```

Like any settings specified at the application level, individual pages can elect to override the default masterPageFile attribute, but adding this to your configuration file will guarantee that no pages will be added to your application accidentally without an associated master page.

Finally, you may find that it is useful to have a "meta" master page, that is, a master page for a set of master pages. Master pages support arbitrarily deep nesting, so you can create whatever level of master pages you decide makes sense for your application. Just like pages that have master pages, master pages that have master pages must consist exclusively of Content controls. Within these Content controls, master pages can then add additional ContentPlaceHolder controls for the actual pages to use. Note that pages that reference a master page which itself has a master page can only provide Content elements for ContentPlaceHolder controls on the immediate parent master page. There is no way to directly populate placeholders on a master page two or more levels up from a particular page. As an example, consider the master page definition (in a file called MetaTemplate.master) in Listing 2-11.

LISTING 2-11: Master page for other master pages (MetaTemplate.master)

```
<%@ Master %>

<html xmlns="http://www.w3.org/1999/xhtml" >
  <head runat="server">
    <title>Default title</title>
  </head>
  <body>
  <form id="_theForm" runat="server">
  <h2>Header</h2>
  <asp:ContentPlaceHolder runat="server"
          id="_mainContentPlaceHolder" />
  <h2>Footer</h2>
 </form>
  </body>
</html>
```

We can now define another master page, which in turn specifies this master page as its master and provides Content elements for each of the ContentPlaceHolder controls in the parent master page, as shown in Listing 2-12.

LISTING 2-12: Master page using another master page

```
<%@ Master MasterPageFile="~/MetaTemplate.master" %>

<asp:Content runat="server"
            ContentPlaceHolderID="_mainContentPlaceHolder">
  <table>
    <tr>
      <td><asp:ContentPlaceHolder ID="_leftContentPlaceHolder"
              runat="server" /></td>
      <td><asp:ContentPlaceHolder id="_rightContentPlaceHolder"
              runat="server" /></td>
    </tr>
  </table>
</asp:Content>
```

You may also find it useful to create alternate master pages based on the user agent string (browser type) sent by the client. If you want to leverage some browser-specific features in your master page, it may make sense to create multiple versions of the master page for the variations across browser types. ASP.NET 2.0 supports device filters to do this declaratively, which are prefix strings that you can apply to the MasterPageFile attribute to indicate which browser type should map to which master page. Prefix strings map to .browser files that have regular expressions defined to determine which browser is being used to access the site from the user agent string. You can include other device filter strings by adding additional .browser files to your local App_Browsers directory. Keep in mind that, as in the earlier example of dynamic master pages, each master page must have the same set of ContentPlaceHolder controls for this technique to work properly. Listing 2-13 shows a sample content page with alternate master page files specified for Internet Explorer (IE) and Mozilla browsers.

LISTING 2-13: Using device filters to declaratively select a master page

```
<%@ Page Language="C#"
    MasterPageFile="~/SiteTemplate.master"
    ie:MasterPageFile="~/IESiteTemplate.master"
    mozilla:MasterPageFile="~/FirefoxSiteTemplate.master" %>
<!-- ... -->
```

Themes and Skins

The other major user interface consolidation feature ASP.NET 2.0 introduces is the ability to create themes for your sites. A **theme** is a collection of user interface elements, like stylesheets, images, and skins, consolidated into a single directory, which can then be applied to an individual page across all pages in a site. Once you have defined a theme for use in your site, you can create a copy of that theme and make changes to the interface elements to create an alternate look and feel that can be applied to pages in your site as well, giving your site the ability to take on different "skins." These skins can be applied statically through Page attributes, or dynamically, often in response to user preferences. Figure 2-7 shows an example of two different skins being applied to a page that alter the appearance of controls on that page.

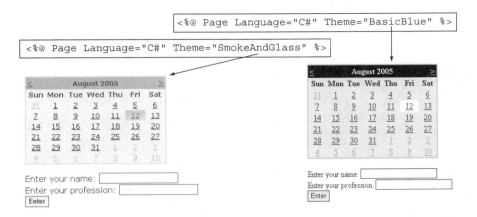

FIGURE 2-7: Theme concept

Themes

Technically, a theme is a subdirectory beneath a site's top level App_Themes directory. The name of each subdirectory becomes a theme available for applications within the site. Inside the directory, you can place .skin files, .css files, other files that may be referenced by .skin or .css files (like image files, JScript files, text files, etc.), and additional subdirectories containing resource files that may be referenced by .skin or .css files (like /images or /scripts). The advantage of including .css files in a theme directory is that every page with this theme applied will have a link added to its <head> element for each .css file in the theme. In addition, references to files contained in subdirectories are implicitly prefixed with the full virtual path to the subdirectory containing the resource, so they are valid from any page in the site. Both .css files as well as .skin files (which we will discuss next) must be placed at the top level of a theme directory to take effect.

Skin files are conceptually like cascading stylesheets for ASP.NET server-side controls. A .skin file consists of a collection of control declarations with properties (you can apply any properties you like, but you can't include an ID attribute). The properties defined by each control will be applied to all instances of that control on pages to which the enclosing theme is applied. For example, Listing 2-14 shows a skin file (Day.skin) that shows three different control declarations with several properties populated. When this skin file is applied to a page, all instances of Button, Calendar, and TextBox controls will take on the properties defined in the skin when the page is prepared for rendering, as shown in Figure 2-8.

```
<%@ Page Language="C#" Theme="Day" %>
...
Enter your name:
<asp:TextBox ID="nameTextBox" runat="server" /><br />
Enter your profession:
<asp:TextBox ID="professionTextBox" runat="server" /><br />
<asp:Calendar runat="server" />
<asp:Button ID="enterButton" runat="server" Text="Enter"
            OnClick="enterButton_Click" />
```

```
Enter your name:
<asp:TextBox ID="nameTextBox" runat="server"
            backcolor="#99ffff" forecolor="#FF3333" /><br />
Enter your profession:
<asp:TextBox ID="professionTextBox" runat="server"
            backcolor="#99ffff" forecolor="#FF3333" /><br />
<asp:Calendar runat="server" borderstyle="Solid"
            borderwidth="2px" bordercolor="#66ff66"
            backcolor="#99ffff" />
<asp:Button ID="enterButton" runat="server" Text="Enter"
        borderstyle="Solid" borderwidth="2px" bordercolor="#66ff66"
        backcolor="#99ffff" OnClick="enterButton_Click" />
```

FIGURE 2-8: Applying skins

LISTING 2-14: Sample skin file for use in a theme

```
<%-- File: Day.skin --%>
<asp:button runat="server" borderstyle="Solid"
            borderwidth="2px" bordercolor="#66ff66"
            backcolor="#99ffff" />

<asp:calendar runat="server" borderstyle="Solid"
            borderwidth="2px" bordercolor="#66ff66"
            backcolor="#99ffff" />

<asp:TextBox runat="server" backcolor="#99ffff" forecolor="#FF3333" />
```

The combination of stylesheets, skin files, and local image references means that themes encapsulate most of the common user interface elements you work with when building Web applications. The ability to group all of these elements together into one location that can be replicated and altered as desired is a powerful feature. Even if you don't plan on using themes as a way of "skinning" your application, the ability to isolate all of these files in one location with support for applying them across your entire site is reason enough to begin using themes.

Figure 2-9 shows a complete picture of how themes consolidate all of these elements together. The theme shown consists of a .css file, a .skin file containing formatting for a Calendar control, and an /images directory. When the page is constructed on the server, the theme is applied and the Calendar control inherits the styles defined by the Calendar control in the MyTheme.skin file. This process all happens on the server as the page and its controls are constructed. Note how the stylesheet (MyTheme.css) is implicitly added using a text/css link element in the <head> portion of the rendered page. Also note that the style attributes applied to the Calendar control impact the rendering of the Calendar as a <table> element to the client.

Working with Themes

At this point you might be wondering, "What happens if a page to which a theme is applied has already defined attributes for a control that is specified in a .skin file of the theme?" It actually depends on how the theme is

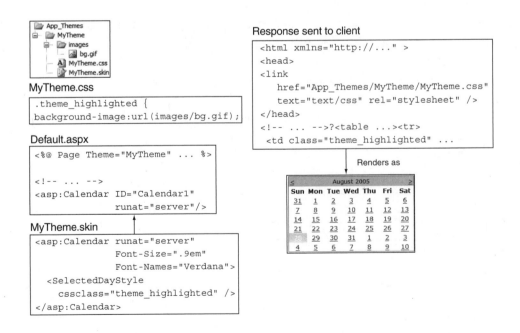

FIGURE 2-9: Theme application

applied. If you use the standard Theme attribute on an @Page directive to apply the theme, the attributes for a control defined in a skin file are applied on top of any attributes defined locally. That is, attributes defined in the theme override attributes defined locally, and in general the two sets of attributes are merged. This can lead to some interesting results if you're not careful, since the designer of the page may not have anticipated that a theme would be augmenting and overriding properties she had defined.

The alternative way to apply a theme to a page is to use the StyleSheetTheme attribute instead. Applying a theme with this attribute will not override local values, and is so named because it behaves more like CSS stylesheets do with HTML elements—they define properties that are applied if no other property has been defined. For example, to apply our Day theme via the StyleSheetTheme attribute, we could write:

```
<%@ Page StyleSheetTheme="Day" %>
```

You can also define multiple skins for a single control in a .skin file if you use the SkinID attribute. This is a convenient way to create an alternate appearance for a particular control and have controls select the skin by using the same SkinID attribute when declared on a page, in much the same way you might define a class attribute for an HTML element to apply the attributes of a stylesheet class. Note that if a control on a page does not specify a SkinID attribute, it will always use the default skin (the one without any SkinID attribute in the .skin file). Listing 2-15 shows a sample .skin file that contains two skins for the TextBox control.

LISTING 2-15: Using SkinID to create multiple control skins

```
<!-- FallTheme.skin -->
<asp:TextBox runat="server" backcolor="DarkRed" />
<asp:TextBox runat="server" backcolor="DarkRed"
             Font-StrikeOut="true" SkinID="strikeOut" />
```

Much like master pages, themes can be applied globally by using the pages element in your configuration file:

```
<!-- file: web.config -->
<configuration>
  <pages theme="Day" />
</configuration>
```

You can also exempt a particular control from having a theme applied to it by using the EnableTheming="false" attribute. Pages can exempt themselves from any global theme application with the same attribute.

Also like master pages, themes can be set programmatically in the PreInit event of the Page class. It is even more likely that you will want to set the theme of a page programmatically, especially if you have created multiple themes and want to let users choose the look and feel of the site themselves.

Listing 2-16 shows an example of setting the theme programmatically in a page. Note that this is really the only place to set a theme; there is no built-in way to programmatically set the theme for an entire site. Unfortunately, this is often what is needed, so it is worth looking at how to accomplish setting the theme globally in code. One way is to create a common base Page-derived class that all of your pages inherit from and set the theme in the PreInit handler of that class. Another way is to trap the Pre-RequestHandlerExecute event in your HttpApplication class and add a handler to the PreInit event to set the theme there. Listing 2-17 shows an example of this latter technique using the global.asax file.

LISTING 2-16: Changing a theme at runtime

```
protected override void OnPreInit(EventArgs e)
{
  this.Theme = "Night";

  base.OnPreInit(e);
}
```

LISTING 2-17: Changing the theme globally at runtime

```
<%--File: Global.asax--%>
<%@ Application Language="C#" %>
<script runat="server">
    void Application_PreRequestHandlerExecute(object src, EventArgs e)
    {
        Page p = this.Context.Handler as Page;
        if (p != null)
        {
            p.PreInit += new EventHandler(page_PreInit);
        }
    }

    void page_PreInit(object sender, EventArgs e)
    {
```

continues

```
            // Note that you could retrieve the theme from
            // anywhere at this point (most likely Profile as shown here).
            //
            Page p = this.Context.Handler as Page;

            if (p != null)
    {
                p.Theme = (string)Context.Profile["theme"];
        }
    }
</script>
```

Fundamentals of Navigation Controls

In addition to the two major platform features of master pages and themes targeted at simplifying user interface development, ASP.NET 2.0 also adds three new controls to aid in building navigational features into your Web applications, collectively called the **navigation controls**. Each of these controls—the TreeView, Menu, and SiteMapPath—are typically populated by an XML file named web.sitemap placed in the root of your application. This file contains the navigational structure of your site described using a predefined schema. The TreeView control provides a standard rendering of a hierarchical collection of items presented as a tree complete with collapsible and expandable nodes. The Menu control renders that same hierarchical data as a menu, with a wide range of options ranging from a static collection of links on a page to a completely dynamic DHTML menu that expands on demand. The SiteMapPath control is the simplest of the three; it displays the current page the client has navigated to, with links to parent pages in the navigational structure of the site to allow easy upward traversal of the site, a feature colloquially called "bread crumbs" in reference to its ability to take you back to where you were.

Each of these controls relies indirectly on the presence of a class called SiteMapProvider, which is an abstract class defining methods for retrieving the navigation information for a site, as well as indicating which node in the navigation information is currently active based on the URL the client has requested. The default SiteMapProvider implementation is the XmlSiteMapProvider, which looks for the web.sitemap file in the root of the application for its navigation information. Figure 2-10 shows sample

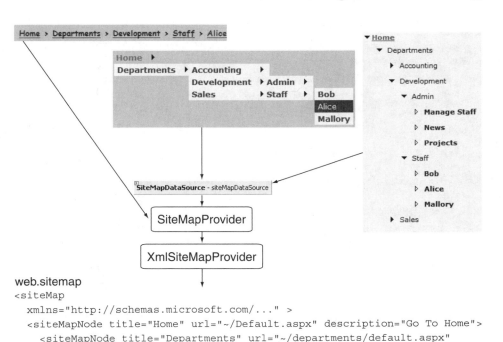

```
web.sitemap
<siteMap
  xmlns="http://schemas.microsoft.com/..." >
  <siteMapNode title="Home" url="~/Default.aspx" description="Go To Home">
    <siteMapNode title="Departments" url="~/departments/default.aspx"
        description="Go To Departments page">  ...
```

FIGURE 2-10: Navigation control architecture

displays of each of these three controls, along with their respective relationship to the web.sitemap file and the provider and data sources that supply the XML content to the controls. Note that the SiteMapPath control communicates directly with the SiteMapProvider, while the Menu and TreeView controls rely on a data source control which talks to the provider.

To take advantage of these three navigation controls, you first need to set up a web.sitemap file that describes the navigational structure of your site. This XML file consists of a top-level siteMap element with siteMapNode elements as children, which can be nested as needed to describe the paths of navigation in your site. Listing 2-18 shows a sample web.sitemap file for a simple site. Note that the organization of these elements need not reflect the physical layout of your site (although they often will), but rather the way in which users navigate from page to page.

LISTING 2-18: Sample web.sitemap file

```xml
<?xml version="1.0" encoding="utf-8" ?>

<siteMap xmlns="http://schemas.microsoft.com/AspNet/SiteMap-File-1.0" >
  <siteMapNode title="Home" url="~/Default.aspx"
                 description="Go To Home">
    <siteMapNode title="Page1.aspx" url="~/Page1.aspx"
                   description="Go to page 1" />
    <siteMapNode title="Page2.aspx" url="~/Page2.aspx"
                   description="Go to page 2" />
    <siteMapNode title="Departments"  url="~/departments/default.aspx"
                   description="Go To Departments page">
      <siteMapNode title="Accounting"
                   url="~/departments/accounting/default.aspx"
                   description="Go to accounting">
        <siteMapNode title="Admin"
                     url="~/departments/accounting/admin/default.aspx"
                     description="Go To accounting administration">
          <siteMapNode title="Manage Staff"
                url="~/departments/accounting/admin/managestaff.aspx"
                description="Go to manage staff"/>
          <siteMapNode title="News"
                       url="~/departments/accounting/admin/News.aspx"
                       description="Go to news"/>
          <siteMapNode title="Projects"
                  url="~/departments/accounting/admin/Projects.aspx"
                  description="Go to projects"/>
        </siteMapNode>
        <siteMapNode title="Staff"
                     url="~/departments/accounting/staff/default.aspx"
                     description="Go To accounting staff">
          <siteMapNode title="Kathy"
                       url="~/departments/accounting/staff/kathy.aspx"
                       description="Go To Kathy"/>
          <siteMapNode title="Joe"
                       url="~/departments/accounting/staff/Joe.aspx"
                       description="Go To Joe"/>
          <siteMapNode title="Lisa"
                       url="~/departments/accounting/staff/Lisa.aspx"
                       description="Go To Lisa"/>
        </siteMapNode>
      </siteMapNode>
    </siteMapNode>
  </siteMapNode>
</siteMap>
```

With the web.sitemap file in place and populated correctly, you can now add any of the three navigation controls to your site. The SiteMapPath control will work without any additional setup; you simply place it on the page and it queries the SiteMapProvider to retrieve the navigational data. The Menu and TreeView controls must be configured using a SiteMap-DataSource control, which in turn will use the SiteMapProvider to retrieve the information. This extra level of indirection makes it possible to use both the Menu and TreeView controls for other tasks besides displaying navigation. Listing 2-19 shows a sample master page with all three controls in place laid out in a table. This example shows each control without any style attributes applied, but be aware that all three controls can be customized extensively to take on whatever appearance you need.

LISTING 2-19: Sample master page with navigation controls

```
<%--File: SimpleSiteTemplate.master--%>
<%@ Master Language="C#" %>

<html xmlns="http://www.w3.org/1999/xhtml" >
<head runat="server">
    <title>My site</title>
</head>
<body>
    <form id="form1" runat="server">

    <table>
      <tr>
        <td>
            <asp:Menu ID="_mainMenu"
                runat="server"DataSourceID="_siteMapDataSource" />
            <asp:SiteMapDataSource ID="_siteMapDataSource"
                runat="server" />
        </td>
      </tr>
      <tr>
        <td>
          <asp:SiteMapPath ID="_mainSiteMapPath" runat="server" />
        </td>
      </tr>
      <tr>
        <td>
          <asp:TreeView ID="_mainTree" runat="server"
                    DataSourceID="_siteMapDataSource" />
        </td>
        <td>
        <asp:ContentPlaceHolder id="_mainContentPlaceHolder"
            runat="server" />
        </td>
      </tr>
```

continues

```
      </table>
    </form>
</body>
</html>
```

Control Adapters

This release of ASP.NET introduces an alternate way to specify renderings of controls through a mechanism called **control adapters**. Originally designed to provide alternate renderings of standard controls for mobile devices, they actually serve a more general purpose of providing a way of completely changing the rendering of a control based on the client's browser type. In 2006, Microsoft released a supplemental set of examples, the **CSS Friendly Control Adapters,** that shows how to change the default tabular rendering of many controls like the Menu and FormView to render without tables and to take all of their style settings from cascading stylesheets. We will explore the control adapter architecture in this section and how you might adapt it to your own uses.

Building Control Adapters

At their core, control adapters are just a way of providing alternative renderings for controls without actually modifying the controls themselves. Because control adapters are designed to provide alternate renderings for different clients, you specify control adapter mappings in a .browser file, which is where associations between User Agent strings and browser capabilities are defined. The control adapter class itself must inherit from the System.Web.UI.Adapters.ControlAdapter, which is an abstract base class that looks much like the Control base class, and includes event methods for Init, Load, PreRender, and Unload, as well as a virtual Render method. Internally, when a control is rendering, the Control base class will first check to see if there is a control adapter currently associated with the control. If there is, it will invoke the Render method of the adapter; if not, it calls the standard Render method of the control. Figure 2-11 shows the control adapter architecture.

To create your own control adapter, you start by creating a new class that inherits from the ControlAdapter base class, or more commonly one of its derivatives, WebControlAdapter. Which control adapter class you

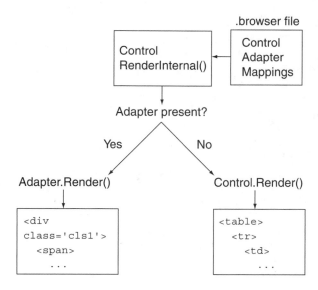

FIGURE 2-11: Control adapter architecture

derive from depends on what control you are building the adapter for. If it is one of the built-in WebControls, you should select the WebControl-Adapter, because it adds virtual RenderBeginTag, RenderEndTag, and RenderContents methods to more closely mirror how WebControls render. There are also more specific control adapters defined for data-bound controls and the Menu control, each of which provides more virtual methods to access and modify features of the controls it is associated with.

As an example of building a control adapter to change the rendering of a particular control, let's use the BulletedList and create a control adapter named BulletedListControlAdapter. BulletedList is a simple control that renders a collection of items as an ordered or unordered list (<ol> or <ul>). To show how flexible the adapter model is, we'll build the control adapter to completely change the rendering to be table-based instead. Since the BulletedList is derived from WebControl, we will start by creating the BulletedListControlAdapter class as a derivative of WebControlAdapter. Next, we'll override the RenderBeginTag and RenderEndTag methods to render the opening and closing tags of the table. Finally, we'll override RenderContents to iterate across the items of the BulletedList control and render each item as a single-cell row in the table prefixed with an asterisk. The full control adapter implementation is shown in Listing 2-20.

LISTING 2-20: Control adapter for the BulletedList control

```
namespace EssentialAspDotNet2.UIElements
{
  public class BulletedListControlAdapter :
                 WebControlAdapter
  {
    protected override void RenderBeginTag(HtmlTextWriter writer)
    {
      writer.WriteLine();
      writer.WriteBeginTag("table");
      writer.Write(HtmlTextWriter.TagRightChar);

      writer.Indent++;
    }

    protected override void RenderEndTag(HtmlTextWriter writer)
    {
      writer.WriteEndTag("table");

      writer.Indent--;
      writer.WriteLine();
    }

    protected override void RenderContents(HtmlTextWriter writer)
    {
      writer.Indent++;

      BulletedList bl = Control as BulletedList;
      if (bl != null)
      {
        foreach (ListItem i in bl.Items)
        {
          writer.WriteLine();
          writer.WriteBeginTag("tr");
          writer.Write(HtmlTextWriter.TagRightChar);
          writer.WriteLine();
          writer.Indent++;
          writer.WriteBeginTag("td");
          writer.Write(HtmlTextWriter.TagRightChar);
          writer.WriteLine();
          writer.Indent++;
          writer.Write("*");
          writer.Write(HtmlTextWriter.SpaceChar);
          writer.Write(i.Text);
          writer.WriteLine();
          writer.Indent--;
          writer.WriteEndTag("td");
          writer.WriteLine();
          writer.Indent--;
```

```
        writer.WriteEndTag("tr");
        writer.WriteLine();
      }
    }

    writer.Indent--;
  }
 }
}
```

The next step is to associate this new BulletedListControlAdapter class with the BulletedList control. As mentioned earlier, this is done by specifying which subset of browsers you want this to apply to. For now, we will simply associate all browsers with this adapter by specifying a refID attribute value of Default in the browser element of a .browser file. The next section covers how to create more granular associations. In this sample, a new file named MyAdapters.browser was created and placed in the application's App_Browsers directory (see Listing 2-21). Any additional browser definitions or control adapters defined in this local file will be added to the collection of browsers and adapters already defined in the system .browser configuration files.

LISTING 2-21: Contents of MyAdapters.browser file

```xml
<!-- File: MyAdapters.browser -->
<browsers>
  <browser refID="Default">
    <controlAdapters>
      <adapter
        controlType="System.Web.UI.WebControls.BulletedList"
        adapterType=
          "EssentialAspDotNet2.UIElements.BulletedListControlAdapter"
      />
    </controlAdapters>
  </browser>
</browsers>
```

The last step is to actually place an instance of the BulletedList control with some items on a page, as shown in Listing 2-22.

LISTING 2-22: Sample page with BulletedList control

```
<%-- File: Default.aspx --%>
<%@ Page Language="C#" %>
```

continues

```
<html xmlns="http://www.w3.org/1999/xhtml" >
<body>
    <form id="form1" runat="server">
    <div>
        <asp:BulletedList ID="_bulletedList" runat="server">
          <asp:ListItem Value="1">Item 1</asp:ListItem>
          <asp:ListItem Value="2">Item 2</asp:ListItem>
          <asp:ListItem Value="3">Item 3</asp:ListItem>
          <asp:ListItem Value="4">Item 4</asp:ListItem>
        </asp:BulletedList>
    </div>
    </form>
</body>
</html>
```

If we first run the page without the control adapter in place (by removing the .browser file or commenting out the control adapter mapping in the .browser file), the BulletedList will render as expected, using a <ul> element with <li> subelements.

```
<ul id="_bulletedList">
  <li>Item 1</li>
  <li>Item 2</li>
  <li>Item 3</li>
  <li>Item 4</li>
</ul>
```

If we then enable the control adapter, the rendering changes to our new table-based rendering defined in our custom adapter, with no changes at all to the actual .aspx page.

```
<table>
<tr>
  <td>
    * Item 1
  </td>
</tr>
  <tr>
  <td>
  * Item 2
  </td>
  </tr>
<tr>
  <td>
  * Item 3
  </td>
</tr>
```

```
<tr>
  <td>
    * Item 4
  </td>
</tr>
</table>
```

As you can see, it is reasonably simple to create an alternate rendering for a control using the control adapter architecture. There are, however, some issues that should be raised at this point. First of all, note that our simplified rendering of the BulletedList did not look at any of the attributes of the BulletedList control except its items collection. This includes the rather important BulletStyle attribute that determines what type of list to render (unordered, numeric, alphabetic, and so on). It is generally important to honor all of the behavioral attributes of a control for which you are writing a control adapter. Style attributes, on the other hand, may or may not make sense to incorporate into your rendering, especially if the target device for which the control adapter is being built does not have a means of displaying a particular style (for example, Back-Color on a black-and-white device). As you will see later in this chapter, the CSS Control Adapters elect to ignore most style attributes of controls they render, providing instead a set of CSS classes that can be modified to control appearance.

The other reason the simplified example of the BulletedListControl-Adapter is not a very realistic one is that we did not actually take advantage of the browser mapping to associate specific user agents with this adapter. Instead, we mapped all browser types (by specifying Default in the refID attribute) to use this control adapter, which means that a site with this control adapter installed would never call the standard rendering of the BulletedListControl, but would always display the rendering supplied by the control adapter. If the only purpose is to create a control that has a different rendering from an existing control, a better approach would probably be to derive a new control class from the existing control and override the necessary methods to change the rendering. The one other potential advantage to using control adapters over custom control derivatives is that they can be applied to a Web application with no modifications to any of the pages (or even the web.config file), so they may be compelling even without browser-contingent rendering for situations where an application is already written and deployed, but a rendering change is needed for a particular control across the entire site.

Browser Recognition

Control adapters are mapped to controls in a particular site by specifying a configuration element in a .browser file. In the 2.0 release of ASP.NET, the browser recognition capability was moved from the <browserCaps> element of the machine.config and web.config files to a collection of .browser files. The <browserCaps> element is still supported, but the preferred way to specify browser capabilities is with a .browser file located either in the local App_Browsers directory of your application or in the machine-wide %SYSTEM%\Microsoft.NET\Framework\v2.0.50727\Config\Browsers directory.

The purpose of browser recognition files, in addition to associating control adapters, is to populate the HttpBrowserCapabilities class for a given request, accessible through the Request.Browser property. Through this class you can find out the name of the requesting browser and whether it supports JavaScript, cookies, and so on. To populate this class, each .browser file contains one or more <browser> elements with a subelement called **identification**, which contains a regular expression that is applied to the User Agent string for each request (with an option to specify an exclusion expression as well). If it matches, the capabilities listed for that browser are used to populate the HttpBrowserCapabilities class. For example, the browser definition for Internet Explorer (found in the machine-wide Browsers directory in the file ie.browser) looks like this:

```
<browsers>
  <browser id="IE" parentID="Mozilla">
    <identification>
      <userAgent
       match="^Mozilla[^(]*\(([C|c]ompatible;\s*MSIE (?'ver-
sion'(?'major'\d+)(?'minor'\.\d+)(?'letters'\w*))(?'extra'[^)]*)" />
      <userAgent nonMatch="Opera|Go\.Web|Windows CE|EudoraWeb" />
    </identification>

    <capabilities>
      <capability name="browser" value="IE" />
      <capability name="extra"    value="${extra}" />
      <capability name="isColor" value="true" />
      <capability name="letters" value="${letters}" />
         . . .
```

Browsers are also grouped hierarchically using the parentID attribute on the <browser> element. In order for a <browser> element to be applied that has a parentID referencing another <browser> element, the regular expression conditions for the parent element must have succeeded. The root of the hierarchy is "Default," which matches all User Agent strings and assumes that the browser has minimal capabilities. All other browser types have either Default or one of its children as a parent. The predefined set of browser definitions located in the machine-wide Browsers directory contains a useful categorization of browser types, with associated names that can be used to identify subsets of browsers. For example, if you wanted to apply a control adapter to all requests made from Internet Explorer versions 6 and higher, you could use the "IE6to9" browser name in the refId attribute of your local browser element. Figure 2-12 shows the hierarchy of browser types defined in the system .browser files (excluding mobile devices, which constitute another hierarchy at least twice this size).

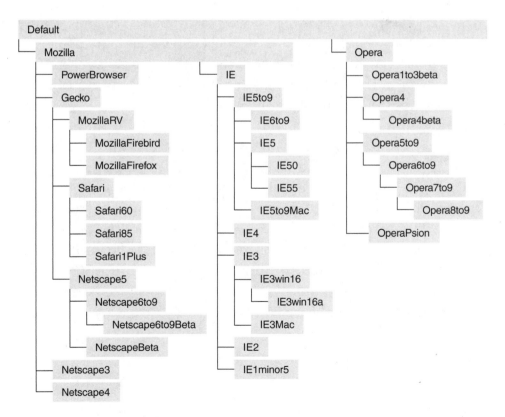

FIGURE 2-12: Browser type hierarchy

You can use any of these browser names in the refID attribute when assigning control adapters. As an example, the CSS Control Adapter toolkit enables their adapters for IE6to9, MozillaFirefox, Opera8to9, and Safari, which covers the subset of browsers that support the CSS features needed by the adapters defined in the toolkit. Other browsers will revert to the standard control renderings.

CSS Friendly Adapters

In April of 2006, Microsoft released a set of samples, CSS-friendly ASP.NET 2.0 control adapters Beta 1.1, which contains a suite of control adapters that change the rendering of several common ASP.NET controls to be more "CSS friendly." This was primarily in response to developers using ASP.NET wanting to specify all of the style attributes, including layout, for their controls using CSS stylesheets instead of primarily server-side attributes of controls. The initial release includes adapters for the Menu, TreeView, DetailsView, FormView, and DataList controls. Future releases of this toolkit (which will undoubtedly be out by the time this book is in print) will include enhancements to the adapters for these controls, plus adapters for additional controls. The toolkit is available for download from www.asp.net/cssadapters/.

SUMMARY

ASP.NET 2.0 introduces several features designed to simplify user interface development for Web applications. In the past, developers had to resort to third-party techniques and controls to create templatized, skinnable sites with full navigation features. Now it is easy to build identical sites with features provided natively in ASP.NET. In addition, each of these features is built in a modular, pluggable way so that replacing part or all of the implementation is entirely possible.

■ 3 ■
Data Binding

I N THIS CHAPTER, we look at the declarative data sources and the new data-bound controls introduced with ASP.NET 2.0. Of all the features introduced in this release, declarative data binding undoubtedly has the most impact on developers. Instead of programmatically populating controls with queries issued through ADO.NET, data source controls provide a way of populating controls with data declaratively. The end result is that developers end up writing much less code to accomplish the same tasks. This model is flexible enough to support many different types of data access as well, ranging from standard parameterized SQL statements to stored procedure calls to full-blown object-oriented data access layers.

Most of the samples shown in this chapter are based on a database called "moviereviews" that contains two tables: movies and reviews. Each table has a single primary key marked as an identity column, and there is a foreign key reference from the reviews table to the movies table. Listing 3-1 shows the creation script for these two tables.[1]

---

1. This script, as well as an accompanying sample data creation script, is available for download as part of the sample collection for this book at http://pluralsight.com/essentialasp.net2/.

LISTING 3-1: Creation script for moviereviews sample database

```
CREATE TABLE movies (
  movie_id              INT IDENTITY(1,1) NOT NULL
                          CONSTRAINT pk_movies PRIMARY KEY CLUSTERED,
  title                 NVARCHAR(64) NOT NULL,
  release_date          DATETIME NOT NULL
)
GO


CREATE TABLE reviews (
  review_id    INT IDENTITY(1,1) NOT NULL
                 CONSTRAINT pk_reviews PRIMARY KEY CLUSTERED,
  movie_id     INT NOT NULL CONSTRAINT fk_reviews_movies
                 FOREIGN KEY (movie_id) REFERENCES movies (movie_id),
  summary      VARCHAR(64) NOT NULL,
  rating       INT NOT NULL,
  review       NVARCHAR(512) NOT NULL,
  reviewer     NVARCHAR(64) NULL
)
GO
```

Declarative Data Binding

This section reviews the fundamentals of data binding in ASP.NET, and then introduces the new declarative model that comes with ASP.NET 2.0.

Data Binding

The core features of data binding remain the same in this release of ASP.NET. Controls that support data binding expose a property named DataSource and a method called DataBind(). When a page is loaded, the user of the control initializes the DataSource property to some collection of data, such as an array, a DataReader, or a DataSet. When the data source is ready to be read from, the user of the control calls the DataBind() method on the control, at which point the control reads in all the data from the data source, making a local copy of it. When the page is ultimately rendered, the control takes the cached data it retrieved from the data source and renders its contents into the response buffer in whatever format the control is built to provide. Figure 3-1 shows the data-binding process for a control.

Several controls support data binding, including simple controls, such as the ListBox, and controls designed exclusively for data binding, such as

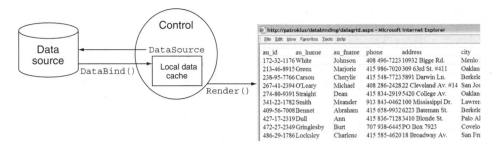

Figure 3-1: Data-binding process

the GridView and DetailsView. As an example of a common use of data binding, Listing 3-2 shows a page that contains a GridView which is data-bound to the "authors" table in the "pubs" database in SQL Server. This example uses a DataReader to retrieve the data, and it takes care to invoke the DataBind() method immediately after the data reader is prepared and before the connection is closed.

Listing 3-2: Imperative data binding

```
<%@ Page Language="C#" %>
<%@ Import Namespace="System.Data.SqlClient" %>

<script runat="server">
  protected void Page_Load(object sender, EventArgs e)
  {
    if (!IsPostBack)
    {
      using (SqlConnection conn =
        new SqlConnection("database=pubs;trusted_connection=yes"))
      using (SqlCommand cmd =
        new SqlCommand("SELECT au_id, au_fname, au_lname FROM authors",
                  conn))
      {
        conn.Open();
        SqlDataReader reader = cmd.ExecuteReader();
        _authorsGridView.DataSource = reader;
        _authorsGridView.DataBind();
      }
    }
  }
</script>
```

continues

```
<html xmlns="http://www.w3.org/1999/xhtml" >
<head runat="server">
    <title>ImperativeDataBinding</title>
</head>
<body>
    <form id="form1" runat="server">
    <div>
      <asp:GridView runat="server" ID="_authorsGridView" />
    </div>
    </form>
</body>
</html>
```

Data Source Controls

While the core concepts of data binding remain unchanged in this release, the way in which you perform data binding has changed. Instead of programmatically populating the DataSource property of a control and invoking the DataBind() method, you typically create the association declaratively using one of the new data source controls. A **data source control** is an abstraction of the retrieval and propagation of data from and to a data repository (typically a SQL database), and it takes care of making the necessary ADO.NET calls to interact with the database. For example, we can rewrite the data-binding example shown in Listing 3-2 using the new Sql-DataSource control to perform the data retrieval in exactly the same way, but without the need to actually write the data access code. Listing 3-3 shows a page that uses declarative data binding with the SqlDataSource control to populate a GridView with the list of authors from the pubs database, as we did earlier.

LISTING 3-3: Declarative data binding with SqlDataSource

```
<asp:GridView ID="_authorsGridView" runat="server"
                 DataSourceID="_authorsDataSource" />

<asp:SqlDataSource ID="_authorsDataSource" runat="server"
     DataSourceMode="DataReader"
     ConnectionString="database=pubs;trusted_connection=yes"
     SelectCommand="SELECT au_id, au_fname, au_lname FROM Authors" />
```

There are two key differences to the way declarative data binding works when contrasted with imperative data binding. First of all, the control to which the data is being bound must specify the DataSourceID property to declaratively associate itself with the data source control. Second, it is no longer necessary to write any code to perform the data retrieval, as the GridView knows when it needs the data and the SqlDataSource knows how to retrieve it; it happens during the course of the page execution. Note that the example in Listing 3-3 specified a DataSourceMode of DataReader to make the example technically identical to our earlier imperative example. You can see that the connection string and the SELECT query contain enough information for the SqlDataSource to perform the ADO.NET calls to retrieve the data for the GridView. Figure 3-2 shows the relationship between a data-bound control, a data source control, and the repository of data being used.

Data Source Control Details

All data source controls implement the IDataSource interface shown in Listing 3-4, which has one important method: GetView(). This returns a

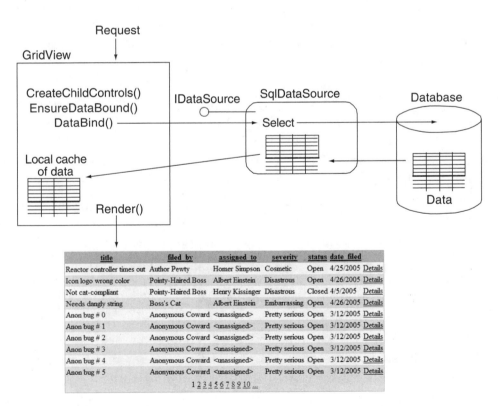

FIGURE 3-2: Relationship between a data-bound control, a data source control, and a database

class deriving from the abstract base class DataSourceView, shown in Listing 3-5, which provides the standard data source operations: Select, Insert, Update, and Delete. Although there is a decoupling between the data source and a particular "view" of that data through this interface, all of the data sources that ship with ASP.NET 2.0 provide only one view of the data. This view can always be retrieved by passing an empty string or null to the GetView method.

In addition, the Select method takes a reference to a DataSourceSelectArguments class, shown in Listing 3-6, which has the following public properties: MaximumRows, RetrieveTotalRowCount, SortExpression, StartRowIndex, and TotalRowCount. These properties can be populated prior to executing a Select to influence the results that are returned. In particular, the SortExpression provides sorting, and the MaximumRows, StartRowIndex, and TotalRowCount provide the ability to implement paging of the data returned from the data source. Before populating these properties on the DataSourceSelectArguments class, you can also query a particular data source for its capabilities. This is used by all of the data-bound controls to enable or disable features based on the capabilities of the data source to which they are bound. The query methods to ask about data source features include: CanDelete, CanInsert, CanPage, CanRetrieveTotalRowCount, CanSort, and CanUpdate.

A good example of these values changing is setting the data retrieval mode of a SqlDataSource from DataSet to DataReader. With a DataSet, there is implicit sorting through the SortExpression property exposed by the underlying DataSet. When you switch to DataReader mode, however, there is no implicit way to implement sorting, so the SqlDataSource will return False from the CanSort property. You will see this in the Visual Studio .NET designer: as you switch data source modes, an associated GridView will disable features that are no longer available through the data source.

Altogether, there are four data source controls provided in ASP.NET 2.0: SqlDataSource, ObjectDataSource, XmlDataSource, and the SiteMapDataSource. The first two are rectangular, returning collections of rows of data; the last two are hierarchical, returning trees of data connected with parent-child relationships. These last two implement IHierarchicalDataSource instead of IDataSource, which we discuss later in this chapter.

LISTING 3-4: IDataSource interface

```
public interface IDataSource
{
    // Events
    event EventHandler DataSourceChanged;

    // Methods
    DataSourceView GetView(string viewName);
    ICollection GetViewNames();
}
```

LISTING 3-5: DataSourceView (abstract) class

```
public abstract class DataSourceView
{
  public event EventHandler DataSourceViewChanged;

  static DataSourceView();
  protected DataSourceView(IDataSource owner, string viewName);

  public virtual void Select(DataSourceSelectArguments arguments,
                        DataSourceViewSelectCallback callback);
  public virtual void Insert(IDictionary values,
                        DataSourceViewOperationCallback callback);
  public virtual void Update(IDictionary keys, IDictionary values,
                        IDictionary oldValues,
                        DataSourceViewOperationCallback callback);
  public virtual void Delete(IDictionary keys, IDictionary oldValues,
                        DataSourceViewOperationCallback callback);

  protected internal abstract IEnumerable ExecuteSelect(
                        DataSourceSelectArguments arguments);
  protected virtual int ExecuteInsert(IDictionary values);
  protected virtual int ExecuteUpdate(IDictionary keys,
                IDictionary values, IDictionary oldValues);
  protected virtual int ExecuteDelete(IDictionary keys,
                        IDictionary oldValues);

  private void OnDataSourceChangedInternal(object sender, EventArgs e);
  protected virtual void OnDataSourceViewChanged(EventArgs e);
  protected internal virtual void RaiseUnsupportedCapabilityError(
                        DataSourceCapabilities capability);

  public virtual bool CanDelete { get; }
  public virtual bool CanInsert { get; }
  public virtual bool CanPage { get; }
  public virtual bool CanRetrieveTotalRowCount { get; }
  public virtual bool CanSort { get; }
  public virtual bool CanUpdate { get; }
```

continues

```
protected EventHandlerList Events { get; }
public string Name { get; }
//...
}
```

LISTING 3-6: DataSourceSelectArguments class

```
public sealed class DataSourceSelectArguments
{
  public DataSourceSelectArguments();
  public DataSourceSelectArguments(string sortExpression);
  public DataSourceSelectArguments(int startRowIndex, int maximumRows);
  public DataSourceSelectArguments(string sortExpression,
                                   int startRowIndex, int maximumRows);
  public void AddSupportedCapabilities(
                              DataSourceCapabilities capabilities);
  public void RaiseUnsupportedCapabilitiesError(DataSourceView view);

  public static DataSourceSelectArguments Empty { get; }

  public int MaximumRows { get; set; }
  public bool RetrieveTotalRowCount { get; set; }
  public string SortExpression { get; set; }
  public int StartRowIndex { get; set; }
  public int TotalRowCount { get; set; }
  //...
}
```

Now that you have an understanding of the interfaces and classes involved with data sources, it is not difficult to see how individual controls use data source controls. In fact, you can even use data source controls yourself programmatically to retrieve data from a data source. Listing 3-7 shows a simple SqlDataSource declaration with an associated Select-Command that could be used to retrieve results from the movies table. To ask the data source to execute its query, you would call its Select method, which returns a generic collection of items in the form of an IEnumerable interface reference. For the SqlDataSource this collection will either be a list of DataRowView classes if it is in the default DataSet retrieval mode, or it will be a collection of DbDataRecord classes if it is in DataReader mode.

Listing 3-8 shows an example of programmatically interacting with a SqlDataSource on a page. Prior to executing the Select method, this example populates a DataSourceSelectArguments object with a sort expression, but only if the data source supports sorting. It also defines a method, ShowDSResults, that takes a generic IEnumerable collection as a parameter and determines whether it is a DataSet- or DataReader-based retrieval, and enumerates the collection, writing the first three columns in each row out to the response. This example, while not something you would probably do in practice, should give you a good idea of how data-bound controls interact with their associated data source controls.

LISTING 3-7: SqlDataSource declaration

```
<asp:SqlDataSource ID="_moviesDataSource" runat="server"
            ConnectionString=
                "<%$ ConnectionStrings:moviereviewsConnectionString %>"
            SelectCommand="SELECT * FROM movies" />
```

LISTING 3-8: Programmatically using a SqlDataSource

```
protected void ShowDSResults(IEnumerable e)
{
  IEnumerator idx = e.GetEnumerator();
  while (idx.MoveNext())
  {
    if (idx.Current is DataRowView) // DataSet used
    {
      DataRowView drv = (DataRowView)idx.Current;
      Response.Output.Write("{0} {1} {2}<br />",
                            drv[0], drv[1], drv[2]);
    }
    else if (idx.Current is DbDataRecord) // IDataReader used
    {
      DbDataRecord dr = (DbDataRecord)idx.Current;
      Response.Output.Write("{0} {1} {2}<br />", dr[0], dr[1], dr[2]);
    }
  }
}

protected void Page_Load(object sender, EventArgs e)
{
  DataSourceSelectArguments dssa = new DataSourceSelectArguments();
  if (((IDataSource)_moviesDataSource).GetView("").CanSort)
    dssa.SortExpression = "release_date DESC";

  ShowDSResults(_moviesDataSource.Select(dssa));
}
```

Tying Together Controls and Data Sources

The true power of declarative data sources becomes clear when you begin wiring a full-featured control like the GridView to a data source with all of

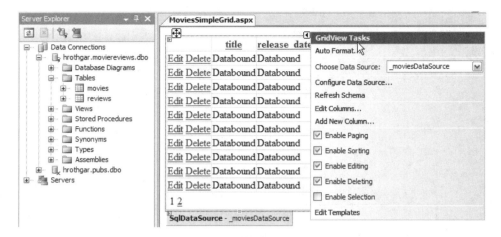

Figure 3-3: Designer support for declarative data sources and data-bound controls

its features enabled. For a true RAD design experience, try dragging a database table from the Server Explorer window of Visual Studio 2005 onto an ASP.NET page's design surface, as shown in Figure 3-3. This will generate a GridView and an associated SqlDataSource pair of controls to display the contents of that table. In addition, the data source is generated with a complete set of select, insert, update, and delete commands and parameters, and is set to the default DataSet mode, which means that all of the advanced features of the GridView control will be enabled. You can quickly turn on the advanced features like paging, sorting, editing, and deleting by using the GridView Tasks menu and selecting the appropriate checkboxes. Without any further work, you have a fully functional grid complete with editing, paging, sorting, and deleting in place. Listing 3-9 shows the generated controls as placed on your .aspx page, and Figure 3-4 shows the runtime rendering of the grid in action.

Listing 3-9: GridView and SqlDataSource with all features enabled

```
<asp:GridView ID="_moviesGrid" runat="server" AllowPaging="True"
             AllowSorting="True"
             AutoGenerateColumns="False" DataKeyNames="movie_id"
             DataSourceID="_moviesDataSource"
             EmptyDataText="There are no data records to display.">
   <Columns>
     <asp:CommandField ShowDeleteButton="True" ShowEditButton="True" />
```

```
    <asp:BoundField DataField="movie_id" HeaderText="movie_id"
                    ReadOnly="True" SortExpression="movie_id"
                    Visible="false" />
    <asp:BoundField DataField="title" HeaderText="title"
                    SortExpression="title" />
    <asp:BoundField DataField="release_date" HeaderText="release_date"
                    SortExpression="release_date" />
  </Columns>
</asp:GridView>

<asp:SqlDataSource ID="_moviesDataSource" runat="server"
ConnectionString="<%$ ConnectionStrings:moviereviewsConnectionString %>"
    DeleteCommand="DELETE FROM movies WHERE movie_id = @movie_id"
    InsertCommand="INSERT INTO movies (title, release_date) VALUES
(@title, @release_date)"
    SelectCommand="SELECT movie_id, title, release_date FROM movies"
    UpdateCommand="UPDATE movies SET title = @title, release_date =
@release_date WHERE movie_id = @movie_id">
    <InsertParameters>
      <asp:Parameter Name="title" Type="String" />
      <asp:Parameter Name="release_date" Type="DateTime" />
    </InsertParameters>
    <UpdateParameters>
      <asp:Parameter Name="title" Type="String" />
      <asp:Parameter Name="release_date" Type="DateTime" />
      <asp:Parameter Name="movie_id" Type="Int32" />
    </UpdateParameters>
    <DeleteParameters>
      <asp:Parameter Name="movie_id" Type="Int32" />
    </DeleteParameters>
  </asp:SqlDataSource>
```

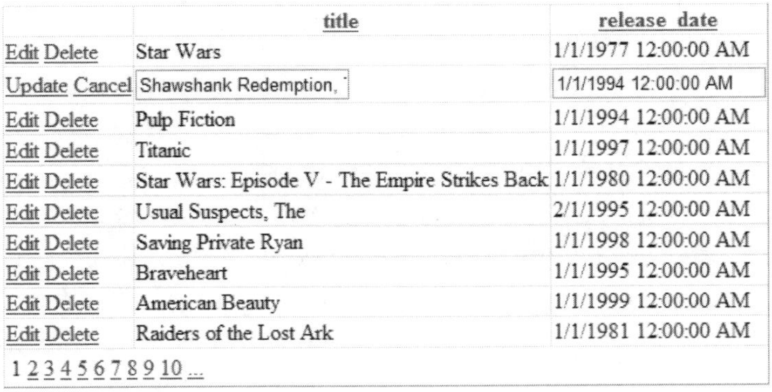

	title	release date
Edit Delete	Star Wars	1/1/1977 12:00:00 AM
Update Cancel	Shawshank Redemption,	1/1/1994 12:00:00 AM
Edit Delete	Pulp Fiction	1/1/1994 12:00:00 AM
Edit Delete	Titanic	1/1/1997 12:00:00 AM
Edit Delete	Star Wars: Episode V - The Empire Strikes Back	1/1/1980 12:00:00 AM
Edit Delete	Usual Suspects, The	2/1/1995 12:00:00 AM
Edit Delete	Saving Private Ryan	1/1/1998 12:00:00 AM
Edit Delete	Braveheart	1/1/1995 12:00:00 AM
Edit Delete	American Beauty	1/1/1999 12:00:00 AM
Edit Delete	Raiders of the Lost Ark	1/1/1981 12:00:00 AM

1 2 3 4 5 6 7 8 9 10 ...

FIGURE 3-4: Default rendering of GridView with attached SqlDataSource with all options enabled

One thing to keep in mind with this example is that most of the advanced features of the SqlDataSource—specifically paging, sorting, and filtering—are provided internally by the DataSet class. If you switch the SqlDataSource mode to use a DataSourceMode of DataReader, these three features will no longer be available in the GridView. This also means that the database itself is not being used to perform the sorting, filtering, or paging, which for large result sets can be very inefficient. Paging in particular is something that you can optimize with little effort to reduce the overall data sent back from the database (we discuss alternatives to using DataSet paging by using the ObjectDataSource later in this chapter).

Data Source Controls, ViewState, and ControlState

The procedure of data binding when using declarative data sources happens in much the same way it does when you do the binding programmatically, except that the association of the data source and the call to DataBind are done implicitly by the control. Specifically, when a control is being constructed, it checks to see if it has an associated declarative data source (indicated by the DataSourceID being populated). If it does, it will implicitly perform the DataBind during the call to the virtual CreateChildControls() method of the control. As in ASP.NET 1.1, controls always keep a local cache of the data to bridge the gap between data binding and rendering. By default, this data will also be stored in ViewState. However, controls that perform data binding implicitly like this realize when ViewState is enabled, and will avoid requerying the data source on postback requests as we did in our earlier example by hand (when we checked for !IsPostBack before calling DataBind). If you disable ViewState on a control, it will retrieve the data again for each request from the data source.

Now this behavior is usually what you want, but you should be aware of it since it can lead to surprising behavior. For example, if you have a button or other postback generating control on a form alongside a GridView, and the effect of the button is to modify the underlying database (say it adds a new row to the table being displayed by the GridView), you won't see the changes made to the database when the page is rendered because the GridView is drawing its state from ViewState and not going back to the database. The solution, of course, is to disable ViewState on the GridView and force it to retrieve the data again with each request.

One of the most frustrating aspects of working with server-side controls in ASP.NET 1.x is the all-or-nothing mentality with respect to view state. Behavioral aspects of controls like pagination in the DataGrid or selection change notifications in text boxes require view state to be enabled to function properly. This was frustrating because controls like the DataGrid (and the new GridView as well) can generate huge amounts of view state, depending on how much data is bound to them. ASP.NET 2.0 addresses this problem by partitioning view state into two separate categories: view state and control state. **Control state** is another type of hidden state reserved exclusively for controls to maintain their core (behavioral) functionality, whereas view state is now only to contain state to maintain the control's contents (UI). Technically, control state is stored in the same hidden field as view state (it is just another leaf node at the end of the view state hierarchy), but if you disable view state on a particular control (or on an entire page), the control state *is still propagated*. This means that you can disable ViewState on a GridView control, and know that all of its behavioral elements, like editing, paging, and so on, will remain functional.

Declarative Data Sources Without Embedded SQL

When developers first see declarative data sources, one common reaction is that embedding SQL queries directly in markup on the .aspx page feels wrong. The .aspx page in general should be kept free of application logic, and the ease with which someone could accidentally alter a query seems to be asking for trouble. There are a couple of strategies to avoiding embedded SQL in your pages, including assigning commands programmatically, storing commands in your web.config file, using stored procedures instead of direct SQL, and using the ObjectDataSource with a data access layer. We will discuss the ObjectDataSource in detail later in this chapter.

To store the SQL commands associated with a declarative data source in web.config, you can add the commands as key-value pairs under the App-Settings element, and then use the resource evaluation syntax to extract the values in the data source declaration. Listing 3-10 shows a sample web.config file with four SQL commands for interacting with the movies table, and Listing 3-11 shows a sample SqlDataSource declaration that uses the resource evaluation syntax to extract the commands from web.config and assign them to the command objects of the data source control.

LISTING 3-10: Storing commands in AppSettings of web.config

```
<configuration>
  <appSettings>
    <add key="MoviesDeleteCommand"
      value="DELETE FROM [movies] WHERE [movie_id] = @movie_id" />
    <add key="MoviesInsertCommand"
      value="INSERT INTO [movies] ([title], [release_date]) VALUES
(@title, @release_date)" />
    <add key="MoviesSelectCommand"
      value="SELECT [movie_id], [title], [release_date] FROM [movies]"/>
    <add key="MoviesUpdateCommand"
      value="UPDATE [movies] SET [title] = @title, [release_date] =
@release_date WHERE [movie_id] = @movie_id" />
  </appSettings>

    ...
</configuration>
```

LISTING 3-11: Extracting commands from AppSettings in a declarative data source control

```
<asp:SqlDataSource ID="_moviesDataSource" runat="server"
        ConnectionString=
            "<%$ ConnectionStrings:moviereviewsConnectionString %>"
        DeleteCommand="<%$ AppSettings:MoviesDeleteCommand %>"
        InsertCommand="<%$ AppSettings:MoviesInsertCommand %>"
        SelectCommand="<%$ AppSettings:MoviesSelectCommand %>"
        UpdateCommand="<%$ AppSettings:MoviesUpdateCommand %>">
  <InsertParameters>
    <asp:Parameter Name="title" Type="String" />
    <asp:Parameter Name="release_date" Type="DateTime" />
  </InsertParameters>
  <UpdateParameters>
    <asp:Parameter Name="title" Type="String" />
    <asp:Parameter Name="release_date" Type="DateTime" />
    <asp:Parameter Name="movie_id" Type="Int32" />
  </UpdateParameters>
  <DeleteParameters>
    <asp:Parameter Name="movie_id" Type="Int32" />
  </DeleteParameters>
</asp:SqlDataSource>
```

Using stored procedures with a declarative data source is not much different from using SQL statements directly. When you specify commands in a SqlDataSource, each command has a corresponding CommandType attribute which determines what type of command will be created under the covers to issue to the database. By default, this command type is set to *Text*, so if you are using stored procedures, you need to explicitly set it to *Stored-Procedure.* Keeping all of your SQL logic embedded in stored procedures is a good way to remove embedded SQL in your pages, and this is common practice in many Web applications today. Listing 3-12 shows four simple stored procedures to manipulate our movies table, and Listing 3-13 shows an example of a SqlDataSource wired up to use these stored procedures.

LISTING 3-12: Sample stored procedures for manipulating movies table

```
CREATE PROCEDURE GetMovies
AS
SELECT movie_id, title, release_date FROM movies
GO


CREATE PROCEDURE DeleteMovie
@movie_id INT
AS
DELETE FROM [movies] WHERE [movie_id] = @movie_id
GO


CREATE PROCEDURE UpdateMovie
    @movie_id INT, @title VARCHAR(64), @release_date DATETIME
AS
UPDATE [movies] SET [title] = @title, [release_date] = @release_date
WHERE [movie_id] = @movie_id
GO


CREATE PROCEDURE InsertMovie
@title VARCHAR(64), @release_date DATETIME
AS
INSERT INTO [movies] ([title], [release_date]) VALUES (@title,
@release_date)
Go
```

LISTING 3-13: Using stored procedures in a SqlDataSource

```
<asp:SqlDataSource ID="_moviesDataSource" runat="server"
    ConnectionString=
            "<%$ ConnectionStrings:moviereviewsConnectionString %>"
    DeleteCommand="DeleteMovie" DeleteCommandType="StoredProcedure"
    InsertCommand="InsertMovie" InsertCommandType="StoredProcedure"
    SelectCommand="GetMovies"   SelectCommandType="StoredProcedure"
    UpdateCommand="UpdateMovie" UpdateCommandType="StoredProcedure" >
  <InsertParameters>
    <asp:Parameter Name="title" Type="String" />
    <asp:Parameter Name="release_date" Type="DateTime" />
  </InsertParameters>
  <UpdateParameters>
    <asp:Parameter Name="title" Type="String" />
    <asp:Parameter Name="release_date" Type="DateTime" />
```

continues

```
    <asp:Parameter Name="movie_id" Type="Int32" />
  </UpdateParameters>
  <DeleteParameters>
    <asp:Parameter Name="movie_id" Type="Int32" />
  </DeleteParameters>
</asp:SqlDataSource>
```

Storing Connection Strings

It is always wise to avoid hard-coding connection strings, whether it's in your code or in a declarative data source control. In the past, developers have typically used the web.config file's appSettings element to store connection strings; this way, the process of changing the data store was as easy as modifying a single element in the configuration file. In ASP.NET 2.0, a new configuration section has been added explicitly for connection strings. In addition, to aid in the retrieval of connection strings from the configuration file, a new evaluation syntax has been introduced. Listings 3-14 and 3-15 show a sample configuration file and a corresponding data source control using the new declarative evaluation syntax to retrieve the connection string.

LISTING 3-14: Storing connection strings in web.config

```
<configuration>
<appSettings/>
<connectionStrings>
    <add name="pubs_dsn" connectionString="server=.;..."
        providerName="System.Data.SqlClient"/>
 </connectionStrings>
</configuration>
```

LISTING 3-15: Referencing a connection string

```
<asp:SqlDataSource
    ConnectionString="<%$ ConnectionStrings:pubs_dsn %>"
    ...
// or programmatically
ConfigurationManager.ConnectionStrings["pubs_dsn"].ConnectionString;
```

As you will see in Chapter 5, it is also possible to encrypt portions of your configuration file, so if you are storing credentials in your connection strings it is wise to use this feature.

Data Source Parameters

So far in our exploration of declarative data sources, we have issued a single select statement to retrieve data, without any option for altering that query. However, it can be necessary to change a query dynamically, often in response to user input. Declarative data sources support modifications to queries in the form of parameter collections. Each data source supports several collections of parameters; for the SqlDataSource these include UpdateParameters, DeleteParameters, InsertParameters, SelectParameters, and FilterParameters. Each collection of parameters must correspond to parameters in the underlying query or stored procedure associated with the command type.

Parameter values can be specified programmatically, either through two-way data binding of controls (more on this later), or through a predefined set of parameter sources that includes

- The value of a property from another control on the same form
- The value of a cookie
- A form parameter
- A query string parameter
- Data stored in the profile associated with a user
- Data stored in the session associated with a user

Each of these is a convenient way to populate parameters of a data source from alternate data sources in your application. For example, if you wanted to let the user specify a search string to constrain the list of movies displayed in a GridView, you could add a TextBox to the form and a button to issue a post-back, and then add a ControlParameter to the list of Filter-Parameters for the SqlDataSource control. Point the ControlParameter class to the identifier of the TextBox you added, and specify a filter expression that constrains the query to list only results whose *title* contains the text typed into the text box. Listing 3-16 shows this example in its entirety, and Figure 3-5 shows the sample running with a search for "star" being performed.

Note that the FilterExpression is only available with the SqlDataSource when running in DataSet mode, and that it expects syntax identical to that required by the RowFilter property of the DataView class, which means

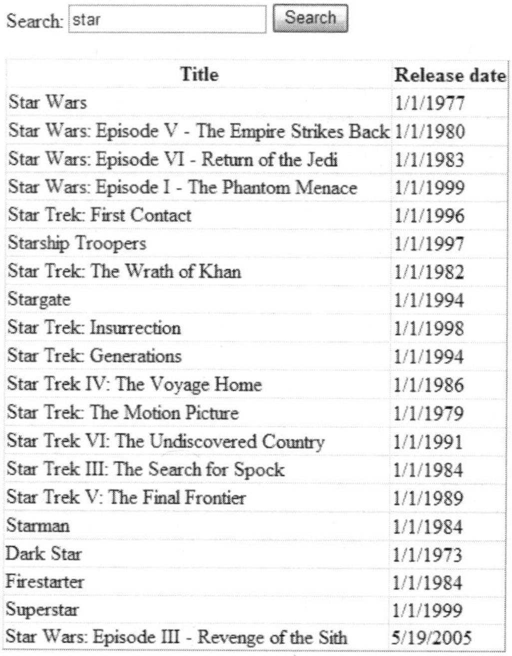

Title	Release date
Star Wars	1/1/1977
Star Wars: Episode V - The Empire Strikes Back	1/1/1980
Star Wars: Episode VI - Return of the Jedi	1/1/1983
Star Wars: Episode I - The Phantom Menace	1/1/1999
Star Trek: First Contact	1/1/1996
Starship Troopers	1/1/1997
Star Trek: The Wrath of Khan	1/1/1982
Stargate	1/1/1994
Star Trek: Insurrection	1/1/1998
Star Trek: Generations	1/1/1994
Star Trek IV: The Voyage Home	1/1/1986
Star Trek: The Motion Picture	1/1/1979
Star Trek VI: The Undiscovered Country	1/1/1991
Star Trek III: The Search for Spock	1/1/1984
Star Trek V: The Final Frontier	1/1/1989
Starman	1/1/1984
Dark Star	1/1/1973
Firestarter	1/1/1984
Superstar	1/1/1999
Star Wars: Episode III - Revenge of the Sith	5/19/2005

FIGURE 3-5: Search feature implemented with a filter parameter

that parameters are specified using string placeholder syntax and are populated in order of declaration. Also remember that this feature is implemented completely by the DataSet, so it will not be as efficient as a WHERE clause in a database query for larger result sets. Note that we could have used any of the parameter types for this filter; for example, if the user navigated to this page with a query string to specify a search, we would have used the QueryStringParameter instead of the ControlParameter.

LISTING 3-16: Specifying a filter parameter for a SqlDataSource with input from a TextBox

```
Search: <asp:TextBox ID="_searchTextBox" runat="server" />
<asp:Button ID="_searchButton" runat="server" Text="Search" /><br />
<br />
<asp:GridView ID="_moviesGrid" runat="server"
            AutoGenerateColumns="False" DataKeyNames="movie_id"
            DataSourceID="_moviesDataSource"
            EmptyDataText="There are no data records to display.">
  <Columns>
 <asp:BoundField DataField="title" HeaderText="Title" />
```

```
<asp:BoundField DataField="release_date" DataFormatString="{0:d}"
                HeaderText="Release date" HtmlEncode="False" />
  </Columns>
</asp:GridView>

<asp:SqlDataSource ID="_moviesDataSource" runat="server"
      ConnectionString=
          "<%$ ConnectionStrings:moviereviewsConnectionString %>"
SelectCommand="SELECT [movie_id], [title], [release_date] FROM [mov-
ies]"
FilterExpression="title LIKE '%{0}%'">
<FilterParameters>
  <asp:ControlParameter ControlID="_searchTextBox"
                        PropertyName="Text" />
</FilterParameters>
</asp:SqlDataSource>
```

Another interesting application of parameters is to create a master-detail relationship between two data-bound controls. The GridView control supports the concept of selecting a row by enabling a CommandField with the ShowSelectButton attribute set to true. With this enabled, the GridView displays a hyperlink column whose default text is *Select*; when the client clicks this, that row is marked as selected. You can then set up a second data-bound control and data source to display details for the currently selected row by adding a parameter to the Select statement and populating the parameter using a ControlParameter set to the GridView's currently selected row (actually the value of the primary key for that row).

For example, we could create a GridView that listed all of the movies from our database, enable selection, and then create a DataList control to display all of the reviews associated with that movie. Listing 3-17 shows the control declarations to accomplish this, and Figure 3-6 shows the Grid-View and associated DataList displaying movies and the selected movie's associated reviews, respectively.

LISTING 3-17: A master-detail relationship between a GridView and a DataList

```
<asp:GridView ID="_moviesGrid" runat="server" AllowPaging="True"
      AllowSorting="True"
      AutoGenerateColumns="False" DataKeyNames="movie_id"
      DataSourceID="_moviesDataSource"
      EmptyDataText="There are no data records to display.">
  <Columns>
    <asp:CommandField ShowSelectButton="True" />
```

continues

```
    <asp:BoundField DataField="movie_id" HeaderText="movie_id"
        ReadOnly="True" SortExpression="movie_id" Visible="False" />
    <asp:BoundField DataField="title" HeaderText="title"
                SortExpression="title" />
    <asp:BoundField DataField="release_date" DataFormatString="{0:d}"
            HeaderText="release_date"
            HtmlEncode="False" SortExpression="release_date" />

  </Columns>
</asp:GridView>

<asp:SqlDataSource ID="_moviesDataSource" runat="server"
    ConnectionString=
        "<%$ ConnectionStrings:moviereviewsConnectionString %>"

    SelectCommand=
        "SELECT [movie_id], [title], [release_date] FROM [movies]"
/><br />

<asp:DataList ID="_reviewsDataList" runat="server" RepeatColumns="2"
            RepeatDirection="Horizontal" DataKeyField="review_id"
            DataSourceID="_reviewsDataSource">
  <ItemTemplate>
    summary: <asp:Label ID="summaryLabel" runat="server"
                    Text='<%# Eval("summary") %>' /><br />
    rating: <asp:Label ID="ratingLabel" runat="server"
                    Text='<%# Eval("rating") %>' /><br />
    review: <asp:Label ID="reviewLabel" runat="server"
                    Text='<%# Eval("review") %>' /><br />
      --
    <asp:Label ID="reviewerLabel" runat="server"
            Text='<%# Eval("reviewer") %>' /><br /><br />
  </ItemTemplate>
</asp:DataList>

<asp:SqlDataSource ID="_reviewsDataSource" runat="server"
    ConnectionString=
        "<%$ ConnectionStrings:moviereviewsConnectionString %>"
    SelectCommand="SELECT review_id, movie_id, summary, rating, review,
reviewer FROM reviews WHERE (movie_id = @movie_id)">
  <SelectParameters>
    <asp:ControlParameter ControlID="_moviesGrid" Name="movie_id"
                        PropertyName="SelectedValue" Type="Int32" />
  </SelectParameters>
</asp:SqlDataSource>
```

	title	release date
Select	Star Wars	1/1/1977
Select	Shawshank Redemption, The	1/1/1994
Select	Pulp Fiction	1/1/1994
Select	Titanic	1/1/1997
Select	Star Wars: Episode V - The Empire Strikes Back	1/1/1980
Select	Usual Suspects, The	2/1/1995
Select	Saving Private Ryan	1/1/1998
Select	Braveheart	1/1/1995
Select	American Beauty	1/1/1999
Select	Raiders of the Lost Ark	1/1/1981

1 2 3 4 5 6 7 8 9 10 ...

summary: Great flick!
rating: 9
review: This movie was a real blast to watch. I highly recommend it to anyone interested in this type of film.
  -- Kent C. Detrees

summary: Mediocre at best
rating: 6
review: I had great expectations for this film, but was disappointed by the uninspired acting and lackluster special effects. I am giving it the rating I am because it was not the absolute worst thing I have seen.
  -- Lisa Carr

summary: Pretty good
rating: 3
review: I enjoyed this film quite a bit, and think you will too. Lots of good action!
  -- Orson Buggy

summary: Lamo!
rating: 8
review: Worst movie since the dawn of time! Avoid at all costs!
  -- Adam Illion

FIGURE 3-6: Master-detail showing reviews associated with the selected film

New Data-Bound Controls

There are several new data-bound controls introduced with this release of ASP.NET 2.0, including most prominently the GridView, DetailsView, and FormView. As you have seen, the GridView is the new grid control, and it is intended to replace the DataGrid (although the DataGrid remains for backward compatibility). It is in general a simpler, more modularly constructed control, and it's easier to use and customize than the DataGrid was. You will notice several differences from the DataGrid when you first start working with the GridView, including the addition of several new column types, including ImageField and CheckBoxField. Most of the features of the GridView are shown throughout the examples in this chapter.

The DetailsView fills the hole of a one-page form display that was missing in ASP.NET 1.1. It supports the ability to show, edit, insert, or delete a single row at a time, and will automatically generate default controls for displaying and updating individual fields based on their type in the underlying data source. The DefaultMode property of the control lets you specify which of the three modes of operation it should initially display: Edit, Insert, or ReadOnly. You typically will include a CommandField that displays hyperlinks to let the user switch between the three modes as well (although you can also restrict the user to only using one or two modes if you like).

Like most data-bound controls, it also supports template fields so that you can customize the appearance of any field as much as needed. Each field has three core templates that are displayed when the control is in each of the possible display modes: ItemTemplate, EditItemTemplate, and InsertItemTemplate. If you find that you are writing a lot of template fields, however, you might instead consider using the FormView control, which we will discuss next. Listing 3-18 shows an example of the DetailsView control being bound to a SqlDataSource, and Figure 3-7 shows the resulting control rendered in each of its three available states of operation.

LISTING 3-18: DetailsView example

```
<asp:DetailsView ID="_moviesDetailsView" runat="server"
     AllowPaging="True" AutoGenerateRows="False"
     DataKeyNames="movie_id" DataSourceID="_moviesDataSource"
     Height="50px" Width="125px">
  <Fields>
    <asp:BoundField DataField="movie_id" HeaderText="movie_id"
                    InsertVisible="False"
                    ReadOnly="True" Visible="False" />
    <asp:BoundField DataField="title" HeaderText="Title" />
    <asp:BoundField DataField="release_date" DataFormatString="{0:d}"
                    HeaderText="Release date" HtmlEncode="False" />
    <asp:CommandField ShowDeleteButton="True" ShowEditButton="True"
                      ShowInsertButton="True" />
  </Fields>
</asp:DetailsView>

<asp:SqlDataSource ID="_moviesDataSource" runat="server"
     ConnectionString=
         "<%$ ConnectionStrings:moviereviewsConnectionString %>"
     DeleteCommand="DELETE FROM movies WHERE movie_id = @movie_id"
     InsertCommand="INSERT INTO movies (title, release_date) VALUES
(@title, @release_date)"
     SelectCommand="SELECT movie_id, title, release_date FROM movies"
     UpdateCommand="UPDATE movies SET title = @title, release_date =
@release_date WHERE movie_id = @movie_id">
  <DeleteParameters>
    <asp:Parameter Name="movie_id" Type="Int32" />
```

```
    </DeleteParameters>
    <UpdateParameters>
      <asp:Parameter Name="title" Type="String" />
      <asp:Parameter Name="release_date" Type="DateTime" />
      <asp:Parameter Name="movie_id" Type="Int32" />
    </UpdateParameters>
    <InsertParameters>
      <asp:Parameter Name="title" Type="String" />
      <asp:Parameter Name="release_date" Type="DateTime" />
    </InsertParameters>
</asp:SqlDataSource>
```

The FormView is very much like the DetailsView—it renders one row at a time and provides the ability to display, edit, insert, and delete rows. The difference is that the FormView has no default rendering of fields, but rather relies on user-defined templates to render the data and the input controls. The choice to use a FormView over a DetailsView usually hinges on how much customization of the default rendering of the DetailsView you anticipate. One scenario that almost always mandates a FormView is if you want to add validation controls to your input controls when the client is updating or inserting a row. To do this in the DetailsView you would have to add a separate EditItemTemplate for each field, but in the Form-View there is only one EditItemTemplate that you populate with all of the input controls and their corresponding validation controls. When working with the InsertItemTemplate and EditItemTemplates in the FormView, you will typically use the new *Bind()* expression to perform two-way data binding to a control's field. This expression is evaluated inside of a data-binding expression, and during updates and inserts it will pull the value from the control field with which it is associated. To retrieve the initial value to populate updateable fields, it will extract the value from the underlying row and set the control field with the value—hence the term two-way binding.

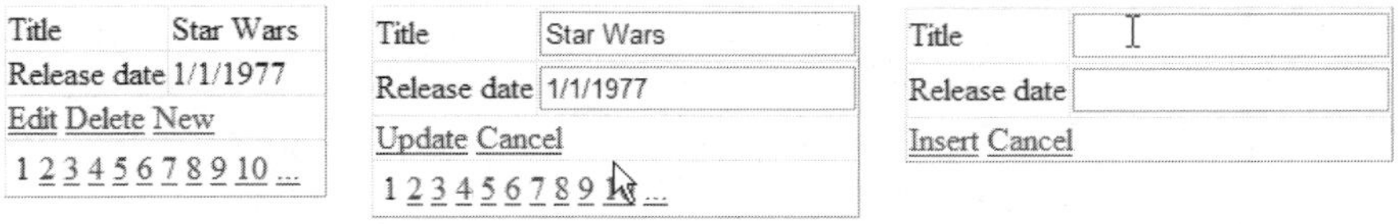

FIGURE 3-7: Default rendering of DetailsView in ReadOnly, Edit, and Insert modes

Listing 3-19 shows an example of a FormView control bound to the same _moviesDataSource as our earlier DetailsView example, complete with validation on all input elements embedded in the EditItemTemplate and InsertItemTemplate.

LISTING 3-19: FormView example

```
<asp:FormView ID="_moviesFormView" runat="server"
    AllowPaging="True" DataKeyNames="movie_id"
    DataSourceID="_moviesDataSource">

  <EditItemTemplate>
    title: <asp:TextBox ID="_titleTextBox" runat="server"
            Text='<%# Bind("title") %>' />
    <asp:RequiredFieldValidator ID="_titleValidator" runat="server"
        ControlToValidate="_titleTextBox"
        ErrorMessage="Please enter a title">**
    </asp:RequiredFieldValidator><br />
    release_date: <asp:TextBox ID="release_dateTextBox" runat="server"
                    Text='<%# Bind("release_date", "{0:d}") %>' />
    <asp:RequiredFieldValidator ID="_releaseValidator" runat="server"
        ControlToValidate="release_dateTextBox"
        ErrorMessage="Please enter a release date">**
    </asp:RequiredFieldValidator>
    <asp:RangeValidator ID="_releaseRangeValidator" runat="server"
        ControlToValidate="release_dateTextBox"
        ErrorMessage="Please enter a valid release date (1/1/2006)"
        MaximumValue="1/1/1600" MinimumValue="1/1/1000" Type="Date">**
    </asp:RangeValidator><br />
    <asp:LinkButton ID="UpdateButton" runat="server"
        CausesValidation="True" CommandName="Update" Text="Update" />
    <asp:LinkButton ID="UpdateCancelButton" runat="server"
        CausesValidation="False" CommandName="Cancel" Text="Cancel" />
  </EditItemTemplate>

  <InsertItemTemplate>
    title: <asp:TextBox ID="_titleTextBox" runat="server"
            Text='<%# Bind("title") %>' />
    <asp:RequiredFieldValidator ID="_titleValidator" runat="server"
        ControlToValidate="_titleTextBox"
        ErrorMessage="Please enter a title">**
    </asp:RequiredFieldValidator><br />
    release_date: <asp:TextBox ID="release_dateTextBox" runat="server"
                    Text='<%# Bind("release_date", "{0:d}") %>' />
    <asp:RequiredFieldValidator ID="_releaseValidator" runat="server"
        ControlToValidate="release_dateTextBox"
        ErrorMessage="Please enter a release date">**
    </asp:RequiredFieldValidator>
```

```
      <asp:RangeValidator ID="_releaseRangeValidator" runat="server"
          ControlToValidate="release_dateTextBox"
          ErrorMessage="Please enter a valid release date (1/1/2006)"
          MaximumValue="1/1/2600" MinimumValue="1/1/1000" Type="Date">**
      </asp:RangeValidator><br />
      <asp:LinkButton ID="InsertButton" runat="server"
          CausesValidation="True" CommandName="Insert" Text="Insert" />
      <asp:LinkButton ID="InsertCancelButton" runat="server"
          CausesValidation="False" CommandName="Cancel" Text="Cancel" />
  </InsertItemTemplate>

  <ItemTemplate>
    Title: <asp:Label ID="titleLabel" runat="server"
              Text='<%# Bind("title") %>' /><br />
    Release date: <asp:Label ID="release_dateLabel" runat="server"
                      Text='<%# Bind("release_date", "{0:d}") %>' />
    <br />
    <asp:LinkButton ID="EditButton" runat="server"
        CausesValidation="False" CommandName="Edit" Text="Edit" />
    <asp:LinkButton ID="DeleteButton" runat="server"
        CausesValidation="False" CommandName="Delete" Text="Delete" />
    <asp:LinkButton ID="NewButton" runat="server"
        CausesValidation="False" CommandName="New" Text="New" />
  </ItemTemplate>
</asp:FormView>
```

Data-Binding Evaluation Syntax

The data-binding syntax used in templates in data-bound controls has been simplified and reduced to just Eval("colname") in this release. The reference to the old Container.DataItem local variable is now implicit. As in the old DataBinder.Eval method, the Eval method takes an optional second parameter, which is a string format for the expression.

The new two-way binding syntax, Bind("colname"), is used mostly by the DetailsView and the FormView in their respective EditItem and InsertItem templates as shown in the previous two examples. This provides a way to populate parameters for update and insertion through data binding as well, not just for selection.

Declarative Data-Binding Techniques

As developers shift from the imperative style of data binding to the declarative one, there is often some confusion about how to accomplish tasks equivalently in the new model. For example, how do you perform a nested data bind to populate a drop-down list with a grid? Or how do you modify a parameter programmatically if there is no corresponding control parameter type? This section looks specifically at how to deal with these two issues in the context of declarative data sources.

Nested Declarative Data Binding

One issue that comes up frequently with dealing with data-bound controls is the asymmetric nature of join queries and their corresponding update statements. These are among the most common types of queries used in Web applications, since you are often presenting data from a table that contains foreign-key references to other tables containing the complete name and description (or whatever the extra data is).

For example, consider the reviews table in our sample database, which contains a foreign key column reference to the movies table. To properly present the data from the reviews table, you might build a query with an inner join to retrieve the titles of the movies instead of displaying the movie_id value itself, which is most likely meaningless to the client.

```
SELECT review_id, m.movie_id, summary, rating, review, reviewer, m.title
FROM reviews AS r INNER JOIN movies as m ON r.movie_id=m.movie_id
```

However, if you are performing an update or an insert into the table, you need to specify the foreign key id fields directly:

```
UPDATE reviews SET summary = @summary, rating = @rating,
       review = @review, reviewer = @reviewer, movie_id=@movie_id
WHERE review_id=@review_id
```

Listing 3-20 shows a sample SqlDataSource that encapsulates these two commands.

LISTING 3-20: SqlDataSource performing a join query with update and insert commands

```
<asp:SqlDataSource ID="_reviewsDataSource" runat="server"
    ConnectionString=
       "<%$ ConnectionStrings:moviereviewsConnectionString %>"
    SelectCommand="SELECT review_id, m.movie_id, summary, rating,
review, reviewer, m.title FROM reviews AS r INNER JOIN movies as m ON
r.movie_id=m.movie_id "
    UpdateCommand="UPDATE reviews SET summary = @summary, rating = @rat-
ing, review = @review, reviewer = @reviewer, movie_id=@movie_id WHERE
review_id=@review_id">
  <UpdateParameters>
    <asp:Parameter Name="summary" />
```

```
    <asp:Parameter Name="rating" />
    <asp:Parameter Name="review" />
    <asp:Parameter Name="reviewer" />
    <asp:Parameter Name="review_id" />
    <asp:Parameter Name="movie_id" />
  </UpdateParameters>
</asp:SqlDataSource>
```

If you attach a GridView to this data source, you typically will want to give the user a drop-down list in update mode so that she can select from the proper list of movie titles. This is where declarative data sources shine, because you can create a template column for the title column, and in its UpdateItemTemplates specify a DropDownList with an associated Data-SourceID attribute pointing to another declarative data source prepared to retrieve all of the movies separately in a nested data bind. Futhermore, you can use a data-binding expression to set the selected element of the Drop-DownList to the currently selected value for that column in the current row.[2] Listing 3-21 shows an example of a GridView pointing to the Data-Source shown in Listing 3-20 with a nested data bind when rendered in Update mode grabbing data from the independent movies DataSource control. Figure 3-8 shows the GridView in update mode when rendered to the client.

LISTING 3-21: Nested declarative data-binding example

```
<asp:GridView ID="_reviewsGrid" runat="server" AllowPaging="True"
        AutoGenerateColumns="False"
        DataKeyNames="review_id" DataSourceID="_reviewsDataSource" >
  <Columns>
    <asp:CommandField ShowEditButton="True" />
    <asp:BoundField DataField="review_id" HeaderText="review_id"
        Visible="False" ReadOnly="True" SortExpression="review_id" />
    <asp:BoundField DataField="summary" HeaderText="summary"
        SortExpression="summary" />
    <asp:BoundField DataField="rating" HeaderText="rating"
        SortExpression="rating" />
    <asp:BoundField DataField="review" HeaderText="review"
        SortExpression="review" />
    <asp:BoundField DataField="reviewer" HeaderText="reviewer"
        SortExpression="reviewer" />
```

continues

---

2. Note that this type of lookup table is an ideal candidate for caching, which is also supported by declarative data sources, as you will see in Chapter 8.

```
  <asp:TemplateField HeaderText="Title" SortExpression="Title">
    <EditItemTemplate>
      <asp:DropDownList runat="server" ID="_movieTitleDropDown"
          DataSourceID="_moviesDataSource" DataTextField="title"
          DataValueField="movie_id"
          SelectedValue='<%# Bind("movie_id") %>' >
      </asp:DropDownList>
    </EditItemTemplate>
    <ItemTemplate>
      <%# Eval("title") %>
    </ItemTemplate>
  </asp:TemplateField>
</Columns>
</asp:GridView>

<asp:SqlDataSource ID="_moviesDataSource" runat="server"
    ConnectionString=
      "<%$ ConnectionStrings:moviereviewsConnectionString %>"
    SelectCommand="SELECT movie_id, title FROM movies ORDER BY title" />
```

Programmatic Parameter Population

Another common scenario is if you have a declarative data source for a
control (let's use an example of a DetailsView with a SqlDataSource) and
you want to implicitly populate one or more of the parameters when the
user inserts a new item. An example of this might be a timestamp field that
should be set to whatever time the new row was inserted, and not some-

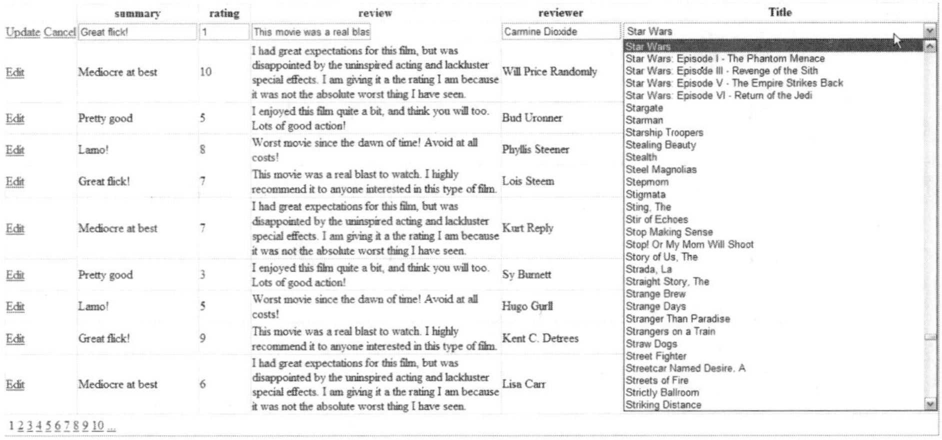

FIGURE 3-8: Nested declarative data binding in action

thing populated by the user, or perhaps a user name that is implicitly filled in based on the credentials of the client. This could equally apply to parameter population for select, update, or delete queries also, but it tends to be most common with inserts.

As you have seen, there are several parameter types available for declarative data sources, including the ability to draw a value from a cookie, a form field, the user's profile data, a query string, and so on. There are occasions, however, where none of these fits the bill and you just need to populate the parameter yourself (like the timestamp case). One solution to this is to add a handler for the appropriate event on the data source control (the events of interest are Inserting, Selecting, Updating, and Deleting, which are all called before the actual SQL call is made). So to complete the example described earlier, imagine having a FormView through which we want our clients to insert new movie reviews into the system, and that we would like the *reviewer* field of the reviews table to be populated implicitly with the current user name of the authenticated client or "anonymous" if the client is not authenticated. Listings 3-22 and 3-23 show how you might accomplish this by adding a handler for the *Inserting* event of the SqlDataSource, retrieving the *@reviewer* parameter from the command's list of parameters, and populating the value with the user name or "Anonymous" depending on whether she is authenticated or not. Note that we are also using the nested declarative data-binding technique to provide a DropDownList control to select the movie.

LISTING 3-22: FormView and associated data source for inserting new reviews with the reviewer field being programmatically populated

```
<h2>Add your own review</h2>
<asp:FormView ID="_insertReviewFormView" runat="server"
    DataSourceID="_reviewsDataSource" DefaultMode="Insert" >
  <InsertItemTemplate>
    <asp:DropDownList runat="server" ID="_movieTitleDropDown"
        DataSourceID="_moviesDataSource" DataTextField="title"
        DataValueField="movie_id"
        SelectedValue='<%# Bind("movie_id") %>' /> <br />
    Summary: <asp:TextBox ID="summaryTextBox" runat="server"
                    Text='<%# Bind("summary") %>' /> <br />
    Rating: <asp:TextBox ID="ratingTextBox" runat="server"
                    Text='<%# Bind("rating") %>' />   <br />
    Review: <asp:TextBox ID="reviewTextBox" runat="server"
                    TextMode="multiLine" Rows="5"
                    Text='<%# Bind("review") %>' /> <br />
```

continues

```
      <asp:LinkButton ID="InsertButton" runat="server"
                      CausesValidation="True"
                      CommandName="Insert" Text="Insert" />
  </InsertItemTemplate>
</asp:FormView>

<asp:SqlDataSource ID="_reviewsDataSource" runat="server"
    ConnectionString=
            "<%$ ConnectionStrings:moviereviewsConnectionString %>"
    InsertCommand="INSERT INTO reviews(movie_id, summary, rating,
review, reviewer) VALUES (@movie_id, @summary, @rating, @review,
@reviewer)"
    OnInserting="_reviewsDataSource_Inserting">
  <InsertParameters>
    <asp:Parameter Name="movie_id" />
    <asp:Parameter Name="summary" />
    <asp:Parameter Name="rating" />
    <asp:Parameter Name="review" />
    <asp:Parameter Name="reviewer" />
  </InsertParameters>
</asp:SqlDataSource>

<asp:SqlDataSource ID="_moviesDataSource" runat="server"
    ConnectionString=
      "<%$ ConnectionStrings:moviereviewsConnectionString %>"
    SelectCommand=
      "SELECT [movie_id], [title] FROM [movies] ORDER BY title" />
```

LISTING 3-23: Event handler for programmatically populating the @reviewer parameter

```
protected void _reviewsDataSource_Inserting(object sender,
                               SqlDataSourceCommandEventArgs e)
{
  e.Command.Parameters["@reviewer"].Value =
      User.Identity.IsAuthenticated ? User.Identity.Name : "Anonymous";
}
```

Hierarchical Data Binding

In addition to the rectangular results modeled by the IDataSource interface, this release of ASP.NET also introduces an interface that models hierarchical data through IHierarchicalDataSource. Like its sibling interface IDataSource, this interface exposes a single method to retrieve a "view" of the data, GetHierarchicalView. All of the hierarchical data source controls defined in this release provide only one "view" of the data, however, so the class of real interest is the HierarchicalDataSourceView class which is returned by GetHierarchicalView. This abstract class exposes a Select method that returns an IHierarchicalEnumerable interface result. IHierarchicalEnumerable in turn exposes a GetHierarchyData method which returns an IHierarchyData interface. IHierarchyData exposes the core methods GetChildren and GetParent, which model the parent-child relationships in a hierarchical data source. The complete set of interfaces and classes involved with hierarchical data sources is shown in Listing 3-24.

LISTING 3-24: Hierarchical data source interfaces

```
public interface IHierarchicalDataSource
{
  event EventHandler DataSourceChanged;

  HierarchicalDataSourceView GetHierarchicalView(string viewPath);
}

public abstract class HierarchicalDataSourceView
{
  protected HierarchicalDataSourceView();
  public abstract IHierarchicalEnumerable Select();
}

public interface IHierarchicalEnumerable : IEnumerable
{
  IHierarchyData GetHierarchyData(object enumeratedItem);
}

public interface IHierarchyData
{
  IHierarchicalEnumerable GetChildren();
  IHierarchyData GetParent();

  bool HasChildren { get; }
  object Item { get; }
  string Path { get; }
  string Type { get; }
}
```

In Chapter 2 we encountered our first hierarchical data source in the form of the SiteMapDataSource, which exposed the navigational structure of a site defined in the web.sitemap file containing XML data. The other hierarchical data source available is the XmlDataSource, which can be bound to any arbitrary XML document. When you create an XmlDataSource control, you specify the XML document in the DataFile attribute.

You can also optionally specify an initial XPath expression to be used to obtain the initial set of nodes from the document with the XPath property, as well as an XSL transform file through the TransformFile property.

What makes this data source even more compelling is the fact that two new data-binding expressions have been added that can be used when binding to a hierarchical data source: XPath and XPathSelect. The XPath data-binding evaluation syntax gives you the ability to declaratively add XPath expressions to be evaluated from the current XmlNode that is being enumerated in a control template, as it is bound to a hierarchical data source. The XPathSelect expression can be used to perform subselections, which can be useful to perform nested bindings, as you will see next.

Listing 3-25 shows an example of binding a DataList to an XmlData-Source, whose data is obtained by specifying an RSS feed as the DataFile. The XPath expression is used to extract a list of *item* elements from the document, which are then bound iteratively to the DataList control. In the DataList control, we are able to specify XPath expressions in an Item-Template to pluck out the XML elements we want to display for each *item* node found in the initial XPath query. Note that this example is using a nonhierarchical data-bound control (the DataList) with a hierarchical Xml-DataSource. This is possible as long as you don't want to do recursive data binding on a node in the result set returned by the data source's initial XPath expression. For true hierarchical data binding, you can use the Xml-DataSource with a hierarchical control like the TreeView control, which we will look at next.

LISTING 3-25: A simple blog reader using XmlDataSource

```
<%@ Page Language="C#" %>
<html xmlns="http://www.w3.org/1999/xhtml" >
<head runat="server" />
<body>
  <form id="form1" runat="server">
  <div>
  <asp:XmlDataSource ID="rssDataSource" Runat="server"
      DataFile="http://pluralsight.com/blogs/fritz/rss.aspx"
      XPath="/rss/channel/item" />

    <asp:DataList ID="rssDataList" Runat="server"
                  DataSourceID="rssDataSource">
      <ItemTemplate>
        <b><%# XPath("pubDate")%> - <%# XPath("title") %></b>
```

```
          <br />
          <%# XPath("description") %>
        </ItemTemplate>
      </asp:DataList>

  </div>
  </form>
</body>
</html>
```

Binding Hierarchical Data Sources to the TreeView Control

To take full advantage of a hierarchical data source like the XmlData-
Source, it is necessary to bind to a control that can represent data hierarchically, like the TreeView control. In Chapter 2 you saw how to bind the
TreeView to the SiteMapDataSource to display a tree structure depicting
the navigational structure of your site. You can also bind an XmlData-
Source to a TreeView control and have it implicitly traverse the XML document, creating nodes and leaves to match the structure of the document.
When you are binding to an XmlDataSource, the TreeView also supports
the concept of tree node bindings, which are a way of describing how you
would like a particular element in the document to be bound to a node,
including an associated image, and which attribute of an element (if any)
to display for the node. Listing 3-26 shows a sample XML file we will use
to bind a TreeView to. Listing 3-27 shows a TreeView bound to an Xml-
DataSource pointing to the sample XML file, and Figure 3-9 shows the
resulting rendering.

LISTING 3-26: Sample XML file with bookstore content

```
<Bookstore>
  <genre name="Business">
    <book ISBN="BU1032" Title="The Busy Executive's Database Guide"
        Price="19.99">
      <chapter num="1" name="Introduction">
        Abstract...
      </chapter>
      <chapter num="2" name="Body">
        Abstract...
      </chapter>
      <chapter num="3" name="Conclusion">
        Abstract...
```

continues

```
      </chapter>
    </book>
    <book ISBN="BU2075" Title="You Can Combat Computer Stress!"
          Price="2.99">
      <chapter num="1" name="Introduction">
        Abstract...
      </chapter>
      <chapter num="2" name="Body">
        Abstract...
      </chapter>
      <chapter num="3" name="Conclusion">
        Abstract...
      </chapter>
    </book>
    <book ISBN="BU7832" Title="Straight Talk About Computers"
          Price="19.99">
      <chapter num="1" name="Introduction">
        Abstract...
      </chapter>
      <chapter num="2" name="Body">
        Abstract...
      </chapter>
      <chapter num="3" name="Conclusion">
        Abstract...
      </chapter>
    </book>
  </genre>
</Bookstore>
```

LISTING 3-27: TreeNodeBinding with the TreeView and the XmlDataSource

```
<asp:TreeView ID="_bookTreeView" runat="server"
              DataSourceID="_bookstoreDataSource" ShowLines="True">
  <DataBindings>
    <asp:TreeNodeBinding DataMember="book"
        ImageUrl="~/img/closedbook.gif" TextField="Title" />
    <asp:TreeNodeBinding DataMember="chapter"
        ImageUrl="~/img/notepad.gif" TextField="name" />
    <asp:TreeNodeBinding DataMember="genre"
        ImageUrl="~/img/folder.gif" Text="." TextField="name" />
  </DataBindings>
</asp:TreeView>

<asp:XmlDataSource ID="_bookstoreDataSource" runat="server"
                   DataFile="~/App_Data/Bookstore.xml" />
```

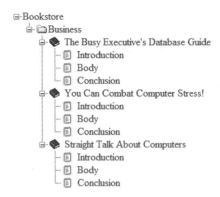

FIGURE 3-9: TreeView with TreeNodeBinding rendering

Nested Hierarchical Data Binding

There are occasions where you don't really want the full hierarchical rendering of a TreeView, but you also need to bind more than one level deep in a rectangular control like the DataList or Repeater. When binding to the XmlDataSource, you can accomplish this by performing a nested data bind using the XPathSelect data-binding expression and assigning the result to a nested control's DataSource property. For example, Listing 3-28 shows a sample DataList control bound to all of the *book* elements in the Bookstore.xml document, but in its ItemTemplate is another DataList declaration, whose DataSource attribute is set to the evaluation of XPathSelect("chapter") to extract all of the chapter elements for that particular book. The resulting (partial) rendering is shown in Figure 3-10.

LISTING 3-28: Nested hierarchical data binding

```
<asp:DataList ID="_bookDataList" runat="server"
            DataSourceID="_bookDataSource">
  <ItemTemplate>
    Title: <%# Eval("Title") %><br />
    <asp:DataList runat="server" ID="_nestedDataList"
        DataSource='<%# XPathSelect("chapter") %>'>
      <ItemTemplate>
        <h4>Chapternum: <%# XPath("@num") %></h4>
        <h4>Chapter name: <%# XPath("@name") %></h4>
        <%# XPath(".") %>
        <br />
```

continues

```
      </ItemTemplate>
    </asp:DataList>
    <br />
  </ItemTemplate>
</asp:DataList>

<asp:XmlDataSource ID="_bookDataSource" runat="server"
                   XPath="/Bookstore/genre/book"
                   DataFile="~/App_Data/Bookstore.xml" />
```

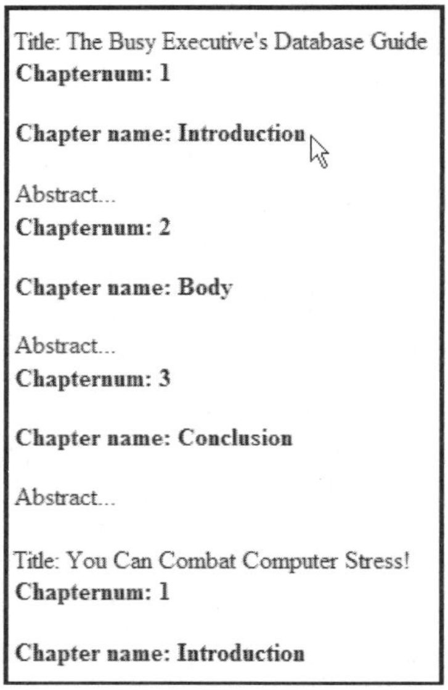

```
Title: The Busy Executive's Database Guide
Chapternum: 1

Chapter name: Introduction

Abstract...
Chapternum: 2

Chapter name: Body

Abstract...
Chapternum: 3

Chapter name: Conclusion

Abstract...

Title: You Can Combat Computer Stress!
Chapternum: 1

Chapter name: Introduction
```

FIGURE 3-10: Rendering of nested hierarchical data binding

Binding to Objects

It is common practice in many applications that deal with data to access the data through a data access layer. Creating a level of indirection between a data source and the elements that consume the data makes for a much more flexible architecture, and opens opportunities in the future for changing details of the data storage without affecting the front end. In the examples of using declarative data sources presented so far in this chapter, we mostly used the SqlDataSource control, which requires that you specify either embedded SQL statements or stored procedures to interact with the database. To work with data access layers instead of direct SQL calls, you can use the ObjectDataSource control instead, with much the same effect.

Instead of a connection string, the ObjectDataSource control is initialized with a type name as the primary object to create, as well as method names for performing select, insert, update, and delete operations. At runtime, the ObjectDataSource will create an instance of the type (if the methods are nonstatic), and using reflection, will invoke the select, update, insert, and/or delete methods as needed in response to control interaction. It is possible to enable sorting, paging, and filtering on an object data source as well, by writing methods with parameters for specifying sort expressions, filter expressions, and methods for performing paging, as you will see shortly. Figure 3-11 shows the role of the ObjectDataSource control, and Listing 3-29 shows the core properties you will set when you work with it.

LISTING 3-29: Core properties of the ObjectDataSource control

```
public class ObjectDataSource : DataSourceControl
  {
    public string TypeName                  { get; set; }
    public string DataObjectTypeName        { get; set; }

    public string DeleteMethod              { get; set; }
    public string InsertMethod              { get; set; }
    public string SelectCountMethod         { get; set; }
    public string SelectMethod              { get; set; }
    public string SortParameterName         { get; set; }
    public string UpdateMethod              { get; set; }
    public string MaximumRowsParameterName  { get; set; }
    public string StartRowIndexParameterName { get; set; }
    //...
```

When you build a class to interact with the ObjectDataSource, there are a few restrictions that you should consider. First of all, if you create a class with nonstatic methods, the ObjectDataSource will create a new instance of your type for each method call made. It is therefore common to create types that expose only static methods to bind to the ObjectDataSource to avoid the overhead of creating and disposing of an object with each method call. This also means that the class you create should be stateless, as any instance of the class will be referred to only once per call. Finally, the method that corresponds to the Select method of your class must return a

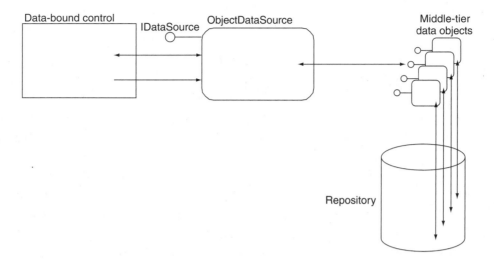

FIGURE 3-11: ObjectDataSource model

collection of items, which at the least implements the IEnumerable or is a DataSet derivative. Listing 3-30 shows a simple static class that returns a list of strings which we can use as a data source. Listing 3-31 shows a sample use of the ObjectDataSource specifying the SimpleDataSource class as the type name and binding the results to a BulletedList control. Figure 3-12 shows the rendered page.

LISTING 3-30: Simple data source for use with ObjectDataSource

```
namespace EssentialAspDotNet2.DataBinding
{
  public static class SimpleDataSource
  {
    public static IEnumerable<string> GetItems()
    {
      for (int i = 0; i < 10; i++)
        yield return "Item " + i.ToString();
    }
  }
}
```

LISTING 3-31: Sample .aspx page using simple data source

```
<%@ Page Language="C#" %>
<html xmlns="http://www.w3.org/1999/xhtml" >
```

```
<head runat="server" />
<body>
  <form id="form1" runat="server"><div>
    <asp:BulletedList ID="_simpleBulletedList" runat="server"
                    DataSourceID="_simpleObjectDataSource" />
    <asp:ObjectDataSource ID="_simpleObjectDataSource" runat="server"
        SelectMethod="GetItems"
        TypeName="EssentialAspDotNet2.DataBinding.SimpleDataSource" />

  </div></form>
</body>
</html>
```

Of course, most of the time the classes you build to interact with the ObjectDataSource will be doing much more than just building an array of strings in memory. As you begin to work with the ObjectDataSource, it is important to keep in mind that its sole purpose is to act as a bridge between data-bound controls and a set of classes providing data. It is not intended as a model for how data access layers should be designed, and in practice you may find that it makes most sense to create a set of "shim" classes that are compatible with the ObjectDataSource control, exposing the methods and parameters needed, but which under the covers invoke methods on classes in a more complete data access layer.

As an example of a slightly more complex data layer, consider the task of building a data access layer for the movies table in our moviereviews database. The first step will be to create an entity class to represent a row from the movies table, exposing property accessors for each of the column types. Listing 3-32 shows the implementation of our Movie entity class.

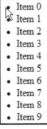

FIGURE 3-12: Simple data source bound to BulletedList with ObjectDataSource

LISTING 3-32: Movie entity class

```
namespace EssentialAspDotNet2.DataBinding
{
  public class Movie
  {
    int _movieId;
    string _title;
    DateTime _releaseDate;

    public Movie() { }
    public Movie(int movieId, string title, DateTime releaseDate)
    {
      _movieId     = movieId;
      _title       = title;
      _releaseDate = releaseDate;
    }

    public int MovieId
    {
      get { return _movieId; }
      set { _movieId = value; }
    }

    public string Title
    {
      get { return _title; }
      set { _title = value; }
    }

    public DateTime ReleaseDate
    {
      get { return _releaseDate; }
      set { _releaseDate = value; }
    }
  }
}
```

Our next task is to build a class that implements the four core access methods to select, update, insert, and delete movies from the database, using instances of our Movie entity class to represent rows in the underlying table. How this class is implemented is completely up to you—you may be calling out to a Web service to retrieve data, or invoking methods in a secondary data access layer, or what have you. The key point is that this class must bridge the gap between the ObjectDataSource control to which it will be bound, and whatever back-end data you are trying to expose. For our example, we will implement the SQL calls directly using ADO.NET. Listing 3-33 shows the MovieReviewsData class with four methods to retrieve and modify movies in our database.

LISTING 3-33: MovieReviewsData class

```
namespace EssentialAspDotNet2.DataBinding
{
  public static class MovieReviewsData
  {
    public static ICollection<Movie> GetMovies()
    {
      string dsn = ConfigurationManager.ConnectionStrings[
                    "moviereviewsConnectionString"].ConnectionString;
      string sql = "SELECT movie_id, title, release_date FROM movies";

      List<Movie> ret = new List<Movie>();

      using (SqlConnection conn = new SqlConnection(dsn))
      using (SqlCommand cmd = new SqlCommand(sql, conn))
      {
        conn.Open();
        SqlDataReader r = cmd.ExecuteReader();
        while (r.Read())
          ret.Add(new Movie(r.GetInt32(0), r.GetString(1),
                            r.GetDateTime(2)));
      }
      return ret;
    }

    public static void UpdateMovie(Movie m)
    {
      string dsn = ConfigurationManager.ConnectionStrings[
                    "moviereviewsConnectionString"].ConnectionString;
      string sql = "UPDATE movies SET title=@title, " +
                   "release_date=@release_date WHERE movie_id=@movie_id";

      using (SqlConnection conn = new SqlConnection(dsn))
      using (SqlCommand cmd = new SqlCommand(sql, conn))
      {
        cmd.Parameters.AddWithValue("@movie_id", m.MovieId);
        cmd.Parameters.AddWithValue("@title", m.Title);
        cmd.Parameters.AddWithValue("@release_date", m.ReleaseDate);

        conn.Open();
        cmd.ExecuteNonQuery();
      }
    }
```

continues

```
public static void DeleteMovie(Movie m)
{
  string dsn = ConfigurationManager.ConnectionStrings[
               "moviereviewsConnectionString"].ConnectionString;
  string sql = "DELETE FROM movies WHERE movie_id=@movie_id";

  using (SqlConnection conn = new SqlConnection(dsn))
  using (SqlCommand cmd = new SqlCommand(sql, conn))
  {
    cmd.Parameters.AddWithValue("@movie_id", m.MovieId);

    conn.Open();
    cmd.ExecuteNonQuery();
  }
}

public static void InsertMovie(Movie m)
{
  string dsn = ConfigurationManager.ConnectionStrings[
               "moviereviewsConnectionString"].ConnectionString;
  string sql = "INSERT INTO movies (title, release_date) " +
               "VALUES (@title, @release_date)";

  using (SqlConnection conn = new SqlConnection(dsn))
  using (SqlCommand cmd = new SqlCommand(sql, conn))
  {
    cmd.Parameters.AddWithValue("@title", m.Title);
    cmd.Parameters.AddWithValue("@release_date", m.ReleaseDate);

    conn.Open();
    cmd.ExecuteNonQuery();
  }
 }
 }
}
```

The last step is to actually wire this data class up to an ObjectData-Source control and bind a control (like a GridView) to that data source. If you are using a GridView, DetailsView, or FormView control to bind to an ObjectDataSource, one thing you will have to take care of by hand is to set the DataKeyNames property of the control to contain the name of the primary key property of your entity class (it could be multiple primary keys if needed, separated by commas). The values of properties in the DataKey-Names collection are cached in the control state of the control, and these values will be used to populate the entity class passed into your update and delete methods (the rest of the entity class will remain empty in the delete method, since you should only need the primary key value(s) to perform the deletion). In our case, we will set the DataKeyNames property in our DataGrid to *MovieId*. As for the ObjectDataSource itself, we need to specify the type name, the names of the four methods, and the name of the type used as the entity class through the DataObjectTypeName so that the control knows what type to reflect on to view the properties.

Listing 3-34 shows a sample use of the ObjectDataSource initialized with our MovieReviewsData class and bound to a GridView with full editing and deleting features enabled. This same data source could be bound to a DetailsView or FormView control as well to perform insertion in the same manner. The rendering of this page will look identical to the GridView paired with a SqlDataSource shown earlier in Figure 3-4.

LISTING 3-34: **Binding a GridView to an ObjectDataSource with a custom data access layer**

```
<asp:GridView ID="_moviesGrid" runat="server" AllowPaging="True"
            AutoGenerateColumns="False"
            DataSourceID="_moviesObjectDataSource"
            DataKeyNames="MovieId">
  <Columns>
    <asp:CommandField ShowDeleteButton="True" ShowEditButton="True" />
    <asp:BoundField DataField="ReleaseDate" DataFormatString="{0:d}"
                HeaderText="ReleaseDate"
                HtmlEncode="False" SortExpression="ReleaseDate" />
    <asp:BoundField DataField="MovieId" HeaderText="MovieId"
                SortExpression="MovieId" Visible="False" />
    <asp:BoundField DataField="Title" HeaderText="Title"
                SortExpression="Title" />
  </Columns>
</asp:GridView>

<asp:ObjectDataSource ID="_moviesObjectDataSource" runat="server"
            TypeName="EssentialAspDotNet2.DataBinding.MovieReviewsData"
            DataObjectTypeName="EssentialAspDotNet2.DataBinding.Movie"
            DeleteMethod="InsertMovie"
            InsertMethod="InsertMovie"
            SelectMethod="GetMovies"
            UpdateMethod="UpdateMovie" />
```

You may have noticed that the previous example had enabled paging on the GridView by default, even though we made no effort to support paging in our data access layer. By default, the GridView is happy to provide paging for you by displaying a particular subset of rows from the underlying query, but this means that it will be retrieving all of the rows with each paginated display, even though it may only be showing a small subset. To implement paging more efficiently in your data layer, you need to build an override of your Select method that takes a maximum row count and a start row index pair of parameters. You also need to provide another method in your data class that returns the total count of items. Finally, in the ObjectDataSource declaration itself, you need to populate the MaximumRowsParameterName, SelectCountMethod, and StartRow-IndexParameterName properties with the names of the parameters and method added to your class.

You must also set the EnablePaging property to true, which will cause the data source control to look for an overload of your Select method with the two parameter names and will use them to expose paging functionality to controls like the GridView. Listing 3-35 shows an updated version of our GetMovies method that uses the ROW_NUMBER function of SQL Server 2005 to implement paging over the movies table, as well as the new Get-MoviesCount method. There are many ways to implement paging over in a query, so the details may well change depending on what features your database supports, but the concepts will be the same. Listing 3-36 shows the updated declaration of the ObjectDataSource control that will take advantage of our custom paging code. No changes are necessary to the GridView in this case.

LISTING 3-35: Enhancements to the MovieReviewsData class to support custom paging

```
public static ICollection<Movie> GetMovies(
              int maxRows, int startRowIndex)
{
  List<Movie> ret = new List<Movie>();

  string dsn = ConfigurationManager.ConnectionStrings[
              "moviereviewsConnectionString"].ConnectionString;

  // This assumes SQL Server 2005 with its new ROW_NUMBER function
  // to assist with pagination.
  //
  string sql = "SELECT movie_id, title, release_date FROM " +
              "(SELECT ROW_NUMBER() OVER (ORDER BY title) As Row, " +
              "movie_id, title, release_date FROM movies)" +
              " As TempRowTable";

  if (startRowIndex >= 0)
  {
```

```
        sql += " WHERE Row >= " + startRowIndex.ToString() + " AND " +
                "Row <= " + (startRowIndex + maxRows).ToString();
    }

    using (SqlConnection conn = new SqlConnection(dsn))
    using (SqlCommand cmd = new SqlCommand(sql, conn))
    {
        conn.Open();
        SqlDataReader r = cmd.ExecuteReader();
        while (r.Read())
            ret.Add(new Movie(r.GetInt32(0), r.GetString(1),
                            r.GetDateTime(2)));
    }

    return ret;
}

public static int GetMovieCount()
{
    int ret = -1;
    string dsn = ConfigurationManager.ConnectionStrings[
                    "moviereviewsConnectionString"].ConnectionString;
    string sql = "SELECT COUNT(*) FROM movies";

    using (SqlConnection conn = new SqlConnection(dsn))
    using (SqlCommand cmd = new SqlCommand(sql, conn))
    {
        conn.Open();
        ret = (int)cmd.ExecuteScalar();
    }
    return ret;
}
```

LISTING 3-36: Updated ObjectDataSource declaration taking advantage of custom paging

```
<asp:ObjectDataSource ID="_moviesObjectDataSource" runat="server"
    TypeName="EssentialAspDotNet2.DataBinding.MovieReviewsData"
    DataObjectTypeName="EssentialAspDotNet2.DataBinding.Movie"
    DeleteMethod="InsertMovie"
    InsertMethod="InsertMovie"
    SelectMethod="GetMovies"
    UpdateMethod="UpdateMovie"
    EnablePaging="true" MaximumRowsParameterName="maxRows"
    SelectCountMethod="GetMovieCount"
    StartRowIndexParameterName="startRowIndex" />
```

You can similarly implement sorting in your Select method by providing a SortExpression parameter which you then specify in the ObjectDataSource declaration using the SortParameterName property. This will make sorting available on controls like the GridView that support it. The samples available for download for this book contain a complete implementation of a data access layer for both the movies and reviews tables, complete with custom paging, sorting, and even filtering.

Typed DataSets

Typed DataSets remain relatively unchanged from their 1.1 incarnation. One significant exception is that the .xsd file now can contain information about a TableAdapter as well as the schema for the typed DataSet. This means that there is now a strongly typed class that is capable of populating the associated typed DataSet, as well as propagating updates, inserts, and deletes.

The easiest way to bind a typed DataSet to a data-bound control is to expose it using an ObjectDataSource. The object data source will pick up on its public properties, notice that its methods return DataTables and DataRows, and enable all of the functionality exposed by the DataSet automatically. It creates an autogenerated type-safe class that acts as an intermediary between the database and the controls on the form. However, it also exposes the database's underlying schema directly to the presentation layer so that changes in the database will directly affect the controls on your forms; hence, it does not have all of the advantages of a custom data access layer (although it is certainly much less work to create).

SUMMARY

Declarative data sources and the new data-binding model of ASP.NET 2.0 are probably the most significant changes introduced in this release. They change the way developers associate data with controls, and force them to think differently about how data is retrieved and propagated. The primary advantage of this model is the removal of data access code from pages, and in general simplifying common tasks like creating a grid to display and edit data from a database. At the same time, this model of data binding works with all types of data access, ranging from direct SQL calls to stored procedure invocations to calling methods in an isolated data access layer.

∎ 4 ∎
State Management

W HERE DO YOU STORE per-client state in a Web application? This question is at the root of many heated debates over how to best design Web applications. The disconnected nature of HTTP means that there is no "natural" way to keep state on behalf of individual clients, but that certainly hasn't stopped developers from finding ways of doing it. Today there are many choices for keeping client-specific state in an ASP.NET Web application, including Session state, View state, cookies, the HttpContext.Items collection, and any number of custom solutions. The best choice depends on many things, including the scope (Do you need the state to last for an entire user session or just between two pages?), the size (Are you worried about passing too much data in the response and would prefer to keep it on the server?), and the deployment environment (Is this application deployed on a Web farm so that server state must be somehow shared?), just to name a few.

ASP.NET 2.0 does not offer a penultimate solution for storing client state, but it does introduce three new features that should be considered any time you are looking for a place to store state on behalf of individual users. The first feature, **cross-page posting**, is actually the resurrection of a common technique used in classic ASP and other Web development environments for propagating state between two pages. This technique was not available in ASP.NET 1.1 because of the way POST requests were parsed and processed by individual pages, but has now been reincorporated into

ASP.NET in such a way that it works in conjunction with server-side controls and other ASP.NET features. The second feature is a trio of new server-side controls that implement the common technique of showing and hiding portions of a page as the user interacts with it. The Wizard control gives developers a simple way to construct a multistep user interface on a single page, and the MultiView and View controls provide a slightly lower-level (and more flexible) way of hiding and displaying panes.

The last feature, Profile, is by far the most intriguing. **Profile** provides a prebuilt implementation that will store per-client state across requests and even sessions of your application in a persistent back-end data store. It ties into the Membership provider of ASP.NET 2.0 for identifying authenticated clients, and generates its own identifier for working with anonymous users as well, storing each client's data in a preconfigured database table. This feature provides a flexible and extensible way of storing client data and should prove quite useful in almost any ASP.NET application.

Cross-Page Posting

This version of ASP.NET reintroduces the ability to perform cross-page posts. Once a common practice in classic ASP applications, ASP.NET 1.x made it nearly impossible to use this technique for state propagation because of server-side forms and view state. This section covers the fundamentals of cross-page posting in general, and then looks at the support added in ASP.NET 2.0.

Fundamentals

One common mechanism for sending state from one page to another in Web applications is to use a form with input elements whose action attribute is set to the URL or the target page. The values of the source page's input elements are passed as name-value pairs to the target page in the body of the POST request (or in the query string if the form's method attribute is set to GET), at which point the target page has access to the values. Listings 4-1 and 4-2 show a pair of sample pages that request a user's name, age, and marital status, and display a customized message on the target page.

LISTING 4-1: sourceform.aspx—sample form using a cross-page post

```
<!-- sourceform.aspx -->
<%@ Page language="C#" %>


<html xmlns="http://www.w3.org/1999/xhtml">
<head>
    <title>Source Form</title>
</head>
<body>
    <form action="target.aspx" method="post">
        Enter your name:
        <input name="_nameTextBox" type="text" id="_nameTextBox" />
        <br />
        Enter your age:
        <input name="_ageTextBox" type="text" id="_ageTextBox" /><br />
        <input id="_marriedCheckBox" type="checkbox"
                name="_marriedCheckBox" />
        <label for="_marriedCheckBox">Married?</label><br />
        <input type="submit" name="_nextPageButton" value="Next page" />
    </form>
</body>
</html>
```

LISTING 4-2: target.aspx—sample target page for a cross-page post

```
<!-- target.aspx -->
<%@ Page language="C#" %>


<html xmlns="http://www.w3.org/1999/xhtml" >
<head>
    <title>Target Page</title>
</head>
<body>
  <h3>
  Hello there
  <%= Request.Form["_nameTextBox"] %>, you are
  <%= Request.Form["_ageTextBox"] %> years old and are
  <%= (Request.Form["_marriedCheckBox"] == "on") ? "" : "not " %>
  married!
  </h3>
</body>
</html>
```

This example works fine in both ASP.NET 1.1 and 2.0, and with a few simple modifications would even work in classic ASP. This technique is rarely used in ASP.NET, however, because the form on the source page cannot be marked with *runat="server"*; thus, many of the advantages of

ASP.NET, including server-side controls, cannot be used. ASP.NET builds much of its server-side control infrastructure on the assumption that pages with forms will generate POST requests back to the same page. In fact, if you try and change the action attribute of a form that is also marked with runat="server", it will have no effect, as ASP.NET will replace the attribute when it renders the page with the page's URL itself. As a result, most ASP.NET sites resort to alternative techniques for propagating state between pages (like Session state or using Server.Transfer while caching data in the Context.Items collection).

In the 2.0 release of ASP.NET, cross-page posting is now supported again, even if you are using server-side controls and all of the other ASP.NET features. The usage model is a bit different from the one shown in Listings 4-1 and 4-2, but in the end it achieves the desired goal of issuing a POST request from one page to another, and allowing the secondary page to harvest the contents from the POST body and process them as it desires. To initiate a cross-page post, you use the new PostBackUrl attribute defined by the IButtonControl interface, which is implemented by the Button, LinkButton, and ImageButton controls. When the PostBackUrl property is set to a different page, the OnClick handler of the button is set to call a JavaScript function that changes the default action of the form to the target page's URL. Listing 4-3 shows a sample form that uses cross-page posting to pass name, age, and marital status data entered by the user to a target page.

LISTING 4-3: SourcePage1.aspx—using cross-page posting support in ASP.NET 2.0

```
<!-- SourcePage1.aspx -->
<%@ Page Language="C#" CodeFile="SourcePage1.aspx.cs"
         Inherits="SourcePage1" %>

<html xmlns="http://www.w3.org/1999/xhtml">
<head runat="server">
    <title>Source page 1</title>
</head>
<body>
    <form id="form1" runat="server">
        <div>
            Enter your name:
            <asp:TextBox ID="_nameTextBox" runat="server" /><br />
            Enter your age:
            <asp:TextBox ID="_ageTextBox" runat="server" /><br />
```

```
        <asp:CheckBox ID="_marriedCheckBox" runat="server"
                    Text="Married?" /><br />
        <asp:Button ID="_nextPageButton" runat="server"
                Text="Next page" PostBackUrl="~/TargetPage.aspx" />
      </div>
    </form>
</body>
</html>
```

Once you have set up the source page to post to the target page, the next step is to build the target page to use the values passed by the source page. Because ASP.NET uses POST data to manage the state of its server-side controls, it would not have been sufficient to expect the target page to pull name/value pairs from the POST body, since many of those values (like __VIEWSTATE) need to be parsed by the server-side controls that wrote the values there in the first place. Therefore, ASP.NET will actually create a fresh instance of the source page class and ask it to parse the POST body on behalf of the target page. This page instance is then made available to the target page via the PreviousPage property, which is now defined in the Page class. Listings 4-4 and 4-5 show one example of how you could use this property in a target page to retrieve the values of the controls from the previous page: by calling FindControl on the Form control, you can retrieve individual controls whose state has been initialized with values from the post's body.

LISTING 4-4: TargetPage.aspx—target page of a cross-page post

```
<!-- TargetPage.aspx -->
<%@ Page Language="C#" AutoEventWireup="true" CodeFile="Tar-
getPage.aspx.cs"
        Inherits="TargetPage" %>

<html xmlns="http://www.w3.org/1999/xhtml">
<head runat="server">
    <title>Target Page</title>
</head>
<body>
    <form id="form1" runat="server">
        <div>
            <asp:Label runat="server" ID="_messageLabel" />
        </div>
    </form>
</body>
</html>
```

LISTING 4-5: TargetPage.aspx.cs—target page of a cross-page post codebehind

```
// TargetPage.aspx.cs
public partial class TargetPage : System.Web.UI.Page
{
    protected void Page_Load(object sender, EventArgs e)
    {
        if (PreviousPage != null)
        {
            TextBox nameTextBox =
                (TextBox)PreviousPage.Form.FindControl("_nameTextBox");
            TextBox ageTextBox =
                (TextBox)PreviousPage.Form.FindControl("_ageTextBox");
            CheckBox marriedCheckBox =
            (CheckBox)PreviousPage.Form.FindControl("_marriedCheckBox");

            _messageLabel.Text = string.Format(
    "<h3>Hello there {0}, you are {1} years old and {2} married!</h3>",
            nameTextBox.Text, ageTextBox.Text,
            marriedCheckBox.Checked ? "" : "not");
        }
    }
}
```

The technique shown in Listing 4-5 for retrieving values from the previous page is somewhat fragile, as it relies on the identifiers of controls on the previous page as well as their hierarchical placement, which could easily be changed. A better approach is to expose any data from the previous page to the target page by writing public property accessors in the codebehind, as shown in Listing 4-6.

LISTING 4-6: SourcePage1.aspx.cs—exposing public properties to the target page

```
// File: SourcePage1.aspx.cs
public partial class SourcePage1 : Page
{
    public string Name
    {
      get { return _nameTextBox.Text; }
    }

    public int Age
    {
      get { return int.Parse(_ageTextBox.Text); }
    }
```

```
  public bool Married
  {
    get { return _marriedCheckBox.Checked; }
  }
}
```

Once the public properties are defined, the target page can cast the PreviousPage property to the specific type of the previous page and retrieve the values using the exposed properties, as shown in Listing 4-7.

LISTING 4-7: TargetPage.aspx.cs—target page using properties to retrieve source page values

```
// TargetPage.aspx.cs
public partial class TargetPage : System.Web.UI.Page
{
    protected void Page_Load(object sender, EventArgs e)
    {
        SourcePage1 sp = PreviousPage as SourcePage1;
        if (sp != null)
        {
            _messageLabel.Text = string.Format(
    "<h3>Hello there {0}, you are {1} years old and {2} married!</h3>",
            sp.Name, sp.Age, sp.Married ? "" : "not");
        }
    }
}
```

Because this last scenario is likely to be the most common use of cross-page posting—that is, a specific source page exposes properties to be consumed by a specific target page—there is a directive called PreviousPage-Type that will automatically cast the previous page to the correct type for you. When you specify a page in the VirtualPath property of this directive, the PreviousPage property that is generated for that page will be strongly typed to the previous page type, meaning that you no longer have to perform the cast yourself, as shown in Listings 4-8 and 4-9.

LISTING 4-8: TargetPage.aspx with strongly typed previous page

```
<!-- TargetPage.aspx -->
<%@ Page Language="C#" AutoEventWireup="true" CodeFile="Tar-
getPage.aspx.cs"
        Inherits="TargetPage" %>
<%@ PreviousPageType VirtualPath="~/SourcePage1.aspx" %>
...
```

LISTING 4-9: TargetPage.aspx.cs—using strongly typed PreviousPage accessor

```
// TargetPage.aspx.cs
public partial class TargetPage : System.Web.UI.Page
{
    protected void Page_Load(object sender, EventArgs e)
    {
        if (PreviousPage != null)
        {
            _messageLabel.Text = string.Format(
    "<h3>Hello there {0}, you are {1} years old and {2} married!</h3>",
            PreviousPage.Name, PreviousPage.Age,
            PreviousPage.Married ? "" : "not");
        }
    }
}
```

Implementation

When you set the PostBackUrl property of a button to a different page, it does two things. First, it sets the client-side OnClick handler for that button to point to a JavaScript method called WebForm_DoPostBackWithOptions, which will programmatically set the form's action to the target page. Second, it causes the page to render an additional hidden field, __PREVIOUSPAGE, which contains the path of the source page in an encrypted string along with an accompanying message authentication code for validating the string. Setting the action dynamically like this enables you to have multiple buttons on a page that all potentially post to different pages and keeps the architecture flexible. Storing the path of the previous page in a hidden field means that no matter where you send the POST request, the target page will be able to determine where the request came from, and will know which class to instantiate to parse the body of the message.

Once the POST request is issued to the target page, the path of the previous page is read and decrypted from the __PREVIOUSPAGE hidden field and cached. As you have seen, the PreviousPage property on the target page gives access to the previous page and its data, but for efficiency, this property allocates the previous page class on demand. If you never actually access the PreviousPage property, it will never create the class and ask it to parse the body of the request.

The first time you do access the PreviousPage property in the target page, ASP.NET allocates a new instance of the previous page type, as determined by the cached path to the previous page extracted from the __PREVIOUSPAGE hidden field. Once it is created, it then executes the page much like it would if the request had been issued to it. The page is not executed in its entirety, however, since it only needs to restore the state from the POST body, so it runs through its life cycle up to and including the LoadComplete event. The Response and Trace objects of the previous page instance are also set to null during this execution since there should be no output associated with the process.

It is important to keep in mind that the preceding page will be created and asked to run through LoadComplete. If you have any code that generates side effects, you should make an effort to exclude that code from running when the page is executed during a cross-page postback. You can check to see whether you are being executed for real or for the purpose of evaluating the POST body of a cross-page post by checking the IsCrossPagePostBack property. For example, suppose that the source page wrote to a database in its Load event handler for logging purposes. You would not want this code to execute during a cross-page postback evaluation since the request was not really made to that page. Listing 4-10 shows how you might exclude your logging code from being evaluated during a cross-page postback.

LISTING 4-10: Checking for IsCrossPagePostBack before running code with side effects

```
public partial class SourcePage1 : Page
{
    protected void Page_Load(object sender, EventArgs e)
    {
        if (!IsCrossPagePostBack)
        {
            WriteDataToLogFile();
        }
    }
}
```

Caveats

While this new support for cross-page posting is a welcome addition to ASP.NET, it does have some potential drawbacks you should be aware of before you elect to use it. The first thing to keep in mind is that the entire contents of the source page is going to be posted to the target page. This includes the entire view state field and all input elements on the page. If you are using cross-page posting to send the value of a pair of TextBox controls to a target page, but you have a GridView with view state enabled on the source page, you're going to incur the cost of posting the entire contents of the GridView in addition to the TextBox controls just to send over a pair of strings. If you can't reduce the size of the request on the source page to an acceptable amount, you may want to consider using an alternative technique (like query strings) to propagate the values.

Validation is another potential trouble area with cross-page posting. If you are using validation controls in the client page to validate user input prior to the cross-page post, you should be aware that server-side validation will not take place until you access the PreviousPage property on the target page. Client-side validation will still happen as usual before the page issues the POST, but if you are relying on server-side validation at all, you must take care to check the IsValid property of the previous page before accessing the data exposed by the PreviousPage property.

A common scenario where this may occur is with custom validation controls. If you have set up a custom validation control with a server-side handler for the ServerValidate event, that method will not be called until you access the PreviousPage after the cross-page posting has occurred. Then there is the question of what to do if the previous page contains invalid data, since you can no longer just let the page render back to the client with error messages in place (because the client has already navigated away from the source page). The best option is probably just to place an indicator message that the data is invalid and provide a link back to the previous page to enter the data again. Listings 4-11 and 4-12 show a sample of a source page with a custom validation control and a button set up to use cross-page posting, along with a target page. Note that the code in the target page explicitly checks the validity of the previous page's data before using it and the error handling added if something is wrong.

LISTING 4-11: Source page with custom validator

```
<!-- SourcePageWithValidation.aspx -->
<%@ Page Language="C#" %>

<script runat="server">
    public int Prime
    {
        get { return int.Parse(_primeNumberTextBox.Text); }
    }
```

```
    private bool IsPrime(int num)
    {
        // implementation omitted
    }

    protected void _primeValidator_ServerValidate(object source,
                        ServerValidateEventArgs args)
    {
        args.IsValid = IsPrime(Prime);
    }
</script>

<html xmlns="http://www.w3.org/1999/xhtml">
<head runat="server">
    <title>Source page with validation</title>
</head>
<body>
    <form id="form1" runat="server">
        <div>
            Enter your favorite prime number:
            <asp:TextBox ID="_primeNumberTextBox" runat="server" />
            <asp:CustomValidator ID="_primeValidator" runat="server"
                ErrorMessage="Please enter a prime number"
              OnServerValidate="_primeValidator_ServerValidate">
                                    **</asp:CustomValidator><br />
            <asp:Button ID="_nextPageButton" runat="server"
                    Text="Next page"
                    PostBackUrl="~/TargetPageWithValidation.aspx"
                     /><br />
            <br />
            <asp:ValidationSummary ID="_validationSummary"
                                runat="server" />
        </div>
    </form>
</body>
</html>
```

LISTING 4-12: Target page checking for validation

```
<!-- TargetPageWithValidation.aspx -->
<%@ Page Language="C#" %>
<%@ PreviousPageType VirtualPath="~/SourcePageWithValidation.aspx" %>

<script runat="server">
    protected void Page_Load(object sender, EventArgs e)
    {
        if (PreviousPage != null && PreviousPage.IsValid)
        {
          _messageLabel.Text = "Thanks for choosing the prime number " +
                    PreviousPage.Prime.ToString();
        }
```

continues

```
        else
        {
            _messageLabel.Text = "Error in entering data";
            _messageLabel.ForeColor = Color.Red;
            _previousPageLink.Visible = true;
        }
    }
</script>

<html xmlns="http://www.w3.org/1999/xhtml">
<head runat="server">
    <title>Target Page With validation</title>
</head>
<body>
    <form id="form1" runat="server">
        <div>
            <asp:Label runat="server" ID="_messageLabel" /><br />
            <asp:HyperLink runat="server" ID="_previousPageLink"
                        NavigateUrl="~/SourcePageWithValidation.aspx"
                        visible="false">
                Return to data entry page...</asp:HyperLink>
        </div>
    </form>
</body>
</html>
```

Finally, it is important to be aware that the entire cross-page posting mechanism relies on JavaScript to work properly, so if the client either doesn't support or has disabled JavaScript, your source pages will simply post back to themselves as the action on the form will not be changed on the client in response to the button press.

Multi-Source Cross-Page Posting

Cross-page posting can also be used to create a single target page that can be posted to by multiple source pages. Such a scenario may be useful if you have a site that provides several different ways of collecting information from the user but one centralized page for processing it.

If we try and extend our earlier example by introducing a second source page, also with the ability to collect the name, age, and marital status of the client, we run into a problem because each page is a distinct type with its own VirtualPath, and the target page will somehow have to distinguish between a post from source page 1 and one from source page 2. One way to solve this problem is to implement a common interface in each source page's base class; this way, the target page assumes only that the posting page implements a particular interface and is not necessarily of one specific type or another. For example, we could write the IPersonInfo interface to model our cross-page POST data, as shown in Listing 4-13.

LISTING 4-13: IPersonInfo interface definition

```
public interface IPersonInfo
{
  string Name { get; }
  int Age { get; }
  bool Married { get; }
}
```

In each of the source pages, we then implement the IPersonInfo on the codebehind base class, and our target page can now safely cast the PreviousPage to the IPersonInfo type and extract the data regardless of which page was the source page, as shown in Listing 4-14.

LISTING 4-14: Generic target page using interface for previous page

```
IPersonInfo pi = PreviousPage as IPersonInfo;
if (pi != null)
{
  _messageLabel.Text = string.Format("<h3>Hello there {0}, you are {1}
years old and {2} married!</h3>",
                   pi.Name, pi.Age, pi.Married ? "" : "not");
}
```

It would be even better if we could use the PreviousPageType directive to strongly type the PreviousPage property to the IPersonInfo interface. In fact, there is a way to associate a type with a previous page instead of using the virtual path, which is to specify the TypeName attribute instead of the VirtualPath attribute in the PreviousPageType directive. Unfortunately, the TypeName attribute of the PreviousPageType directive requires that the specified type inherit from System.Web.UI.Page. You can introduce a workaround to get the strong typing by defining an abstract base class that implements the interface (or just defines abstract methods directly) and inherits from Page, as shown in Listing 4-15.

LISTING 4-15: Abstract base class inheriting from Page for strong typing with PreviousPageType

```
public abstract class PersonInfoPage : Page, IPersonInfo
{
  public abstract string Name { get; }
  public abstract int Age { get; }
  public abstract bool Married { get; }
}
```

This technique then requires that each of the source pages you author change their base class from Page to this new PersonInfoPage base, and then implement the abstract properties to return the appropriate data. Listing 4-16 shows an example of a codebehind class for a source page using this new base class.

LISTING 4-16: Codebehind class for a sample source page inheriting from PersonInfoPage

```
public partial class SourcePage1 : PersonInfoPage
{
  public override string Name
  {
    get { return _nameTextBox.Text; }
  }
  public override int Age
  {
    get { return int.Parse(_ageTextBox.Text); }
  }
  public override bool Married
  {
    get { return _marriedCheckBox.Checked; }
  }
}
```

Once all source pages are derived from our PersonInfoPage and the three abstract properties are implemented, our target page can be rewritten with a strongly typed PreviousPageType directive, which saves the trouble of casting, as shown in Listing 4-17.

LISTING 4-17: Strongly typed target page using TypeName

```
<%@ PreviousPageType TypeName="PersonInfoPage" %>

<script runat="server">
protected void Page_Load(object sender, EventArgs e)
{
  if (PreviousPage != null)
```

```
  {
    _messageLabel.Text = string.Format(
 "<h3>Hello there {0}, you are {1} years old and {2} married!</h3>",
              PreviousPage.Name, PreviousPage.Age,
              PreviousPage.Married ? "" : "not");
  }
}
</script>
<!-- ... -->
```

The effort required to get the strong typing to work for multiple source pages hardly seems worth it in the end. You already have to check to see whether the PreviousPage property is null or not, and casting it to the interface using the *as* operator in C# is about the same amount of work as checking for null. However, both ways are valid approaches, and it is up to you to decide how much effort you want to put into making your previous pages strongly typed.

Wizard and MultiView Controls

This section covers a new collection of controls in ASP.NET 2.0 that simplify the process of collecting data from the user by using a sequence of steps that are all on a single page. The controls include the new Wizard control as well as the View and MultiView controls.

Same Page State Management

Another alternative to storing per-client state across requests is to have the user post back to the same page instead of navigating from one page to another. You can achieve the same sequential set of steps for data collection that you can using multiple pages with this technique by toggling the display of various panels, showing only one of several panels at any given time based on the user's progress. Instead of placing input controls on separate pages, you place them all on the same page, but separate them with Panel (or Placeholder) controls as shown in Figure 4-1. When the user selects the Next button in one panel, the handler for that button sets the visibility of the current panel to false and of the next panel to true.

This technique works well because all of the state for all the controls is kept on a single page, and even when the controls in a particular panel are

CollectInfo.aspx

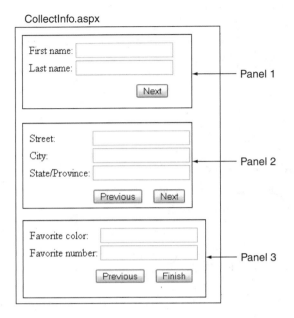

FIGURE 4-1: Multipanel page

not displayed, their state is maintained in view state, so programmatically it is just like working with one giant form. It is also quite efficient, since the contents of invisible panels are not even sent to the client browser; just the state of the controls is sent through view state.

Wizard Control

In the 2.0 release of ASP.NET this technique has been standardized in the form of the Wizard control. Instead of laying out the Panel controls yourself and adding the logic to flip the visibility of each panel in response to button presses, you can use the Wizard control to manage the details for you and focus on laying out the controls for each step. The control itself consists of a collection of WizardSteps which act as containers for any controls you want to add. Listing 4-18 shows a sample Wizard control populated with the input elements described in Figure 4-1 (also included is an adjacent Label control to display the data on completion).

LISTING 4-18: Sample Wizard control with three steps

```
<asp:Wizard ID="_infoWizard" runat="server" ActiveStepIndex="0"
        OnFinishButtonClick="_infoWizard_FinishButtonClick"
        DisplaySideBar="False">
    <WizardSteps>
      <asp:WizardStep ID="_step1" runat="server" Title="Name">
      <table>
        <tr>
          <td>First name:</td>
          <td><asp:TextBox ID="_firstNameTextBox" runat="server" /></td>
        </tr>
        <tr>
          <td>Last name:</td>
          <td><asp:TextBox ID="_lastNameTextBox" runat="server" /></td>
        </tr>
      </table>
      </asp:WizardStep>
      <asp:WizardStep ID="_step2" runat="server" Title="Address">
        <table>
          <tr>
            <td>Street:</td>
            <td><asp:TextBox ID="_streetTextBox" runat="server" /></td>
          </tr>
          <tr>
            <td>City:</td>
            <td><asp:TextBox ID="_cityTextBox" runat="server" /></td>
          </tr>
          <tr>
            <td>State/Province:</td>
            <td><asp:TextBox ID="_stateTextBox" runat="server" /></td>
          </tr>
        </table>
      </asp:WizardStep>
      <asp:WizardStep ID="_step3" runat="server" Title="Preferences">
        <table>
          <tr>
            <td>Favorite color:</td>
            <td><asp:TextBox ID="_colorTextBox" runat="server" /></td>
          </tr>
          <tr>
            <td>Favorite number:</td>
            <td><asp:TextBox ID="_numberTextBox" runat="server" /></td>
          </tr>
        </table>
      </asp:WizardStep>
    </WizardSteps>
  </asp:Wizard>
  <asp:Label ID="_summaryLabel" runat="server" />
```

Like most controls in ASP.NET, both the appearance and behavior of the Wizard control are extremely customizable. In the previous example, the control's SideBar portion, which generates a set of navigation hyperlinks on the left side to let the user jump between steps in the wizard without using the Next/Previous buttons, was not displayed. Figure 4-2 shows two different renderings of the Wizard control: the first is exactly how the Wizard control shown in Listing 4-18 would appear, and the second shows the same control with a different formatting applied and with the ShowSideBar attribute set to true. This control also supports templates so that you can completely customize the look and feel of it as desired.

The advantage of working with the Wizard control like this is that it manages all of the details of the sequential interaction with the user, and you can treat all of the input elements in each of the separate steps as if they were all part of a single page. For example, in our OnFinishButton-Click handler for the Wizard control we can easily use all of the data the user has entered. Listing 4-19 shows an example of printing a message back to the user in the form of a label and then hiding the Wizard control as an indicator that the input sequence is complete.

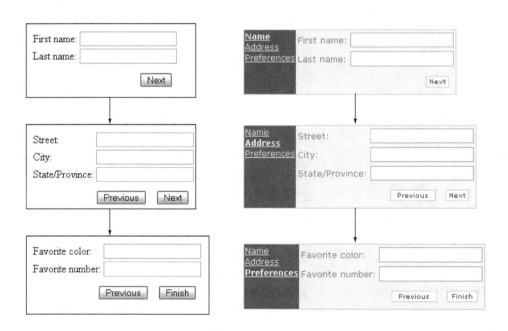

FIGURE 4-2: Wizard control, unadorned, and with SideBar and formatting

LISTING 4-19: Handler for the Wizard's Finish button click event

```
protected void _infoWizard_FinishButtonClick(object sender,
                                    WizardNavigationEventArgs e)
{
  _summaryLabel.Text = string.Format(
            "<h2>Thank you for submitting your information!</h2>" +
            "Name: {0} {1}<br /><br/>Address: {2}<br/>" +
            "{3}, {4}<br /><br />Prefs: {5} {6}<br />",
                        _firstNameTextBox.Text,
                        _lastNameTextBox.Text, _streetTextBox.Text,
                        _cityTextBox.Text, _stateTextBox.Text,
                        _colorTextBox.Text, _numberTextBox.Text);
  _infoWizard.Visible = false;
}
```

MultiView and View Controls

If you want the ability to toggle among multiple panels on a page but find the Wizard control too constraining, you might instead consider using the MultiView control. A MultiView control consists of several child View controls, and it maintains an active index indicating which of those child views should be visible. In fact, the WizardStep control used by the Wizard control inherits from the View class used by the MultiView, so the similarity is not a coincidence. Unlike the Wizard control, the MultiView renders nothing but the contents of the active view—there are no buttons, links, or titles of any kind. This means that it is up to you to determine how the user switches between the various views. Listings 4-20 and 4-21 show a sample MultiView with three embedded views to collect data from the user. This example uses three link buttons to let the user toggle among the three views by setting the ActiveViewIndex of the MultiView depending on which button was selected.

LISTING 4-20: MultiView with LinkButtons

```
        <asp:LinkButton ID="_view1LinkButton" runat="server"
            OnClick="_view1LinkButton_Click">
            View 1</asp:LinkButton>  
        <asp:LinkButton ID="_view2LinkButton" runat="server"
            OnClick="_view2LinkButton_Click">
            View 2</asp:LinkButton>  
        <asp:LinkButton ID="_view3LinkButton" runat="server"
            OnClick="_view3LinkButton_Click">
            View 3</asp:LinkButton><br />
```

continues

```
<asp:MultiView ID="_infoMultiView" runat="server"
            ActiveViewIndex="0">
    <asp:View ID="_view1" runat="server">
     <table>
        <tr>
          <td>First name:</td>
          <td><asp:TextBox ID="_firstNameTextBox"
                            runat="server" /></td>
        </tr>
        <tr>
          <td>Last name:</td>
          <td><asp:TextBox ID="_lastNameTextBox"
                            runat="server" /></td>
        </tr>
      </table>
    </asp:View>
    <asp:View ID="_view2" runat="server">
        <table>
          <tr>
            <td>Street:</td>
            <td><asp:TextBox ID="_streetTextBox"
                              runat="server" /></td>
          </tr>
          <tr>
            <td>City:</td>
            <td><asp:TextBox ID="_cityTextBox"
                              runat="server" /></td>
          </tr>
          <tr>
            <td>State/Province:</td>
            <td><asp:TextBox ID="_stateTextBox"
                              runat="server" /></td>
          </tr>
        </table>
    </asp:View>
    <asp:View ID="_view3" runat="server">
        <table>
          <tr>
            <td>Favorite color:</td>
            <td><asp:TextBox ID="_colorTextBox"
                              runat="server" /></td>
          </tr>
          <tr>
            <td>Favorite number:</td>
            <td><asp:TextBox ID="_numberTextBox"
                              runat="server" /></td>
          </tr>
        </table>
    </asp:View>
</asp:MultiView>
```

LISTING 4-21: LinkButton handlers for MultiView switching

```
protected void _view1LinkButton_Click(object sender, EventArgs e)
{
    _infoMultiView.ActiveViewIndex = 0;
}
protected void _view2LinkButton_Click(object sender, EventArgs e)
{
    _infoMultiView.ActiveViewIndex = 1;
}
protected void _view3LinkButton_Click(object sender, EventArgs e)
{
    _infoMultiView.ActiveViewIndex = 2;
}
```

Profile

Profile provides a simple way of defining database-backed user profile information. With just a few configuration file entries, you can quickly build a site that stores user preferences (or any other data, for that matter) into a database, all with a simple type-safe interface for the developer. In many ways, Profile looks and feels much like Session state, but unlike Session state, Profile is persistent across sessions and is also tied into the Membership provider, so authenticated clients have data stored associated with their real identities instead of some arbitrary identifier. Anonymous clients will have an identifier generated for them, stored as a persistent cookie so that subsequent access from the same machine will retain their preferences as well. In addition, Profile is retrieved on demand and written only when modified, so unlike out-of-process Session state storage, you only incur a trip to the database when you actually use Profile, not implicitly with each request.

Fundamentals

The first step in using Profile is to declare the properties you would like to store on behalf of each user in your web.config file under the <profile> element. Your first decision is whether you want to allow anonymous clients to store profile data or only authenticated clients. If you elect to support anonymous clients, you must enable anonymous identification by adding the anonymousIdentification element in your web.config file with its enabled attribute set to true. This will cause ASP.NET to generate a unique identifier (a GUID) to associate with each anonymous user via a persistent cookie. If the user is authenticated, the membership identifier for that user will be used directly and no additional cookie will be created. You also have control over whether individual properties are stored on behalf of anonymous users through the allowAnonymous attribute of the add element. Listing 4-22 shows a sample web.config file with anonymous identification enabled, and three property declarations, one each for the user's favorite color, favorite number, and favorite HTTP status code. Note that all properties in this example allow anonymous access.

LISTING 4-22: Defining three Profile properties in web.config

```
<configuration>
  <system.web>
    <anonymousIdentification enabled="true" />

    <profile enabled="true">
      <properties>
        <add name="FavoriteColor" defaultValue="blue"
                 type="System.String"
                 allowAnonymous="true" />

        <add name="FavoriteNumber" defaultValue="42"
                 type="System.Int32"
                 allowAnonymous="true" />

        <add name="FavoriteHttpStatusCode"
                 type="System.Net.HttpStatusCode"
                 allowAnonymous="true" serializeAs="String"
                 defaultValue="OK" />
      </properties>
    </profile>
  </system.web>
</configuration>
```

When ASP.NET compiles your site, it creates a new class that derives from ProfileBase with type-safe accessors to the properties you declared. These accessors use the Profile provider to save and retrieve these properties to and from whatever database the provider is configured to interact with. Listing 4-23 shows what the generated class would look like for the three profile properties defined in Listing 4-22.

LISTING 4-23: Generated ProfileCommon Class

```csharp
public class ProfileCommon : ProfileBase {
    public virtual HttpStatusCode FavoriteHttpStatusCode {
        get {
            return ((HttpStatusCode)(this.GetPropertyValue(
                    "FavoriteHttpStatusCode")));
        }
        set {
            this.SetPropertyValue("FavoriteHttpStatusCode",
                    value);
        }
    }

    public virtual int FavoriteNumber {
        get {
            return ((int)(this.GetPropertyValue(
                        "FavoriteNumber")));
        }
        set {
            this.SetPropertyValue("FavoriteNumber", value);
        }
    }

    public virtual string FavoriteColor {
        get {
            return ((string)(this.GetPropertyValue(
                            "FavoriteColor")));
        }
        set {
            this.SetPropertyValue("FavoriteColor", value);
        }
    }

    public virtual ProfileCommon GetProfile(string username)
    {
        return ((ProfileCommon)(ProfileBase.Create(
                        username)));
    }
}
```

The second thing that happens is ASP.NET adds a property declaration to each generated Page class in your site named *Profile*, which is a type-safe accessor to the current Profile class (which is part of the HttpContext), as shown in Listing 4-24.

LISTING 4-24: Type-safe property added to Page-derived class for profile access

```
public partial class Default_aspx : Page
{
   protected ProfileCommon Profile {
      get {
          return ((ProfileCommon)(this.Context.Profile));
      }
   }
   //...
}
```

This lets you interact with your profile properties in a very convenient way. For example, Listing 4-25 shows a snippet of code that sets the profile properties based on fields in a form.

LISTING 4-25: Setting profile properties

```
void enterButton_Click(object sender, EventArgs e)
{
  Profile.FavoriteColor = colorTextBox.Text;
  Profile.FavoriteNumber  = int.Parse(numberTextBox.Text);
  Profile.FavoriteHttpStatusCode = (HttpStatusCode)
                  Enum.Parse(typeof(HttpStatusCode),
                      statusCodeTextBox.Text);
}
```

If you look in the database used by the Profile provider (by default a local SQL Server 2005 Express database in your application's App_Data directory), you will see a table called aspnet_Profile with 5 columns:

```
UserId
PropertyNames
PropertyValuesString
PropertyValuesBinary
LastUpdatedDate
```

In the example shown in Listings 4-22, 4-23, and 4-25 these columns were populated with the following values:

```
405A7333-2C8D-4E63-AB56-BA54398D47DF
FavoriteColor:S:0:3:FavoriteNumber:S:3:2:FavoriteHttpStatusCode:S:5:16:
red42MovedPermanently
2006-1-1 09:00:00.000
```

So you can see that by default the Profile provider uses a string serialization with property names and string lengths carefully stored as well on a per-user basis. In our example the user was anonymous, so a GUID was generated and used to index the property values in the aspnet_Profile table. The UserId column is actually a foreign key reference to the UserId column of the aspnet_Users table, where the membership system keeps user information (anonymous user information is also stored in this table).

Migrating Anonymous Profile Data

If your application supports both anonymous and authenticated clients, you may find that clients are frustrated when they store data as an anonymous user only to find it disappear when they log in and become authenticated. You can take steps to migrate their anonymous data to their authenticated identity by using the MigrateAnonymous event of the Profile-Module. This event, which you would typically add as a handler in global.asax, is triggered when an anonymous client with profile information transitions to an authenticated user. Listing 4-26 shows a sample global.asax file with a handler for this event transferring all profile state to the new profile data store for the newly authenticated client.

LISTING 4-26: Sample global.asax file migrating anonymous profile data

```csharp
<%@ Application Language="C#" %>

<script runat="server">
  void Profile_MigrateAnonymous(object sender,
                                ProfileMigrateEventArgs e)
  {
    ProfileCommon prof = Profile.GetProfile(e.AnonymousID);
    Profile.FavoriteColor = prof.FavoriteColor;
    Profile.FavoriteNumber = prof.FavoriteNumber;
    Profile.FavoriteHttpStatusCode = prof.FavoriteHttpStatusCode;
  }
</script>
```

Note that the anonymous identifier previously associated with the client is available through the ProfileMigrateEventArgs parameter, and the actual profile for that identity is accessible using the static GetProfile method of the Profile class. In most cases it would be wise to prompt the user before migrating her anonymous data, since that user may have profile data already associated with her account and might elect to not have the data she entered as an anonymous client overwrite the data that was stored previously on her behalf.

Managing Profile Data

Once you start using Profile in a live site, you will quickly discover that the number of entries in your profile database can grow without bound, especially if you have enabled anonymous storage. To deal with this, there is a class called ProfileManager which you can use to periodically clean up the profile database. Listing 4-27 shows the core static methods of this class, which tie into the current Profile provider.

LISTING 4-27: The ProfileManager class

```
public static class ProfileManager
{
  public static int DeleteInactiveProfiles(
        ProfileAuthenticationOption authenticationOption,
        DateTime userInactiveSinceDate);
  public static bool DeleteProfile(string username);

  public static ProfileInfoCollection FindProfilesByUserName(...);
  public static ProfileInfoCollection GetAllProfiles(...);
  public static int GetNumberOfInactiveProfiles(...);
  public static int GetNumberOfProfiles(...);

    //...
}
```

This class is accessible both in an ASP.NET Web application as well as in any .NET application that links to the System.Web.dll assembly. You can use the static methods in this class to build an administrative page in your site that lets the administrator clean up the profile database from time to time, perhaps giving her the option of specifying an inactive lower bound above which all profiles should be deleted (using the last parameter to DeleteInactiveProfiles method). If you prefer to automate the process, you could also write a Windows service that ran continuously on the server, deleting inactive profiles periodically, or perhaps a command line program that was run as part of a batch script periodically. Whichever technique you use is unimportant, but making sure you have a plan to clear out unused profile data from time to time is critical, especially if you allow anonymous clients to store data.

Storing Profile Data

The default Profile provider in ASP.NET 2.0 stores profile data in a local SQL Server 2005 Express database located in the App_Data directory of your application. For most production sites, this will be insufficient, and they will want to store the data in a full SQL Server database along with the rest of the data for their application. You can change the default database used by the Profile provider class by changing the value of the LocalSqlServer connection string in your web.config file. Prior to doing this, you must ensure that the target database has the profile and membership tables installed, which you can do using the aspnet_regsql.exe utility. Running this utility without any parameters brings up a user interface which walks you through installing the schema into an existing database, or creating a new default database, aspnetdb, to store all of ASP.NET 2.0's application services (membership, roles, profiles, Web part personalization, and the SQL Web event provider).

You can also use the command line parameters to install the database in an automated fashion (for example, if you are writing an install script for your application). For instance, to install all of the ASP.NET 2.0 application services into a new database named aspnetdb on the local machine (using Windows credentials to access the database), you would run the command:

```
aspnet_regsql -A all -C server=.;database=aspnetdb;trusted_connection=yes
```

Then, to change your ASP.NET application to use this new database to store Profile data (along with all other Application Service data), you would remove the LocalSqlServer connection string and then add it with a connection string pointing to your new database, as shown in Listing 4-28.

LISTING 4-28: Changing the default database for Profile storage

```
<configuration>
 <connectionStrings>
  <remove name="LocalSqlServer" />
  <add name="LocalSqlServer"
       connectionString=
                "Server=.;Database=aspnetdb;trusted_connection=yes"/>
 </connectionStrings>
 <!--...-->
```

Serialization

As you saw earlier, the default serialization for properties stored in Profile is to write them out as strings, storing the property names and substring

indices in the PropertyNames column. You can control how your properties are serialized by changing the serializeAs attribute on the add element
in web.config. This attribute can be one of four values:

```
Binary
ProviderSpecific
String
Xml
```

The default is ProviderSpecific, which might better be called Type-
Specific since the type of the object will determine the format of its serialization. ProviderSpecific with the default SQL Provider implementation
writes the property as a simple string if it is either a string already or a
primitive type (int, double, float, etc.). Otherwise it defaults to XML serialization, which is a natural fallback because it will work with most types
(even custom ones) without any modification to the type definition itself.
So what ProviderSpecific really means is StringForPrimitiveTypesAnd-
StringsOtherwiseXml, which is obviously quite a mouthful, so it's under-
standable they went with something shorter. This can lead to some
confusing behavior if you're not aware of it, however. For example, consider the two Profile property definitions shown in Listing 4-29.

LISTING 4-29: Sample Profile property definitions with invalid default values

```
<add name="TestCode" type="System.Net.HttpStatusCode"
    defaultValue="OK" /> <!-- defaultValue invalid -->
<add name="TestDate" type="DateTime"
    defaultValue="1/1/2006"/> <!-- defaultValue invalid -->
```

After using integer and string profile properties, adding an enum and a
DateTime in this manner seems reasonable. Because the default serialization is ProviderSpecific, we now know that these two types will be serialized with the XmlSerializer, so specifying default values as simple strings
is not going to fly (as you will find out quickly once you try accessing the
properties). You have two ways of dealing with this problem. One is to
specify the XML-serialized value directly in the configuration file (taking
care to escape any angle brackets), as shown in Listing 4-30.

LISTING 4-30: Specifying XML-serialized default values

```
<add name="TestCode" type="System.Net.HttpStatusCode"
    defaultValue=
       "&lt;HttpStatusCode&gt;OK&lt;/HttpStatusCode&gt;" />
```

```
<add name="TestDate" type="DateTime"
    defaultValue=
        "&lt;dateTime&gt;2006-01-01&lt;/dateTime&gt;" />
```

The other (and perhaps more appealing) option is to change the serialization from ProviderSpecific (which we know turns into XML) to String. String serialization only works for types that have TypeConversions defined for strings, which in our case is true since both enums and the DateTime class have string conversions defined (we discuss how to write your own string conversions in the next section). If you look carefully at Listing 4-22, you will notice that it specifies a serializeAs attribute of String for the HttpStatusCode so that a simple string default value of "OK" could be used, as shown in Listing 4-31.

LISTING 4-31: Specifying string default values

```
<add name="TestCode" type="System.Net.HttpStatusCode"
    serializeAs="String"
    defaultValue="OK" />
<add name="TestDate" type="DateTime"
    serializeAs="String"
    defaultValue="2006-01-01" />
```

The other option for serialization is Binary, which will use the BinaryFormatter to serialize the property. With the default SQL provider, this will write the binary data into the database's PropertyValuesBinary column. This is a useful option if you want to make it difficult to tweak the profile values directly in the database, or if you are storing types whose entire state is not properly persisted using the XmlSerializer (classes with private data members that are not accessible through public properties fall into this category, for example). Before you can use the binary option, the type being stored must be marked with the Serializable attribute or must implement the ISerializable interface. Keep in mind that selecting the binary serialization option makes it impossible to specify a default value, so it is typically used only for complex types for which a default value doesn't usually make sense anyway. If you ever do need to specify a default value for binary serialization, it is technically possible by base64 encoding a serialized instance of the type and using the resulting string in the defaultValue property.

User-Defined Types as Profile Properties

One of the advantages of the Profile architecture is that it is generic enough to store arbitrary types and, as we have seen, it supports several different persistence models. This means that it is quite straightforward to write your own classes to store user data and then store the entire class in Profile. Suppose, for example, we wanted to provide a shopping cart for users to let them collect items to purchase. We might write a class to store an individual item containing a description and a cost, and another class that keeps a list of all of the items in the current cart as well as exposing a property that calculates the total cost of all items in the cart, as shown in Listing 4-32.

LISTING 4-32: Sample ShoppingCart class definition

```
namespace PS
{
    [Serializable]
    public class ShoppingCart
    {
        private List<Item> _items = new List<Item>();

        public Collection<Item> Items
        {
            get { return new Collection<Item>(_items); }
        }

        public float TotalCost
        {
            get
            {
                float sum = 0F;
                foreach (Item i in _items)
                    sum += i.Cost;
                return sum;
            }
        }
    }

    [Serializable]
    public class Item
    {
        private string _description;
        private float  _cost;

        public Item() : this("", 0F) { }

        public Item(string description, float cost)
```

```
        {
            _description = description;
            _cost = cost;
        }

        public string Description
        {
            get { return _description;  }
            set { _description = value; }
        }

        public float Cost
        {
            get { return _cost;  }
            set { _cost = value; }
        }
    }
}
```

Note that our classes are marked with the [Serializable] attribute in anticipation of using binary serialization (although the XmlSerializer will work fine with these classes as well, so we have both options at our disposal). We can then add a profile property of type ShoppingCart to our collection, and we have a fully database-backed per-client persistent shopping cart implemented!

```
<profile enabled="true">
  <properties>
    <add name="ShoppingCart" type="PS.ShoppingCart"
        allowAnonymous="true" />
  </properties>
</profile>
```

Using the shopping cart in our application is as simple as accessing the ShoppingCart property in Profile and adding new instances of the Item class as needed (the sample available for download has a complete interface for users to shop using this class as the storage mechanism).

```
Profile.ShoppingCart.Items.Add(
        new Item("Chocolate covered cherries", 3.95F));
```

Optimizing Profile

You may be wondering at this point what sort of cost is incurred by leveraging Profile to store your per-client data, especially if you start using complex classes like the ShoppingCart, which may end up storing significant amounts of information on behalf of each user. Those of you who have taken advantage of the SQL Server-backed Session state feature introduced in ASP.NET 1.0 may be especially leery, since by default each request for a page incurred two round trips to the state database to retrieve and then flush session from and to the database. The good news is that by default, the profile persistence mechanism is reasonably efficient. Unlike out-of-process Session state, it performs lazy retrieval of the profile data on behalf of a user (loading on demand only), and only writes the profile data back out if it has changed.

Unfortunately, if you are storing anything besides strings, DateTime classes, or primitive types, it becomes impossible for the ProfileModule to determine whether the content has actually changed, and it is forced to write the profile back to the data store every time it is retrieved. This is obviously true for custom classes as well, so be aware that adding any types beside string, DateTime, and primitives will force Profile to write back to the database at the end of each request that accesses Profile. Internally there is a dirty flag used to keep track of whether a property in Profile has changed or not. You can explicitly set the IsDirty property for a profile property to false. If you do this for all properties associated with a specific provider instance, then when that provider instance is asked to save the profile data, it will see that all the properties passed to it are not dirty and it will skip communication with the database. This approach relies on knowledge of the underlying SettingsBase, SettingsProperty, and Settings-PropertyValue types (all in System.Configuration). For a profile property called Nickname, you could force it to not be considered dirty, as shown in Listing 4-33.

LISTING 4-33: Setting the IsDirty attribute for a property in a custom class

```
Profile.PropertyValues["Nickname"].IsDirty = false;
```

Note that you can disable automatic profile saving using the automaticSaveEnabled attribute on the <profile/> element in the configuration file (this attribute defaults to true). You can set automaticSaveEnabled to false to stop ProfileModule from storing the Profile on your behalf automatically. It is then up to you to call Profile.Save if you want to store data back to the database. Alternatively, you can hook the ProfileModule's ProfileAutoSaving event. If you set the ContinueWithProfileAutoSave property on the event argument to false, then the ProfileModule will not call Profile.Save.

As you saw earlier, it is possible to specify String, Binary, or Xml as the serialization mechanism for your properties. If you are storing your own custom classes like our ShoppingCart example, you can take steps to reduce the amount of space used to store instances of your class in one of two ways: writing your own TypeConverter for the class to support conversion to string format, or implementing the ISerializable interface to control the format of the binary data used by the BinaryFormatter. Listing 4-34 shows the default serialization of our ShoppingCart class with four items in it in XML format. The equivalent binary serialization occupies 678 bytes of space.

LISTING 4-34: XML-serialized shopping cart with four items (590 characters)

```xml
<?xml version="1.0" encoding="utf-16"?>
<ShoppingCart xmlns:xsi="http://www.w3.org/2001/XMLSchema-instance"
  xmlns:xsd="http://www.w3.org/2001/XMLSchema">
  <Items>
<Item>
  <Description>Chocolate covered cherries</Description>
  <Cost>3.95</Cost>
</Item>
<Item>
  <Description>Toy Train Set</Description>
  <Cost>49.95</Cost>
</Item>
<Item>
  <Description>XBox 360</Description>
  <Cost>399.95</Cost>
</Item>
<Item>
  <Description>Wagon</Description>
  <Cost>24.95</Cost>
</Item>
  </Items>
</ShoppingCart>
```

By default, you cannot use the serializeAs="String" option for custom types, since there is no way to convert the types to and from a string format in a lossless way. You can provide such a conversion yourself by implementing a TypeConverter for your class. This involves creating a class that inherits from TypeConverter, implementing the conversion methods, and then annotating your original class with the TypeConverter attribute that associates it with your conversion class. You must also decide on how to persist your class as a string (and then parse it from a string), which can be a nontrivial task, so make sure it's worth the effort before taking this approach. As an example, here is a TypeConverter class for the Item class that represents items in our shopping cart. In this case I chose to use a non-printable character as a delimiter, and since the Item class consists of two pieces of state which are easily rendered as strings, the parsing becomes trivial using the Split method of the string class. The converter class is then associated with the Item class using the TypeConverter attribute, both of which are shown in Listing 4-35.

LISTING 4-35: Writing a custom type converter

```
public class ItemTypeConverter : TypeConverter
{
    private const char _delimiter = (char)10;

    public override object
        ConvertFrom(ITypeDescriptorContext context,
                CultureInfo culture, object value)
    {
        string sValue = value as string;
        if (sValue != null)
        {
            string[] vals = sValue.Split(_delimiter);
            return new Item(vals[0],
                    float.Parse(vals[1]));
        }
        else
            return base.ConvertFrom(context,
                            culture, value);
    }

    public override object
        ConvertTo(ITypeDescriptorContext context,
                    CultureInfo culture,
                object value, Type destinationType)
    {
        if (destinationType == typeof(string))
        {
            Item i = value as Item;
            return string.Format("{0}{1}{2}",
                    i.Description, _delimiter, i.Cost);
        }
        else
        {
```

```
                return base.ConvertTo(context, culture,
                        value, destinationType);
        }
    }

    public override bool CanConvertFrom(
                    ITypeDescriptorContext context,
                    Type sourceType)
    {
        if (sourceType == typeof(string))
            return true;
        else
            return base.CanConvertFrom(
                        context, sourceType);
    }

    public override bool CanConvertTo(
                    ITypeDescriptorContext context,
                    Type destinationType)
    {
        if (destinationType == typeof(string))
            return true;
        else
            return base.CanConvertTo(
                        context, destinationType);
    }
}

[Serializable]
[TypeConverter(typeof(ItemTypeConverter))]
public class Item
{
    ...
```

With these classes in place, our Item class can be used with string serialization in a profile property. Note that for our shopping cart to be completely serializable as a string, we also need to write a type converter for our ShoppingCart class, a sample of which can be found in the downloadable samples for this book. The advantage of controlling the persistence in this way is that the serialization of the same shopping cart filled with four items now only takes 79 characters!

Going the Custom Route

Any time you find yourself spending a lot of time trying to make an architecture do what you want, it is important to step back and make sure that the work necessary to customize the architecture to do what you want is less than what it would take to do it entirely yourself. Profile is a great example of a feature that is convenient and easy to use but that may be too constraining as your design evolves. Let's look at what features Profile specifically gives us.

- Support for anonymous and authenticated clients
- Anonymous users identified through a new cookie (or alternatively through embedded id with URL mangling, including support for autodetect cookieless mode)
- Arbitrary type storage, strongly typed through configuration file
- Per-client persistent data store
- Management class for cleaning up unused profile data

One of the drawbacks to using Profile to store client data is that it stores all of the data in one column (or two columns if you are using both string and binary serialization) of the database table. This means that it is practically impossible to make modifications to the profile data without going through the profile API. It's also impractical to generate any reports from the data or otherwise collect information from the database directly.

If you find yourself wanting more control over the storage of per-client state in your application, you have two choices: build a custom Profile provider or forget Profile and just write data yourself. Building a custom Profile provider gives you the ability to retarget where Profile actually writes the data, but because of the nature of the provider interface, it doesn't really make it any easier to write property values to specific columns in a table. For more information and samples on building custom Profile providers, take a look at the ASP.NET provider model toolkit (http://msdn.microsoft.com/asp.net/downloads/providers/default.aspx).

If you decide to forget Profile and just write the serialization of client data yourself, be aware that you can still leverage the identification features of Profile even if you aren't using the storage features. Specifically, there is a UserName property on the ProfileBase class that will contain either the name of the current authenticated user or the GUID that was generated for an anonymous user. You can use this UserName property as a unique index into a custom database table of your own construction to easily store and retrieve user data. Just make sure that Profile and anony-mousIdentification are enabled in your application, and you can use the same client identification mechanism as Profile.

```
<anonymousIdentification enabled="true"/>
        <profile enabled="true" />
```

By writing your own client persistence backend using the unique iden-tifier provided by Profile, you gain several unique advantages over the generic profile implementation.

- The ability to write stored procedures against client data
- The ability to retrieve only the portions of data you need for a client at any given time (instead of relying on Profile to just load the whole chunk into memory)
- The ability to cache per-client data across requests for efficiency
- Complete control over the serialization, and the ability to map onto existing tables instead of creating new data stores that you may already have in place

The sample available for download contains an alternate implementa-tion of the shopping cart described earlier, using a custom database table to store cart items and leveraging the unique client identifier available through the ProfileBase class. In general, you may even consider starting out by using Profile for convenience to get things started, and then later migrate some of the profile data into custom tables with a separate data access layer. In this sense, Profile fills a convenient role as an easy way to store per-client data, with an obvious path forward to factoring data out into a more strongly typed schema.

SUMMARY

With the reintroduction of cross-page posting and the introduction of Pro-file and the Wizard, View, and MultiView controls to the ASP.NET devel-oper's toolbox, ASP.NET 2.0 should make the discussion of where to store client state in Web applications even more interesting. Cross-page posting brings back the common technique of parsing the POST request from a source page in a different target page. The Wizard, MultiView, and View controls provide an easy-to-use implementation of a common technique of showing and hiding parts of a page as the client interacts with it. Profile gives developers a complete solution for persisting client data across sessions, for both authenticated and anonymous users.

■ 5 ■
Security

SECURITY IS AN IMPORTANT FEATURE of most Web applications, and thinking about it earlier rather than later can save you heartache and money down the road. That's why this chapter doesn't come at the end of this book!

ASP.NET 2.0 shipped with a number of new security features and improvements. If you're using Forms authentication, you'll be happy to know that it's gotten a lot of attention in this new version, with a robust provider model making it easy to track user accounts and roles. We'll explore the Membership and Role providers in depth in this chapter, and talk about real-world security issues you should consider when configuring them. We'll also explore the role of machine keys and some other features such as cookieless Forms authentication and web.config file encryption.

How Much Security Do I Need?

This is an excellent question to start with. Every security countermeasure trades off against *something*. That something could be ease of use, cost, ease of deployment, ease of administration, and so on. For example, consider password complexity requirements. If your Web application is simply giving people access to publicly available weather information, the tradeoff of requiring strong passwords is probably not worth it. In fact, you may not need to annoy your users with a login at all. On the other hand, if you are protecting company assets or personally identifiable information for your users, then having a strong password policy is a critical step toward making your Web application *secure enough*.

Ultimately, that's your job: to build your Web application to be secure enough considering the real threats that it faces. Choosing an appropriate security posture means thinking about how valuable the assets you have are to an attacker, how far he'd be willing to go to get at those assets, and how much you're willing to pay (or trade off) to protect those assets. A great way to approach this problem is to build a threat model, which you can learn more about at the Microsoft patterns & practices Web site.[1] With a threat model in place, you can streamline your effort because you'll have a prioritized list of threats and vulnerabilities. There is never enough time or resources to implement all of the security features you would like, and it's wise to use whatever precious time you *do* have to address the highest priority security issues first.

This chapter covers many of the new security features in ASP.NET 2.0, but ironically most of the worst security breaches have nothing to do with security features at all. The common SQL injection vulnerability that allows an attacker to pilfer private information from your database (or even worse, make subtle changes or destroy your database entirely) is introduced not by the person building security features, but by the new hire who is simply writing naïve database access logic. Consider the filename canonicalization bug that allows an attacker to download your entire membership database or, even worse, your security accounts manager (SAM) database that contains the password hashes for the Windows accounts on your server. Cross-site scripting is another nasty vulnerability that allows an attacker to completely change the look and functionality of your Web site and to create virtually undetectable phishing attacks against legitimate users (this is especially dangerous if the attacker knows how to write grammatically correct sentences).

All of the developers on your team need to have a basic understanding of these coding errors, so be sure to educate them by giving them good

---

1. Start at msdn.com/securityengineering and look for guidance on threat modeling Web applications. Another great resource is the ACE threat modeling tool that is in version 2.0 as of this writing. You can find this latter tool by visiting http://msdn.microsoft.com/security/securecode/threatmodeling/acetm/ or http://blogs.msdn.com/threatmodeling/.

security guidance. The patterns & practices Web site has some excellent guidance you can use, including some free security training modules[2] that can help your team learn about some of the common input validation issues in Web applications. The book *Writing Secure Code*, 2nd edition, by Michael Howard and David LeBlanc is also an excellent resource.

Getting Started with Membership

By far, the biggest new security feature in ASP.NET 2.0 is **membership**, which makes it easy to implement user accounts and get started authenticating your users using Forms authentication. To get things started quickly, we'll begin with a five-minute demo that you can follow along with if you are sitting in front of a computer.[3] This will quickly show you the power of membership and introduce you to some of the new login controls. Once you have a feel for what membership is all about, we'll drill down and show you the nuts and bolts so that you can squeeze the most out of it in your own applications.

After opening Visual Studio, we begin by creating a new Web application in a temporary file system folder. We add a web.config file and enable Forms authentication, and require that everyone log in by denying all anonymous requests (*?* is a wildcard that matches all anonymous requests), as shown in Listing 5-1.

LISTING 5-1: web.config

```
<configuration>
    <system.web>
      <compilation defaultLanguage="C#"/>
      <authentication mode="Forms" />
      <authorization>
        <deny users="?"/>
      </authorization>
    </system.web>
</configuration>
```

---

2. See http://pluralsight.com/blogs/keith/archive/2006/02/22/18995.aspx, or search for "Keith Brown input validation modules."

3. Note that for this demo we're using a machine with Visual Studio 2005 on which SQL Server 2005 is also installed. We've already run aspnet_regsql to create the ASP.NET membership database, as was described in Chapter 4.

We can then put together a default Web page using a couple of the membership controls that are new on the toolbar in Visual Studio 2005 (see Figure 5-1). We use the LoginName control to welcome the user by name, and the LoginStatus control to allow the user to log out when finished with the application. Listing 5-2 shows the code for this page.

LISTING 5-2: default.aspx

```
<html>
<body>
<form id="form1" runat="server">
    <h1>Getting Started with Membership</h1>
    <p>Welcome, <asp:LoginName ID="LoginName1" runat="server" /></p>
    <p><asp:LoginStatus ID="LoginStatus1" runat="server" /></p>
</form>
</body>
</html>
```

Next, we create the simplest possible login form, using the new login control. By default, Forms authentication assumes the name of the login page is login.aspx, so that's what we name the login form, shown in Listing 5-3.

LISTING 5-3: login.aspx

```
<html>
<body>
<form id="form1" runat="server">
    <asp:Login ID="Login1" runat="server"/>
</form>
</body>
</html>
```

FIGURE 5-1: Login controls in the toolbox

At this point, believe it or not, we've got a functioning Web application that authenticates its users with a form. But at the moment there are no users who are allowed to log in, so we need to populate the membership database for this application with some users. To do this, we'll use the built-in administration tool in Visual Studio via the Website | ASP.NET Configuration menu. This pops up a Web page with several options: we choose the Security tab and select Create User, at which point we can fill out a form to add a user (Alice, in Figure 5-2) to the membership database for the application.

Once this new user is created, we can test the application. If we navigate to the default.aspx page, we are immediately redirected to the login page, where we can enter Alice's user name and password, as shown in Figure 5-3.

After pressing the Log In button, we will be redirected back to the originally requested page, default.aspx, which welcomes the user by name and

FIGURE 5-2: Creating a new user

FIGURE 5-3: Logging in

offers a way to log out, shown in Figure 5-4. If we press the Logout link, we are redirected back to the login page.

It's a testament to the efficiency of ASP.NET 2.0 that we can build a full database-backed site with Forms authentication in so few steps. For most "real" Web applications, however, a more thorough understanding of each component we just used is necessary, both for possible customization and to know if your particular solution is "secure enough" as we discussed earlier. Let's start by tracking down how all of this "magic" happened. If you open machine.config, you'll see a new <membership> section that provides a number of default settings (see Listing 5-4). The default Membership provider is based on SQL Server, and there is a connectionStringName

FIGURE 5-4: Logged in

property that points to the <connectionStrings> section, where the default connection string uses integrated security to connect to the local SQL server instance using a database called ASPNETDB. This is the database that aspnet_regsql creates by default.

LISTING 5-4: Machine.config

```
<connectionStrings>
    <add name="LocalSqlServer"
        connectionString="Integrated Security=SSPI;database=aspnetdb"
        providerName="System.Data.SqlClient" />
</connectionStrings>

<system.web>
  <membership>
    <providers>
      <add name="AspNetSqlMembershipProvider"
          type="System.Web.Security.SqlMembershipProvider, ..."
          connectionStringName="LocalSqlServer"
          enablePasswordRetrieval="false"
          enablePasswordReset="true"
          requiresQuestionAndAnswer="true"
          applicationName="/"
          requiresUniqueEmail="false"
          passwordFormat="Hashed"
          maxInvalidPasswordAttempts="5"
          minRequiredPasswordLength="7"
          minRequiredNonalphanumericCharacters="1"
          passwordAttemptWindow="10"
          passwordStrengthRegularExpression="" />
    </providers>
  </membership>
</system.web>
```

Note that if you're running as an administrator when you launch this Web application in Visual Studio, you'll have full permission to the membership database by default, and your demo will work smoothly. If you're running as a normal user[4] and try the same thing, you'll find that things don't work until you grant yourself permission to use the Membership features of the ASPNETDB database, as you'll see later in this chapter.

---

4. Good for you! It's tough to run as a nonadmin, but there are lots of benefits, not the least of which is that you'll be safer from viruses and worms that threaten to install root kits, key loggers, and so on. For more information, check out items 8 and 9 in Keith's book at winsecguide.net, and also Aaron Margosis' list of articles on the topic at http://tinyurl.com/ge7f2.

If you drill into the ASPNETDB database, you'll see some tables that relate to the membership functionality being used here. The aspnet_Applications table allows multiple Web applications to use a single database, which is convenient for people who give trade show demos on a regular basis, but in a production scenario you'll usually be better off giving your application its own private database, as opposed to sharing it with other applications that you might not trust. The aspnet_Users and aspnet_Membership tables store data for each user account, including details like the user's name, password verifier, e-mail address, and so on.

At this point you might be wondering exactly how the login controls interact with the database, but to understand that, you'll first need to see how the new provider architecture in ASP.NET 2.0 works.

Provider Architecture

Instead of hardwiring these controls to talk directly to the membership database, the ASP.NET team decided to introduce a provider model to abstract the data source from the controls that use it. You'll find this model in a lot of different places in ASP.NET,[5] but to make things more concrete, Figure 5-5 illustrates how the Membership provider works.

This model is common in software design. It decouples the consumer of a service from the implementation of that service, or as the ASP.NET team refers to it, the **provider** of the service. In this case, we're talking about user accounts, or **membership**. ASP.NET includes an abstract base class, MembershipProvider, from which all concrete implementations must derive in order to plug into this architecture. The default Membership provider is SqlMembershipProvider, which sits on top of a SQL Server database. ASP.NET also ships with an Active Directory (AD) provider, which can be configured to use an Active Directory domain or an Active Directory Application Mode (ADAM) instance as the source of user accounts. You can also create your own implementation by deriving a class from MembershipProvider. The feature set you get will differ slightly across providers, and we will point out many of the differences in this chapter.

---

5. Check out the list of classes that derive from System.Configuration.Provider.ProviderBase if you're interested in finding other places where this pattern is used. The MSDN documentation for the class is a great way to do this.

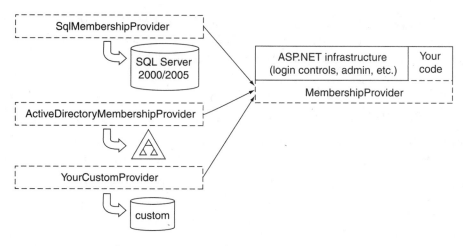

FIGURE 5-5: Provider architecture

The ASP.NET infrastructure (such as the membership controls and the administration Web application) knows how to use the Membership-Provider base class, but doesn't care about the details of how it's implemented, which makes it much easier to swap out different stores for your user accounts. For example, you might choose to use the AD provider if you must use a forms-based login but want users to be authenticated against accounts in Active Directory. This would make sense for an Intranet application designed for use with browsers that don't support integrated authentication, where you are forced to use a forms-based login. Another instance in which pluggable providers are useful is when you have an existing user store that isn't supported by ASP.NET out of the box. You can write your own provider in this case, as many people already have.[6]

Another nice benefit of this model is that you can write your own code that uses the Membership provider. We've included a tool called the ASP.NET Administration Console as an example with this book that does just this. You will find this code helpful in learning more about how the

---

6. As of this writing, a quick search reveals a MySql provider (at http://codeproject.com), a web.config provider (search for "WebConfigMembershipProvider" at http://leastprivilege.com), a Web service-based provider (search for "Membership-Provider and Web Services" at http://codeproject.com), among others. These are only referenced as examples and have not been tested by, nor are they endorsed by, the authors.

Membership and Role providers work. Besides finding it a helpful learning tool, you'll probably find that it performs better than the built-in Web administration application that comes with Visual Studio.

MembershipProvider

This abstract base class defines the interface for accessing a user account store through the membership feature in ASP.NET. Refer to Listing 5-5 and familiarize yourself with this interface, as this is a great way to get a quick introduction to the features that membership offers.

LISTING 5-5: MembershipProvider

```
public abstract class MembershipProvider : ProviderBase {

   // user management
   public abstract MembershipUser CreateUser(string username,
                                             string password,
                                             string email,
                                             string passwordQuestion,
                                             string passwordAnswer,
                                             bool isApproved,
                                             object providerUserKey,
                                         out MembershipCreateStatus s);
   public abstract void UpdateUser(MembershipUser user);
   public abstract bool DeleteUser(string username,
                                   bool deleteAllRelatedData);
   public abstract bool UnlockUser(string userName);

   // user identification and authentication
   public abstract string GetUserNameByEmail(string email);
   public abstract bool ValidateUser(string username,
                                     string password);

   // user credential management
   public abstract string GetPassword(string username,
                                      string answer);
   public abstract string ResetPassword(string username,
                                        string answer);
   public abstract bool ChangePassword(string username,
                                       string oldPassword,
                                       string newPassword);
   public abstract bool ChangePasswordQuestionAndAnswer(
                        string username,
                        string password,
                        string newQuestion,
                        string newAnswer);
```

```
public event MembershipValidatePasswordEventHandler
                 ValidatingPassword;

// finding users (some details omitted for brevity)
public abstract MembershipUserCollection FindUsersByEmail(...);
public abstract MembershipUserCollection FindUsersByName(...);
public abstract MembershipUserCollection GetAllUsers(...);
public abstract int GetNumberOfUsersOnline();
public abstract MembershipUser GetUser(string name, bool isOnline);
public abstract MembershipUser GetUser(object key, bool isOnline);

// configuration properties
public abstract string ApplicationName { get; set; }
public abstract bool EnablePasswordReset { get; }
public abstract bool EnablePasswordRetrieval { get; }
public abstract int MaxInvalidPasswordAttempts { get; }
public abstract int MinRequiredNonAlphanumericCharacters { get; }
public abstract int MinRequiredPasswordLength { get; }
public abstract int PasswordAttemptWindow { get; }
public abstract MembershipPasswordFormat PasswordFormat { get; }
public abstract string PasswordStrengthRegularExpression { get; }
public abstract bool RequiresQuestionAndAnswer { get; }
public abstract bool RequiresUniqueEmail { get; }
}
```

The CreateUser method gives you a good idea of the type of user data tracked by membership. Each user has a name and password and an e-mail address. To allow users to reset their own passwords, there is also an optional question and answer that can be used as a secondary form of authentication for the user. Each user has a flag that indicates whether they are approved to log in. To ban a user, you can clear this flag and they will no longer be allowed to log in (the AD provider is serious about this; it disables the user account if you do this). If you ever call CreateUser directly, pass a null argument to indicate a missing parameter (providerUserKey, password question and answer, etc.), as opposed to an empty string, which the provider may interpret as a value you want it to use.

UpdateUser and DeleteUser are pretty self-explanatory, except perhaps for the deleteRelatedData argument. If you pass true, SqlMembershipProvider deletes all records related to the user, including role memberships and profile, and so on. If you pass false, the only thing that is deleted is the membership record, which contains items like the user's e-mail address and password verifier, making it impossible for that user to log in again.

The presence of the UnlockUser method indicates that accounts can be locked out after a certain number of failed logon attempts. Account lockout policy depends on the provider. Under the AD provider, the number of failed password attempts is controlled by password policy in AD, while the SQL provider relies on the maxInvalidPasswordAttempts attribute specified in web.config.

ValidateUser is perhaps the most important method: this is how the login control (or even your own code) attempts to log on a user, supplying the user name and password. While the AD provider forwards this request on to a directory service, the SQL provider must actually perform the password validation itself against a password verifier stored in the membership database. We'll devote a section to password verification later in this chapter, as it's an important configuration choice you have to make if you're going to use the SQL provider. If a valid password is supplied, the current time is recorded for the user account, which helps the membership system make an educated guess as to which members are actively online.[7] On the other hand, if ValidateUser is called with an invalid password for a particular user in rapid succession, the user's account may be locked out, a feature we'll discuss in more detail. After all this takes place, ValidateUser updates performance counters and fires a health monitoring event, which helps you track the number of successful versus failed login attempts for your Web application.

Given that a user is much more likely to remember her e-mail address than to remember the user account name she chose to use at your Web site, the GetUserNameByEmail method can really come in handy. If the user can't figure out her user name, you can look it up for her based on her e-mail address. You could use this in conjunction with the events fired by the login control to allow the user to enter either a user name *or* an e-mail address in order to log in.

You've now seen enough Membership plumbing to understand the login control, so let's digress for a moment to examine it in more detail.

The Login Control

The login control is very useful, as it allows you to crank out a login page with a single line of markup, as you saw at the beginning of this chapter, but you can use it other places as well. Imagine dropping a login control

---

7. You can tweak this with the userIsOnlineTimeWindow attribute in the <membership> config element. The default is 10 minutes.

onto your master page that would let anonymous users browse your Web site and log in if they want more personalized service. Many Web sites work this way.

The login control is infinitely customizable. Using the designer, you can autoformat an instance of the control to give it a look you like, or you can centralize the look of all your login controls with a skin (see Chapter 2). You can also customize each bit of text shown, orient the control so that it lies horizontally instead of vertically, and use images instead of buttons. Figure 5-6 shows the default login control above the one that we customized by tweaking some of these settings and adding an image to replace the Log In button. You can find the code for this page in the LoginControlCustomization sample available for download with this book.

Besides controlling the look and feel of this control, you'll need to make some important decisions about what features you want to expose to your users. The "Remember me next time" checkbox is convenient for users, but it also persists the forms login cookie on the user's hard drive. In ASP.NET 1.x this persistent cookie was set to last for 50 years! Fortunately in ASP.NET 2.0, the cookie expires based on the timeout you configure for

FIGURE 5-6: Customizing the login control

Forms authentication.[8] Keep in mind that an attacker who steals a forms login cookie can replay it at his leisure and impersonate the legitimate user from whom it was stolen, and allowing cookies to be stored on the user's hard drive may increase the feasibility of this attack. If this is a concern, you can effectively disable this feature in the customized control by setting the control's DisplayRememberMe to false.

The login control will optionally display links to other membership-related pages for performing tasks such as creating users, recovering passwords, or getting help. And if all else fails, you can choose the "Convert to Template" task from the Designer view, which will let you lay out the control however you like. In this mode, you can reposition any of the existing controls, or even add and remove controls if you like.

The login control fires a sequence of events when the user presses the Login button. The first is the LoggingIn event, where you can preprocess the request and choose to allow or cancel the login before it's even attempted. The next event fired, Authenticate, is the core event for this control; it contacts the Membership provider and authenticates the user. If you handle this event, the default processing won't happen, so you'll have to authenticate the user yourself (which isn't hard with a Membership provider using its ValidateUser method). If your handler returns an event arg indicating success, the control sets up the Forms authentication cookie and then fires the LoggedIn event. Otherwise it fires the LoginError event, which by default informs the user of the login failure.

User Account Lockout: Blessing or Curse?

SqlMembershipProvider has a user account lockout feature that is designed to thwart password guessing attacks. Here's how it works: for a given user account, the first time ValidateUser is given an invalid password, a counter in the user's membership record (FailedPasswordAttemptCount) is bumped up, and the time of this first failed login is recorded (FailedPassword-AttemptWindowStart). If this happens five times in rapid succession (within ten minutes by default), the user's account will be locked out. You

---

8. If you're upgrading to ASP.NET 2.0, this may surprise you: by default, users who check the "Remember me" box will only be remembered for 30 minutes after they stop using your Web application. You can change this by adjusting the timeout attribute on the <forms> element in your web.config file.

can modify these thresholds in web.config via the maxInvalidPassword-Attempts and passwordAttemptWindow attributes on the provider.

ActiveDirectoryMembershipProvider indirectly provides the same service, because directory services typically provide optional account lockout features. For example, if you're using AD as your user store, you can use the account lockout features in AD to lock user accounts after a certain number of failed login attempts. In both the SQL and AD provider cases, an administrator must intervene and unlock the user's account before she will be allowed to log in again. This is when the UnlockUser method comes in handy.

Before you get too excited about account lockout, consider the dark side. While it's hard for an attacker to guess a correct password for a user, it's trivial to guess an incorrect password. If I don't like Alice, and I want to make sure she can't log in to your Web site, all I have to do is use an incorrect password in several login attempts in rapid succession. And this attack can be automated. Imagine the pain you'd be in if an attacker learned the names of all of your users, and used that in a script that locked them all out each evening!

You can effectively turn off account lockout if you're worried about this. Just change the configuration to increase those threshold values to very large numbers or turn off the feature in your directory service.[9] Unfortunately this also makes you more vulnerable to password guessing attacks, because there seems to be no delay built into the SqlMembership-Provider. I wrote a little program that turned off the account lockout feature and then dropped it into a loop calling ValidateUser with a known bad password. On my box at home, I was able to make about 530 guesses each second. Obviously, with network latency a remote attacker wouldn't be able to go this fast, but given a dictionary of commonly used passwords, it wouldn't take long to crack a weak password.

A more useful feature might be a delay, as you see when you try to interactively log in to Windows. If you supply around five bad passwords

---

9. If you're using Active Directory, you can turn off account lockout in security policy. The setting, called Account lockout threshold, is found under Security Settings | Account Policies | Account Lockout Policy. By setting this value to zero, you effectively turn off account lockout. But before making this change, I'd recommend reading Chapter 11 of Jesper Johansson and Steve Riley's excellent book *Protect Your Windows Network* to help you understand more about problems with passwords and account lockout.

to the interactive Windows login screen, you'll have to wait a little bit before you can try again. The system simply slows you down every four or five tries. A delay like this can significantly reduce the effectiveness of a brute force password guessing attack. The built-in login control and SqlMembershipProvider don't support this, so you'd have to write a bit of code in the login control or build a custom provider if you wanted to add this feature. But it'd be a worthwhile effort.

Password Complexity Policy

Ultimately the best protection against password guessing attacks is to require strong passwords. There are several ways to enforce this password policy with the membership system. The first is through the configuration of your Membership provider. You can modify the following provider attributes to provide some general constraints on password complexity.

* minRequiredPasswordLength (the default is 7)
* minRequiredNonAlphanumericCharacters (the default is 1)

There's also a passwordStrengthRegularExpression attribute if you're comfortable using regular expressions. You can find an example of a regular expression that controls password length and requires the use of upper and lower alphanumeric characters and numeric digits in the patterns & practices guidance document *How to Protect Forms Authentication in ASP.NET 2.0.*[10]

Each time a password is updated via the membership service, the ValidatingPassword event is fired. Don't let the name confuse you: this event isn't fired when a user is authenticated, only when his password is being changed. If you handle this event, you will be given the proposed new password, and you can decide whether or not it is acceptable. You could plug in code to do your own dictionary attack against the password, or add in a password history database to ensure that users aren't reusing old passwords.

If you are using the AD provider, your directory service's password policy will act as a yet another complexity check. Passwords will only be accepted if they pass both the membership password complexity constraints and the directory service's constraints.

---

10. See http://msdn.microsoft.com/library/en-us/dnpag2/html/PAGHT000012.asp.

The MembershipProvider class includes several methods that help to automate user credential management, which are shown in Listing 5-5. Not all of these functions will be available to you; it depends on the provider you use and how you configure that provider. For example, the AD provider will throw a NotSupportedException if GetPassword is called. Most directory services don't support retrieval of user passwords because the cleartext password is simply not available most of the time. For example, unless you explicitly mark an account in Active Directory as storing its password reversibly encrypted, AD will only store a hash of the password. Which brings us to another critical topic: password format.

Choosing a Password Format

If you use the SqlMembershipProvider, you have three choices for how user passwords (and password answers, which we'll talk about in the next section) should be stored. The MembershipPasswordFormat enumeration provides three options: Clear, Encrypted, and Hashed. The first option, Clear, should obviously be avoided in production scenarios. If you are forcing your users to take the time to log into your Web application, you'd better take the time to protect their passwords on the backend. For better or worse, many naïve users use the same password everywhere, and you need to take some basic steps to prevent passwords from casually leaking, even to authorized administrators.

So the choice really comes down to using Encrypted or Hashed password storage. If you choose the former, you need to supply an encryption key,[11] and if you ever lose that key, you won't be able to authenticate your users anymore, which is a bit of a drawback. There *is* one usability benefit to using Encrypted password storage: the password can be retrieved if the user forgets what it is, although how you communicate that password to the end user depends on your security posture (many Web sites e-mail passwords to forgetful users, which drives Keith bonkers). The Password-Recovery control automates this if you decide you want this feature.

The most secure option is to choose Hashed password storage. In this case, whenever a user's password is set, SqlMembershipProvider computes a

---

11. Discussed further in the section titled A Word about Machine Keys.

one-way hash of the new password along with a random salt, and stores the hash and the salt value in the user's record in the membership database. That means there's no need for an encryption key, which ironically is a huge benefit: the fewer secrets you have, the better off you are!

When you choose Hashed, all you really have is a **password verifier**; there's no way to reverse that hash to retrieve the password. This means that if a user forgets her password, retrieving it is not an option; the Get-Password method will throw an exception. Of course, this doesn't mean that your membership database is uncrackable. Unless you're requiring users to have *very* long passwords, you must assume that an attacker who steals your membership database will eventually guess the passwords via a brute force or dictionary attack. This just buys you a bit of time to inform your users of the compromise. It'll also frustrate the administrator who decides to go poking around the membership database late at night when nobody is looking, and it'll do so without requiring a secret key.

With encrypted passwords, if the user forgets her password, you could use GetPassword to retrieve it for her. If you're storing hashed passwords, ResetPassword is what you should use instead. This method generates a random password for the user, hashes it, and stores the verifier in the user's record. It then returns the new password to you so that you can communicate it to the user. If the user doesn't like the password you've generated, she can always change her password, which is why the ChangePassword method exists. There's also a ChangePassword control that automates this, shown in Figure 5-7.

There are additional configuration settings on the Membership provider that impact credential management. The first is PasswordFormat, which defaults to Hashed. Next is enablePasswordRetrieval, which is set to false by default, causing GetPassword to throw an exception if called. Note that if you want to avoid configuration exceptions, this attribute *must* be set to false if you're using the AD provider, or the SQL provider with

Change Your Password	
Password:	
New Password:	
Confirm New Password:	
Change Password	Cancel

FIGURE 5-7: The ChangePassword control

PasswordFormat="Hashed". The enablePasswordReset attribute defaults to true. Setting it to false causes ResetPassword to throw an exception. When coupled with enablePasswordRetrieval="false", you get a Web site that forces the user to create a new account if she forgets her password. And finally, there's the requiresQuestionAndAnswer setting, which warrants its own discussion.

Password Questions and Answers

I recently reset my password at PayPal's Web site. It was automated by a Web form that first challenged me to answer a couple of questions to prove my identity. One of them was, "What are the last four digits of your U.S. Social Security Number?" My first reaction was shock and outrage! How did PayPal discover my SSN? But after poking around a little bit, it turned out that when I first registered for my PayPal account (over eight years ago), I was asked to supply answers to a couple of security questions. I got to choose from a list of four questions, and apparently back then I figured that the last four digits of my SSN was something I'd remember easily, and seemed more palatable than giving away my mother's maiden name, which was one of the other choices. Ask any IT helpdesk worker, and they'll tell you that password reset is *the* most common ailment of users around the world. Automating password reset like PayPal does saves a lot of money.

Recall that the MembershipProvider.CreateUser method takes a question and answer. This is exactly what it's for: providing an alternative means to authenticate the user in case she misplaces her password. You may have also noticed that GetPassword and ResetPassword both take two arguments: username and answer. If a user forgets her password and wants to retrieve it or reset it, you can challenge her to answer a question the same way she answered it when she first created the account. The answer is really just an alternate password, if you think about it.

This feature is on by default for the SqlMembershipProvider, and if you rely on it, you need to make sure you get a question and answer from the user when she registers an account. The CreateUserWizard control (see Figure 5-8) will automate this for you, but it allows the user to supply any question she wants. What if, annoyed by your request, she supplies a question like, "What's two plus two?" Her account may very well be easy to

FIGURE 5-8: The CreateUserWizard control

compromise, or at least disrupt, if you allow an attacker to reset her password by answering this simple question. Questions like "What's my favorite color" are also bad news. How long would it take a hacker to guess the answer to *that* question?

Don't let the CreateUserWizard control fool you into thinking that the user must supply the question; keep in mind that just like PayPal does, you also can control the questions that a user must answer. (Here's another feature request in case the ASP.NET team is reading: allow me to easily switch the Security Question text box into a drop-down list where I get to control the questions!) Of course, if you decide to be responsible for the questions, don't force the user to supply personally identifiable information like his full Social Security Number. Security and privacy are a delicate balance.

If you require questions and answers, you'll probably want to allow the user to change her question and answer if she so desires. That's what the ChangePasswordQuestionAndAnswer method is for. Note that in this case, the user must supply her password before the Membership provider will allow the question and answer to be changed. As of this writing, there's no built-in control in ASP.NET 2.0 for automating this, but such a form is trivial to create.

Configuring a Membership Provider

The example at the beginning of this chapter, the trade show demo approach, simply used the default Membership provider supplied in machine.config. After reading this far, you should have a much better understanding of the configuration options on the provider.

While you can live a full and happy life using the default provider configuration, we strongly advise you to use your own web.config file to specify provider settings, especially if you're going to use the SqlMembershipProvider, which is very popular. To do this, you'll need to add a <membership> section to your web.config file, and add a provider of your own. To avoid confusion, we like to start by clearing the provider list so that we don't accidentally use the default provider from machine.config. Listing 5-6 shows an example.

LISTING 5-6: MyMembershipProvider

```
<connectionStrings>
  <clear/>
  <add name="asp"
      connectionString="integrated security=sspi;
                        database=myaspnetdb"
      providerName="System.Data.SqlClient" />
</connectionStrings>

<system.web>
  <!-- other entries omitted for brevity -->
  <membership defaultProvider="MyProvider">
    <providers>
      <clear/>
      <add name="MyProvider"
        type="System.Web.Security.SqlMembershipProvider"
        connectionStringName="asp"
        applicationName="MyApplication"
        enablePasswordRetrieval="false"
        enablePasswordReset="true"
        requiresQuestionAndAnswer="true"
        requiresUniqueEmail="false"
        passwordFormat="Hashed"
        maxInvalidPasswordAttempts="5"
        minRequiredPasswordLength="7"
        minRequiredNonalphanumericCharacters="1"
        passwordAttemptWindow="10"
        passwordStrengthRegularExpression="" />
    </providers>
  </membership>
</system.web>
```

Here we've created a new connection string so that we can have our own private membership database for this application. We also cleared out any inherited connection strings for clarity, since we're not using them.

Note how we set the defaultProvider attribute on the <membership> element. This is important: it tells the login controls and other ASP.NET infrastructure which provider to use by default. Controls that rely on membership (like Login and CreateUserWizard) expose a property called ProviderName that allows you to override this default and hardwire to a particular provider, but generally you'll use a single provider for your entire application, so setting the defaultProvider attribute should suffice.

When you're using SqlMembershipProvider, another important attribute to set is applicationName. This is because the SQL provider supports multiple Web applications in a single membership database, each of which can have its own unique user accounts. Each application is scoped by the applicationName attribute in its provider's configuration. Applications sharing the same applicationName will share the same set of users, whereas an application with a unique applicationName will see its own private set of users. If you look back at Listing 5-4, you'll see that the machine-wide default provider (whose name is AspNetSqlMembership-Provider) uses an applicationName of "/", so all applications that use this machine-wide default (like my trade show demo) end up seeing the same set of users. This is good to know when you're experimenting with membership.

Don't omit the applicationName attribute on your provider definition. If you do, the SQL provider will look at your Web application's virtual root and construct an application name from that. This can lead to trouble: If your application is moved to a new virtual directory, suddenly it can no longer see any users in its membership database. So be sure to set this value up front (even using a simple value of "/" is better than not setting it at all). Note that if you're using the AD provider, this value is ignored—all applications that use the AD provider with the same connection string see the same set of users.

Custom Providers

The type attribute names the class you want to use to implement Membership Provider. In Listing 5-6 above, it's set to the SqlMembershipProvider, but it could easily be set to a class that you write. For example, if you wanted to replace the account lockout feature of SqlMembershipProvider with a login delay, you could do that by starting with the source code for

SqlMembershipProvider, modifying it however you like, and giving it a new name. (Although for this particular feature, you'll probably spend most of your time changing the stored procedures in the membership database.) You might be surprised to learn that the source code for all of the Microsoft providers for ASP.NET 2.0 are available to you royalty free,[12] and you are allowed to create derivative works under that license.

Here's another helpful tip if you're planning on replacing the SQL provider or just learning more about how it works. You can ask aspnet_regsql to give you a dump of the SQL required to construct the provider tables, views, stored procedures, and so on. Here's the command (replace *file.sql* with the name of the output file that you want aspnet_regsql to create for you):

```
aspnet_regsql -A all -sqlexportonly file.sql
```

This creates a text file with all table, view, and stored procedure definitions, and you can search it to find out how things work under the covers. This is invaluable for the SqlMembershipProvider, as much of the actual functionality is provided by these stored procedures.

Using the Membership Class to Access Your Provider

Once you've configured a default Membership provider for your Web application, it's trivial to program against it. There's a helper class called Membership that exposes much of the functionality of the Membership-Provider class, along with several overloaded methods that make certain methods easier to use (by passing default values for unused arguments). For example, if you want to get a list of users, you can simply call Membership.GetAllUsers(). Under the hood, this accesses the default provider and calls its GetAllUsers method, passing in the three arguments the provider expects to see, indicating that you don't care about paging; rather, you just want a collection of all the possible users.

For some reason, the Membership class doesn't expose all of the functionality of MembershipProvider. For example, if you're implementing a

---

12. If you'd like to download the source code, see http://msdn.microsoft.com/asp.net/ downloads/providers/ or search for "ASP.NET Provider Toolkit."

form to allow the user to change her password question and answer, you'll quickly find that the Membership class doesn't expose the ChangePassword-QuestionAndAnswer method. But don't fret; you can just reach down and talk directly to the provider, and there's absolutely no harm in doing this. The easiest way to get your hands on the default provider for your application is to use the Membership.Provider property. This will load your provider based on the class name in web.config (if it's not already been loaded), and give you a reference to it. This is how the Membership class itself dispatches calls to the provider.

The Membership class doesn't seem to be critical in this version of ASP.NET; it seems more of a convenience. You could live a full and rich life programming against MembershipProvider without ever using the Membership class. The only nonobvious thing is how to load the default provider, and as you can see in Listing 5-7, even that is not difficult, and can actually come in handy if you want to change some of the configuration settings before loading the provider.[13]

LISTING 5-7: LoadMembershipProvider

```
using System.Configuration;
using System.Web.Configuration;
using System.Web.Security;
// ...
public MembershipProvider LoadMembershipProvider(string name) {
  MembershipSection ms = (MembershipSection)
    WebConfigurationManager.GetSection("system.web/membership");
  foreach (ProviderSettings ps in ms.Providers) {
    if (name == ps.Name) {
      return (MembershipProvider)ProvidersHelper.InstantiateProvider(
        ps, typeof(MembershipProvider));
    }
  }
  return null; // not found
}
```

---

13. Most provider settings are read-only once the provider is loaded, but you can use the ProviderSettings.Parameters collection to tweak the settings from config. Just be sure to make all your changes before calling ProvidersHelper.InstantiateProvider(). Also be aware that any tweaks you make may limit an administrator's ability to configure your application by changing your web.config file.

SQL Database Permissions

When you launch (or debug) a Web application from Visual Studio, you're actually using its built-in Web server, which was originally code-named Cassini. This is a really useful tool, as it allows you to test a Web site without even having IIS installed, but it also can give you some false expectations. For one thing, Cassini runs in the same security context as Visual Studio, which naturally runs under your interactive logon. When I log in as Keith and run my Web application under Cassini, it's running as *Keith*; it's not running as Network Service, or whatever user account I plan on using in a production scenario.

If you run Visual Studio using an account that is a member of the Administrators group, your Web application will run with very high privilege under Cassini. This means it'll have no problem accessing the membership, role, profile, or personalization databases in SQL Server, assuming you connect to SQL Server using integrated security (a good idea in general). But it also means that your code is running in a very different environment than it will in production.

In a production scenario (or simply running your application in IIS under the ASPNET or Network Service accounts, which are low privilege), your application will probably fail to access these databases at first, as the stored procedures required to access them are locked down with SQL Server's role-based security. You'll need to do two things to solve this problem: give your application's identity permission to access the ASPNETDB database and grant it appropriate database roles. Figure 5-9 shows the various database roles you can use.

Note that each feature exposes three levels of authorization: Basic, Reporting, and Full. The Full role always includes the Basic and Reporting roles, and typically adds a few more features that are often reserved for administrators. Nothing stops you from adding more roles that are a superset of these, though. For example, if you let users self-register using the SqlMembershipProvider, Basic access won't be enough. You normally need Full access to call the CreateUser stored procedure. But nothing stops you from adding a new role called MyAccess that includes the Basic role (fortunately, roles can be nested in SQL Server) and adds the CreateUser sproc. The same goes for allowing users to reset their own passwords or update their membership information, such as their e-mail address.

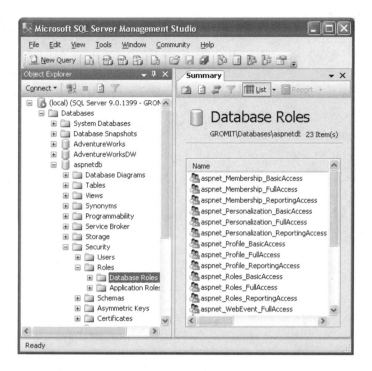

FIGURE 5-9: Security roles in the ASPNETDB database

In general, you should start by trying to give your application the least possible privileges and work up from there. While things will work great for you by blindly cranking up all access levels to Full, you've probably granted yourself more privilege than your application really needs, and that can be catastrophic if an attacker discovers and exploits, say, a SQL injection vulnerability in your application.

Play it safe and spend a few minutes figuring out what permissions your application really needs to do its job. One approach is to use the aspnet_regsql -sqlexportonly trick mentioned earlier to dump the SQL for the database, and then search for the word "rights" so that you can quickly find the permission grants that these various database roles imply.

Another consideration mentioned early in this chapter is that you will typically be better off giving each of your applications a separate membership database entirely, unless those applications need to share data (such as user accounts). Imagine if you put two applications that didn't trust one another into the same membership database. You might even scope them differently using the applicationName attribute, but it turns out that it's trivial for one application to access the other application's data. In fact, the ApplicationName property on the SqlMembershipProvider is writable, which means in theory I can simply change that property to the name used by my sibling and instantly enumerate all of her user accounts! The database roles shown here don't prevent this rather rude (if not outright malicious) behavior, so this is a good reason to consider using separate databases for each application, unless they trust one another and have a good reason to share data.

The LoginView and Other Controls

There are a few other security-related controls that ship with ASP.NET 2.0 that help to automate security-related tasks. This section shows how to use the LoginView, LoginName, and LoginStatus controls.

The LoginView control is designed to show different content depending on the authentication and authorization level of the user making the request. It's independent of Membership; it only cares about the current IPrincipal and IIdentity that are being held in the HttpContext of the request, so it can be used with any authentication strategy, including integrated authentication.

The control is similar to a MultiView, which displays different templates that you can switch between programmatically (see Chapter 4). The LoginView control determines which template should be shown automatically based on the information known about the user making the request. This is really convenient if you want your user interface to change a bit depending on whether the user is anonymous, authenticated, or even in a particular role.

One convenient place to use this control is when you have a Web site that allows anonymous users, but that provides specialized services for authenticated users. There are many Web sites like this—you can browse around all you want, but at some point you might need to log in to access a particular feature.

Listing 5-8 shows how to use the LoginView control to display a login control if the user is anonymous (thus allowing them to log in). If the user has already been authenticated, there's no need to display the login control, so a welcome message is displayed instead. The welcome message uses the LoginName control, an extremely simple control whose output is the name of the user (or blank if the user is not authenticated).

Below the welcome message, I display a LoginStatus control. You'll find this control very useful on a master page, as it allows an authenticated user to log off and an anonymous user to log on. Because I'm already showing a login control to anonymous users in Listing 5-8, there's no need for a "login" button, which is why I only show the LoginStatus control to authenticated users, allowing them to log out.

LISTING 5-8: The LoginView, LoginName, and LoginStatus controls

```
<asp:LoginView ID="loginView" runat="server">
   <LoggedInTemplate>
      <h1>Welcome, <asp:LoginName ID="ln" runat="server" /></h1>
      <p><asp:LoginStatus ID="ls" runat="server" /></p>
   </LoggedInTemplate>
   <AnonymousTemplate>
      <asp:Login ID="login" runat="server"/>
   </AnonymousTemplate>
</asp:LoginView>
```

If you are using role-based security, you can add templates to the Login-View control that will be shown to users based on their role. Each role-based template is called a **RoleGroup**, which is a bit of a funky name, but just think of it as a template that will only be shown if the user is in the associated role. For example, managers might be shown an extra set of links to pages that require higher privileges. Keep in mind that simply hiding links from a user won't stop a reasonably intelligent attacker from getting to those pages by simply guessing their URLs. You'll want to lock down those restricted pages you're linking to in order to ensure that any direct requests will be denied unless the user is authorized. Use the <authorization> section to do this, as described in *Essential ASP.NET*.

In Visual Studio designer mode, the LoginView control only shows one template at a time. You can use the LoginView tasks pane to flip between templates in the designer, which is convenient for editing the templates visually. Press the Edit RoleGroups button to add templates that will be displayed based on roles (see Figure 5-10).

The order of the RoleGroups you define can be important. If a user is in more than one RoleGroup, the first match wins, and the matching template will be displayed. So it is wise to arrange RoleGroups in order from high to

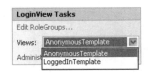

FIGURE 5-10: Switching views

low privilege, top to bottom. If none of the RoleGroups match, the Logged-InTemplate will be displayed, unless the user has not been authenticated, in which case the AnonymousTemplate will be shown.

The LoginView control fires two events as it switches between templates at runtime. ViewChanging fires before the controls from the old template are torn down, giving you a chance to extract their state. ViewChanged fires after the controls for the new template are created, giving you a chance to data bind or otherwise initialize them.

One thing that might surprise you if you're new to templated controls like the LoginView is that you cannot access its child controls directly by name. For example, the login control in the AnonymousTemplate shown in Listing 5-8 is not added to your Web form as a member variable. If you want to access this control, you'll need to use the FindControl method on the LoginView control to look for the child control by name, as shown in Listing 5-9.

LISTING 5-9: Accessing child controls

```
if (!User.Identity.IsAuthenticated) {
  Login loginControl = (Login)loginView.FindControl("login");
  // ...
}
```

Note the check against User.Identity.IsAuthenticated to ensure that the anonymous template is actually showing. If it wasn't being shown, FindControl would not find any control named "login" and would return null.

And finally, there's the CreateUserWizard control (illustrated in Figure 5-8), which is convenient if you're building a user-management page or if you allow users to self-register. This wizard by default has only two steps, although you can easily add more. The first step collects enough information to create a user in the Membership system, and the second step is simply a success indicator after the user has been created.

The Role Manager

If you tried implementing role-based security with Forms authentication back in ASP.NET 1.x, you were pretty much on your own. Many people wrote code in global.asax to handle the Authorize event, replacing the IPrincipal implementation with a GenericPrincipal filled with a set of roles typically looked up in a database. But there were many others who didn't know enough about the Forms authentication mechanism to implement this, and those who did often weren't happy with the performance implications of hitting the database to look up roles for every single authenticated request.[14]

Fortunately, ASP.NET 2.0 ships with a role manager and Role provider infrastructure that solves these problems. If you don't already have a role-based infrastructure, you can simply use the SqlRoleProvider that ships with ASP.NET. This class builds on the services provided by SqlMembership-Provider, allowing you to put users into roles that you can then use for authorizing requests.

The role database behind SqlRoleProvider is really straightforward. It simply adds a table of roles (aspnet_Roles) and a second table that links users to their roles (aspnet_UsersInRoles). The RoleProvider base class exposes the methods you'd expect, allowing you to create and delete roles, add and remove users from those roles, and check to see if a user is a member of a role. There's nothing surprising there.

If this were all the role infrastructure did, it would be really useful. But the ASP.NET team took this a bit further and provided an optional solution for the performance problem mentioned earlier. Their solution was to cache the roles for a user in an HTTP cookie. By caching these roles, the role manager doesn't have to hit the database for each request, since the cookie can be used to do a quick lookup instead. To prevent the cookie from being manipulated by a user who wants to modify her roles, the cookie is crypto-graphically protected with tamper detection and encryption by default. The user would need to learn the secret key stored on the Web server to be able to modify her cookie without being detected, which is the exact same protection that ASP.NET provides on the Forms login cookie by default.

---

14. See www.pluralsight.com/articlecontent/efficientRoleBasedAuthentication.pdf for a discussion of the issues involved.

Sophisticated applications can have lots of roles, which may not be feasible for storing in a cookie. To account for practical limitations on cookie size, the role manager has a configurable limit to the number of roles it'll cache in a cookie (maxCachedResults), which defaults to 25. While there was some talk early on about optimizing the use of this space by caching the most recently checked roles in the cookie, this code got too complicated for the ASP.NET team to manage and test properly, which is a really bad situation for a security feature. So in the released implementation, once the number of roles reaches this threshold, the cookie is simply cleared and not used at all.

Just as the Membership provider infrastructure comes with a Membership class, there is a Roles class that makes it easy to access roles. This class has a Provider property that lets you access the provider directly, although unlike the Membership class, the Roles class exposes 100 percent of the functionality of the underlying provider, which means you can use it exclusively without ever having to talk to the provider directly. The ASP.NET Administration Console sample that comes with this book is a good place to look for code that uses the Roles class, as it provides a Windows Forms interface for managing roles and member lists.

Once you've enabled the role manager, you can look up roles for the logged on user programmatically. The easiest way to do this is with the User property on your page or the HttpContext.User property. This refers to an instance of IPrincipal, and if you're using the role manager, the concrete class you'll see here will be RolePrincipal. So a simple call to User.IsInRole(string roleName) will tell you whether the logged-on user is in a particular role, or you can call RolePrincipal.GetRoles() to get an array of strings representing all the roles in which the user is a member. This latter technique is great for debugging, and don't forget about the LoginView control, which is a convenient way to display different content depending on the user's roles.

Configuring the Role Manager and Provider

Like the Membership provider, a **Role provider** is simply a class that extends an abstract base class (in this case, RoleProvider). But in order to implement the optional cookie cache, ASP.NET also includes an HttpModule called RoleManagerModule. This module is wired into the pipeline by default, but it does nothing unless you enable it via web.config. Listing 5-10 is an example that does just that. (Note that just like <membership>, the <roleManager> element should be placed under <system.web>.)

LISTING 5-10: RoleManager configuration

```
<roleManager enabled="true"
             defaultProvider="MyRoleProvider"
             cacheRolesInCookie="true"
             maxCachedResults="25"
             cookieName=".ASPXROLES"
             cookiePath="/"
             cookieTimeout="30"
             cookieSlidingExpiration="true"
             cookieRequireSSL="false"
             cookieProtection="All"
             createPersistentCookie="false"
             domain="">
  <providers>
    <clear/>
    <add name="MyRoleProvider"
         type="System.Web.Security.SqlRoleProvider"
         connectionStringName="aspnetdb"
         applicationName="MyApplication"/>
  </providers>
</roleManager>
```

The first thing Listing 5-10 does is "turn on" the RoleManagerModule by setting enabled="true". I've configured a default Role provider, and defined it in the <providers> section. Note that the provider specifies an application name and a connection string, just like with Membership. It's important that these values be the same for both your Membership provider and your Role provider if you're using the SQL providers.

The rest of the role manager configuration is all about cookie caching, so you only need to worry about these settings if you're going to use that feature. The first thing I've done is enable the feature by setting cacheRolesInCookie="true". This is false by default. I've shown the rest of the role cookie-related settings just so you can get a feel for what's available for tweaking. These are the default settings you'll get if you simply omit these attributes, and if you're familiar with the Forms authentication configuration, they should look familiar. Unless you really know what you're doing, you should leave all of these settings at their default values (the easiest way is to simply omit them from web.config), with the exception of cookie-RequiresSSL.

If you're running your Web application over SSL (which you really should be doing if you're using Forms authentication), I recommend setting cookieRequiresSSL="true" (more importantly, you should also set requiresSSL="true" in the <forms> configuration element as well). This prevents the cookie from being sent over a nonsecure connection and potentially being stolen by an eavesdropper. This is particularly important for the forms login cookie, because if it's stolen, it can be replayed by an attacker, allowing him to impersonate the user from which the cookie was stolen. This is a very nasty attack, and it's surprisingly easy to pull off. Most Web developers (and hackers) have cookie editors[15] that make it easy to use any cookie they want with your application.

Other Role Providers

Besides the SqlRoleProvider, there is also an AuthorizationStoreRoleProvider which uses Authorization Manager (AzMan)[16] as the backing store for roles. Unless you're already using AzMan elsewhere, this isn't going to buy you much if you're using SqlMembershipProvider, as it only uses a small subset of the features of the AzMan product. The biggest benefit in this case is the fact that roles can be nested, unlike SqlRoleProvider. For example, say you have a role called Administrators, and you'd like anyone in that role to be treated as though they are a member of all other roles. Using AzMan you could make the Administrators role a member of all those other roles. This nesting feature simplifies role management when you have a lot of roles, but it isn't really necessary for simpler applications with only a few roles.

AuthorizationStoreRoleProvider really shines when you use it coupled with Windows' integrated authentication, where groups are normally used directly as roles via WindowsPrincipal. One of the troublesome things I've found with WindowsPrincipal is that you can easily be lured into hardcoding group names into your code. User.IsInRole("MyDomain\Managers")

---

15. My favorite cookie editor plugin for Firefox is called Add & Edit Cookies, which you can download from http://addneditcookies.mozdev.org/.

16. AzMan is beyond the scope of this chapter, but if you want to learn more about it, see http://pluralsight.com/wiki/default.aspx/Keith.GuideBook/WhatIsAuthorizationManager.html, or search for "WhatIsAuthorizationManager."

isn't going to work well if you deploy your application in a different domain or in a nondomain environment. By using the AuthorizationStore-RoleProvider, you'll now be using RolePrincipal, which relies on AzMan roles instead of Windows groups, and all the details of which groups are being used can be isolated into your AzMan policy (which can be stored in a directory service or a simple XML file). Now you can simply write User.IsInRole("Managers") and defer to your AzMan policy to determine which users and groups the Managers role should map onto.

And finally, there's the WindowsTokenRoleProvider, which allows you to use the ASP.NET role manager infrastructure directly with Windows' integrated authentication without AzMan in the picture. I haven't come up with a compelling reason to use this class, but perhaps you might find a corner case where it's really useful. Keep in mind that unlike the other two providers, this one is read-only; you cannot use it to add or remove Windows groups, or to change their membership lists.

A Word about Machine Keys

Since its inception, ASP.NET has allowed you to configure two cryptographic keys that control its validation and encryption of state—like the Forms authentication cookie, the hidden view state field in a Web form, and so on. By default, the <machineKey> element that controls this via configuration is set to AutoGenerate, which is why you may never have needed to think about it, unless you were implementing a Web farm. In a Web farm scenario, if Web server A issues state to a client that is encrypted with its autogenerated key, Web server B isn't going to be able to decrypt that state because its autogenerated key is going to be different. Generating a good, random key becomes important when you have a Web farm, and there are many tools available that can help you do it, including the ASP.NET Administration Console sample that comes with this book.

With the arrival of SqlMembershipProvider, the machine key becomes even more important. If you choose to store passwords encrypted with a key (see the earlier section titled Choosing a Password Format), it's critical that you choose that key yourself instead of allowing ASP.NET to autogenerate it. The reason for this is that if you lose the key, all of your user password verifiers become useless. With an autogenerated <machineKey>, moving your Web application from one Web server to another or reinstalling the operating system on your Web server would cause you to lose the ability to authenticate all of your users.

Because of this, if you choose Encrypted password storage, the SqlMembershipProvider will fail to initialize if you haven't explicitly chosen a <machineKey> (the ASP.NET team didn't want you to accidentally run with an autogenerated key and end up paying for it later!).

There's an unfortunate irony when it comes to cryptographic keys: the longer you use a key, the weaker it gets, and over time you're protecting more and more data with that same key, thus the damage potential (if the key is compromised) continues to increase over time as well. *Any system that requires cryptographic keys should make it easy to change those keys on a regular basis; otherwise, you're effectively relying on hardcoded keys, which is bad news.* Consider this: How comfortable are you going to feel when your system administrator quits and starts working for your competitor, potentially taking knowledge of your applications' secrets with her?

Sadly, <machineKey> doesn't ease the pain at all by making key versioning easy. For example, if you decide to swap out your key, you'll be in a real pickle if you're using Encrypted password storage (you'd need to write custom code to rekey those user password verifiers, for one thing). Also, any users with existing view state or forms login cookies will receive errors the next time they connect. So, assuming you aren't using the Encrypted password format, if you decide to change your <machineKey> settings in production, be sure not to do it during peak traffic time. I hope the ASP.NET team considers making key versioning a priority in the next release.

On the plus side, in ASP.NET 2.0 you have more control over the algorithms and key lengths used by <machineKey>. You can now generate a 256-bit encryption key that uses the Advanced Encryption Standard (AES), and that is exactly what you should do to ensure that your attackers don't even bother trying to crack the cryptography you're using. The ASP.NET Administration Console sample will create a strong key like this for you by default using the cryptographic random number generator that's provided by the Windows CryptoAPI.

Cookieless Forms Authentication

In version 1.x, if you wanted to use Forms authentication, your clients had to support cookies; if a user turned off cookies, she would be denied access to any page that required Forms authentication. Many Web sites would simply inform the user that she needed to "turn on cookies" in order to allow her to log on, but smarter Web sites actually took the time to explain to the user what cookies are and how to enable them for specific, trusted Web sites. But for many mobile devices, cookies simply aren't an option at all. Because of this, the ASP.NET team decided to provide a cookieless alternative (which uses URL mangling) in version 2.0.

This new feature can be enabled by setting the cookieless attribute on the <forms> configuration element. There are four options, the default being UseDeviceProfile, which looks at the User-Agent header to determine whether the browser being used supports cookies at all. For browsers that are known not to support cookies, the cookieless option will be used. The next two options are pretty obvious: UseCookies and UseUri, which indicates that cookies or URL mangling should be used all the time, respectively. The last option, AutoDetect, will attempt to set a cookie, and if that fails, it automatically switches to using URL mangling.

If you end up using URL mangling, the URL for a Web page changes from looking like this:

```
http://www.pluralsight.com/foo/bar.aspx
```

. . . to something like this:

```
http://www.pluralsight.com/foo/(F(Cvc...A1))/bar.aspx
```

The parenthesized section of the URL (which I've shortened quite a bit—the ellipses are mine) contains the data that would normally be stored in the Forms authentication cookie. It has tamper detection and encryption built in just like the cookie would, but because it is now part of the URL, it's easier for the user to accidentally share this URL with someone else (one benefit of cookies is that it's difficult to *accidentally* share them).

Let's say Alice logs in and copies the resulting mangled URL to her friend Bob via instant messenger. If Bob clicks that link, he's effectively (if not knowingly) conducting a replay attack against Alice's logon, and the Web server will treat his request as if it came from Alice. And if you think about it, SSL isn't going to stop this sort of thing from happening, although you should still use SSL even with cookieless authentication to protect these URLs from being stolen by an adversary who is sniffing packets on the network.

One approach you can take to reduce the risk of this kind of attack is to reduce the timeout value for each logon in the <forms> element. This reduces the window of time that any given mangled URL is valid; if an attacker submits an expired URL, he'll be asked to log in like any anonymous user. Another approach is to educate your users not to share URLs. Some Web sites make this easier by providing explicit hyperlinks with unmangled URLs that users can copy if they want to share or bookmark a Web page (you can use Request.Path to get an unmangled URL for this purpose).

SiteMapProvider Security Trimming

Here's a nice little feature worth mentioning. If you are using the site map provider, you can now turn on a new feature called **security trimming**. This adds an extra step when constructing the site map: it checks to see whether the user has permission to visit the page in question, and if not, trims that page from the site map. There's no point listing a Web page in a site map that will only fail when the user clicks it.

There is a new public method on the base SiteMapProvider called IsAccessibleToUser, that takes an HttpContext and a SiteMapNode. This checks to see if the user has permission to access the page by checking with both the FileAuthorizationModule and the UrlAuthorizationModule. The former checks to make sure the user has permission based on the access control list (ACL) on the file, while the latter checks the <authorization> section in web.config to verify that the user is allowed permission to the file.

To enable this new feature, modify your configuration as shown in Listing 5-11.

LISTING 5-11: Enabling security trimming

```
<siteMap defaultProvider="AspNetXmlSiteMapProvider">
  <providers>
    <remove name="AspNetXmlSiteMapProvider" />
    <add name="AspNetXmlSiteMapProvider"
         type="System.Web.XmlSiteMapProvider, System.Web, ..."
         siteMapFile="Web.sitemap"
         securityTrimmingEnabled="true" />
  </providers>
</siteMap>
```

In your site map, you can also further restrict visibility of nodes in the map based on roles. The example in Listing 5-12 requires you to be in the "admin" role in order to access the CreateUser.aspx page.

LISTING 5-12: Restricting node visibility with security roles

```
<siteMapNode url="~/CreateUser.aspx"
            title="Create user"
            description="" roles="admin" />
```

Remember that just hiding a site map node from a user isn't enough to guarantee she'll never be able to see that page. You should start by restricting access to resources using ACLs or the <authorization> section in web.config.

Configuration File Encryption

It never fails: At some point in your career as a Web application designer or developer you're going to end up with a secret that your application needs to store somewhere, and that's never fun. The most common secret is a connection string that has a password in it, or a user name and password that you need to access a remote resource. Of course your first intuition should be to try to eliminate the secret. For example, you might be able to use integrated security to connect to your database instead of using a connection string with a password in it. Integrated security can often reduce the number of secrets that your application needs to manage, and it is a good place to start. But sometimes that's simply not an option.

When faced with this problem, most people will look for a place on the machine to hide the secret. "Maybe the registry would work, or perhaps I could use a file with an obfuscated name on a different drive than my virtual directory. And I can protect it even further by locking down the access control list, so only my Web application has permission to read the secret."

The next phase is to start thinking about encryption: "Perhaps I can encrypt the secret! Oh wait, now I've got an encryption key that I must hide somewhere. I know—I'll encrypt that key as well! Oh, wait . . ." If you go down this road, you'll quickly discover that encryption doesn't eliminate secrets; it merely transfers them into keys. Ultimately, there's still a secret to worry about.

There's no foolproof way to hide a secret on a machine if your application needs to be able to use that secret on a regular basis. Any resource that's available to your application is available to an attacker who has taken control of your application by exploiting some vulnerability that you missed, be it a buffer overrun, SQL injection vulnerability, or whatever. But that doesn't mean you should just give up and leave secrets in cleartext hardcoded in your ASPX pages, web.config file, or elsewhere. ASP.NET 2.0 helps by providing a standard technique for encrypting sections of your configuration files; stuff that sometimes needs to be encrypted, such as the <connectionStrings> section. There's even a provider model that allows you to decide on the encryption and key management technique.

The simplest way to get started is to use the Data Protection API (DPAPI) provider. DPAPI is a facility built into modern versions of Windows that lets you ask the Local Security Authority Subsystem (LSASS.EXE) to encrypt data for you with a set of keys that it manages. Yes, there's still a secret key, but at least it's one that's being managed by the most secure process on the machine.

To encrypt a section of your web.config file using DPAPI, just run the aspnet_regiis tool and point it at your virtual directory, naming the section you wish to encrypt:

```
aspnet_regiis -pef connectionStrings e:\web\myVirtualDir
  -prov DataProtectionConfigurationProvider
```

The -pef switch indicates you want to use the **p**rotection facility, **e**ncrypt a section, and provide a **f**ile path that points to the directory where your web.config file lives. There are many different flavors of protection switches; just run aspnet_regiis -? to get a listing of all the options.

The –prov switch indicates which provider you want to use. Providers are listed under the <configProtectedData> section of machine.config. There are two, and I'll explain why you might want to use the other one shortly.

What's nice about this technique is that the code you use to access encrypted configuration sections doesn't change at all. At runtime, you don't need to worry about whether a section is encrypted or not: it'll automatically be decrypted in memory for you when you need it, while anyone who looks at web.config directly will see ciphertext.

So what if the administrator needs to change the connection string? She can either replace the entire section with a normal <connectionStrings>

section, or more likely run aspnet_regiis using the -pef switch to decrypt the file on disk, make her change, then run aspnet_regiis with the -pef switch to reencrypt the section.

As an example, I encrypted an empty <connectionStrings/> element using DPAPI, and Listing 5-13 shows what it ended up looking like (the ellipses are mine; the ciphertext is rather long).

LISTING 5-13: Encrypted connection strings

```
<configuration>
 <connectionStrings configProtectionProvider=
   "DataProtectionConfigurationProvider">
  <EncryptedData>
   <CipherData>
     <CipherValue>AQAAANCMnd8...Cin</CipherValue>
   </CipherData>
  </EncryptedData>
 </connectionStrings>
</configuration>
```

Since DPAPI uses a key that's hidden away on the machine, it makes xcopy deployment pretty much impossible. Web farms become a nightmare, because each server has its own Local Security Authority with its own key, and you can't synchronize these like you can with the ASP.NET <machineKey> element. If this is a problem, you should use the RSA provider instead. This provider uses a public/private key pair, so it's not quite as fast, but since you can export the key pair, you can synchronize keys across a Web farm.[17]

Note that if the section you want to encrypt isn't a direct child of the root <configuration> element, you should specify a path to get to it. For example, if you want to encrypt the <machineKey> element, you would do so by specifying "system.web/machineKey" as the section name.

Keep in mind that none of this is foolproof, but if an attacker manages to download your web.config file, he'll need to do more if he wants to decrypt your secrets. He'll either need to run code on your server to decrypt the data or find a way to steal the encryption key. It's all about defense in depth, and it's so easy to do that it's really a no-brainer.

---

17. To learn how to synchronize keys in a Web farm, see http://msdn.microsoft.com/library/ en-us/dnpag2/html/paght000006.asp or search for "How To: Encrypt Configuration Sections in ASP.NET 2.0 Using RSA."

SUMMARY

The ASP.NET team gave Forms authentication a lot of love in version 2.0. A new provider model now gives you direct support for managing users and roles in SQL Server. And if you don't want to use SQL Server, you can rely on Active Directory or write your own providers to hook up with a user store of your own making, or use one built by a third party. You can even download the source code for the existing providers to help you get started.

Be sure to test your application using IIS under a least-privileged user account. Do this early and often, as it will help you quickly discover potential problems, such as restricted access to resources. Encrypt sensitive sections of your web.config and machine.config files, including <machineKey> and <connectionStrings> using the aspnet_regiis tool. Try to eliminate as many secrets as you can—using integrated security really helps with this.

You'll find that implementing security-related UI features such as login and self-registration pages is much easier with the new login controls in ASP.NET 2.0, and since these controls know about the provider model, you probably won't have to write much code (if any at all) to get started using them.

Keep in mind that cookieless Forms authentication is now available, and use it if necessary, but if you do, be certain to take steps to reduce the dangers of sharing URLs with login details in them. And keep an eye on the wisdom provided by the patterns & practices group at Microsoft: there's some great advice on building secure ASP.NET 2.0 applications at http://msdn.com/securityguidance. Remember, security is a feature!

■ 6 ■
Web Parts

W EB-BASED PORTAL APPLICATIONS have become a popular platform for all types of products, ranging from Intranet sites used internally at a company to popular Internet sites supporting millions of users. Microsoft made great strides in adding a scalable portal framework to the Windows Server 2003 platform when they released Windows SharePoint Services (WSS) in September of 2003. WSS provides the basic elements required by a portal framework by including support for site membership, content and document management, and the modular presentation of data through the use of Web Parts.

Web Parts provide WSS with its foundation for both customization and personalization. A user with the proper permissions can easily customize a page in a WSS site using a browser by adding, reconfiguring, and removing Web Parts. Customization changes will be seen by all site members. Individual site members can further personalize pages by adding, reconfiguring, and removing Web Parts. Developing custom Web Parts has provided an easy and powerful way to extend WSS sites. When you create a custom Web Part for WSS in which you want support for customization and personalization, you simply add properties to your Web Part class and apply a few special attributes. What's nice is that the Web Part infrastructure of WSS manages all of the details of serializing, storing, and retrieving the data associated with site customization and member personalization.

ASP.NET 2.0 introduces a Web Part infrastructure that is similar yet distinct from that of WSS. The new Web Part infrastructure of ASP.NET 2.0 is similar to WSS in the sense that it was designed to deal with the serialization, storage, and retrieval of customization and personalization data behind the scenes. It's different and far more flexible in that it's not tightly coupled to either SQL Server or Active Directory. That's great news for companies that want to build portal applications using Forms-based authentication and non-Microsoft DBMSs such as Oracle and DB2. The next release of WSS, SharePoint 2007, is based on the ASP.NET 2.0 infrastructure as well, so going forward, all portal development on Microsoft platforms will be based on the technology presented in this chapter.

Web Part Fundamentals

ASP.NET 2.0 introduces a collection of components and controls that provide the building blocks for constructing a customizable portal site. These components manage the details of storing the user customization data, providing the interface for customization, and managing the Web Parts you define as components for users to work with. You are left with the task of placing the various zones on your portal page (Web Part zones, editor zones, catalog zones, and connection zones), building customizable Web Parts, and instructing the WebPartManager when to transition among the various editing modes. These components make it easy to build a portal site in any format, layout, or design that you can imagine, taking care of the difficult elements of constructing a portal for you automatically. Figure 6-1 shows a sample portal site in action, with the user dragging a Web Part from one zone on the page to another.

Portal Components

There are three core conceptual components to building portal pages in ASP.NET 2.0: Web Parts, zones, and the Web Part manager. **Web Parts** are the UI components you build as pieces of functionality for clients to use. Web Parts can be custom classes that inherit from the WebPart base class (which in turn inherits from the Panel control), or they can be any control-derived class in ASP.NET (controls are implicitly wrapped by a generic Web Part class). **Zones** are regions on a page, typically embedded in an HTML layout element like a table cell or DIV, that contain the Web Parts. When a client customizes the page, she can elect to move Web Parts from

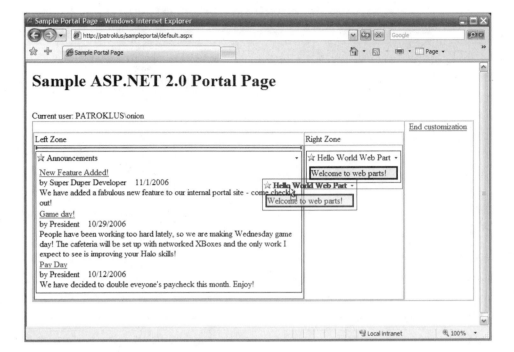

FIGURE 6-1: Sample portal page running

one zone to another, so the more zones you provide in your interface, the more flexibility the client will have with the page's layout. You will also typically include an editor zone and a catalog zone, which will display the properties of a Web Part that can be modified and a collection of available Web Parts, respectively. Finally, the **Web Part manager** is a nonvisual control that orchestrates the interaction of all of the zones and Web Parts on a page, providing methods for entering modes of customization and for exporting, importing, and saving Web Parts. Figure 6-2 shows one possible layout of a portal page using Web Parts, zones, and the Web Part manager.

Building a Minimal Portal Page

The first task in putting together a portal page with ASP.NET 2.0 is to add a WebPartManager control, which orchestrates the interaction of Web Parts and Web Part zones on the page. This control must be placed before any other Web Part components on the page, so it is usually a good idea to place the WebPartManager control right at the top of the page (just inside

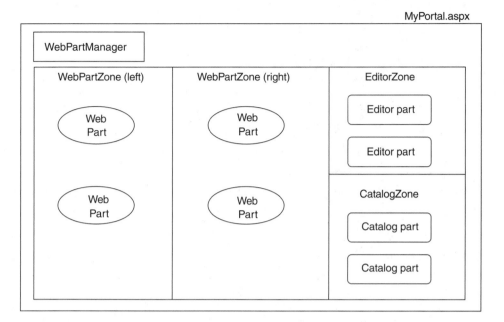

FIGURE 6-2: Portal components in ASP.NET 2.0

the opening server-side form tag). Next you'll want to add a few WebPart-Zone controls so that there is a place to put Web Parts. Listing 6-1 shows a minimal portal page with two zones laid out in an HTML table and the accompanying WebPartManager.

LISTING 6-1: Minimal portal page

```
<%--File: MinimalPortalPage.aspx--%>
<%@ Page Language="C#" AutoEventWireup="true"
        CodeFile="MinimalPortalPage.aspx.cs"
        Inherits="MinimalPortalPage" %>

<html xmlns="http://www.w3.org/1999/xhtml" >
<head runat="server">
    <title>Minimal Portal Page</title>
</head>
<body>
  <form id="form1" runat="server">
  <asp:WebPartManager runat="server" ID="_webPartManager" />

  <div>
    <table width="100%">
```

```
      <tr><td>
        <asp:WebPartZone ID="_leftWebPartZone" runat="server"
                       HeaderText="Left Zone">
          <ZoneTemplate>
            <!-- Web Parts go here -->
          </ZoneTemplate>
       </asp:WebPartZone>
    </td><td>
        <asp:WebPartZone ID="_rightWebPartZone" runat="server"
                       HeaderText="Right Zone">
          <ZoneTemplate>
              <!-- Web Parts go here -->
          </ZoneTemplate>
        </asp:WebPartZone>
    </td></tr>
    </table>
  </div>

  </form>
</body>
</html>
```

The next task is to build some Web Parts to place in the Web Part zones. There are several ways of doing this, as you shall soon see, but we will start by writing a pair of Web Parts in code, much like you would write any custom control in ASP.NET. Instead of inheriting from Control or WebControl, however, you inherit from System.Web.UI.WebControls.WebParts.WebPart, and override the virtual RenderContents method to supply the user interface. Listing 6-2 shows a minimal pair of "Hello world" Web Parts.

LISTING 6-2: "Hello world" Web Parts

```
// File: HelloWorldWebParts.cs
using System;
using System.Web.UI;
using System.Web.UI.WebControls.WebParts;

namespace EssentialAspDotNet2.WebParts
{
    public class HelloWorldWebPart : WebPart
    {
        protected override void RenderContents(HtmlTextWriter writer)
        {
            writer.Write("Welcome to web parts!");

            base.RenderContents(writer);
        }
    }
```

continues

```
public class HelloWorldWebPart2 : WebPart
{
    protected override void RenderContents(HtmlTextWriter writer)
    {
        writer.RenderBeginTag(HtmlTextWriterTag.H1);
        writer.Write("Hello world!");
        writer.RenderEndTag();

        base.RenderContents(writer);
    }
}
}
```

To add our new Web Parts to our portal page, we need to register the namespace and assembly in the page, as you would with any custom control, and then declare instances of the Web Parts in the ZoneTemplate elements in each WebPartZone. Web Parts placed in this template will appear in that zone when the page is first accessed prior to any customization by the user (or administrator). If you would prefer not to have a particular Web Part displayed on a page when it is first shown, you could opt to include it in the declarative catalog for a page, as you will see. Listing 6-3 shows our updated portal page with an @Register directive referencing our Web Parts and an instance of each of our custom Web Parts placed in each of the page's zones. This example assumes that the HelloWorldWeb-Parts.cs file is deployed in the App_Code directory of this site so that the Assembly attribute of the @Register directive can be omitted.

LISTING 6-3: **Minimal portal page with Web Parts**

```
<%--File: MinimalPortalPage.aspx--%>
<%@ Page Language="C#" AutoEventWireup="true"
        CodeFile="MinimalPortalPage.aspx.cs"
        Inherits="MinimalPortalPage" %>

<%@ Register Namespace="EssentialAspDotNet2.WebParts"
             TagPrefix="eadn2" %>

<html xmlns="http://www.w3.org/1999/xhtml" >
<head runat="server">
    <title>Minimal Portal Page</title>
</head>
<body>
  <form id="form1" runat="server">
  <asp:WebPartManager runat="server" ID="_webPartManager" />
```

```
<div>
  <table width="100%">
  <tr><td>
      <asp:WebPartZone ID="_leftWebPartZone" runat="server"
                       HeaderText="Left Zone">
          <ZoneTemplate>
            <eadn2:HelloWorldWebPart runat="server" ID="_wp1" />
          </ZoneTemplate>
    </asp:WebPartZone>
  </td><td>
      <asp:WebPartZone ID="_rightWebPartZone" runat="server"
                       HeaderText="Right Zone">
          <ZoneTemplate>
             <eadn2:HelloWorldWebPart2 runat="server" ID="_wp2" />
          </ZoneTemplate>
      </asp:WebPartZone>
  </td></tr>
  </table>
  </div>

  </form>
</body>
</html>
```

At this point we can actually run our portal page, and the Web Parts will show up in their respective zones. It's not much to look at so far, and there is no customization available, but it will indeed run, as shown in Figure 6-3.

The reason there is no customization yet in our site is that the site is running with anonymous access enabled, so there is no authentication for clients. The Web Part infrastructure depends on uniquely identifying clients by their user name and thus requires all clients to be authenticated to support customization. Note that by default if an anonymous client is accessing the site, she will see the Web Parts and be able to interact with them, but she will not be able to change their attributes or modify the page layout. You can use any of the supported authentication mechanisms in ASP.NET or IIS (Windows, Forms, Passport, etc.) as long as the user is forced to authenticate when she visits the page. In this example, we will enable Windows authentication and disallow anonymous users by modifying the web.config file, as shown in Listing 6-4.

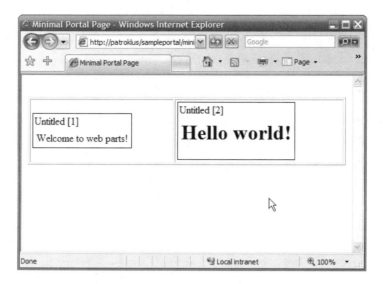

FIGURE 6-3: Minimal portal page running

LISTING 6-4: Forcing authentication for our portal site using web.config

```
<configuration>
  <system.web>
    <authentication mode="Windows" />
    <authorization>
      <deny users="?"/>
    </authorization>
  </system.web>
</configuration>
```

Once our users are authenticated, the Web Parts on the page take on a slightly different appearance by enabling a menu in the upper right corner. By default, this menu lets you minimize or close a Web Part, persisting the state of the Web Part on behalf of the current client (so when a new client visits the site, she will still see the Web Parts in their original state even though a different client may have minimized or closed them). Figure 6-4 shows the default menu that appears once the page is displayed to an authenticated client. When you minimize a Web Part it displays only the title portion, but if you close it, it is removed from the form altogether. To give users the ability to add back closed Web Parts, we will need to add a catalog zone, which we will do shortly.

FIGURE 6-4: Web Parts with menu (displayed for authenticated clients)

Display Mode

The ability to minimize and close individual Web Parts is a good first step at providing customization for our site, but ideally we want to provide users with much more than that. Web Parts also support the ability to change the layout of a page (by letting users drag and drop parts between zones), modify properties of individual Web Parts, connect multiple Web Parts together (by sharing data), and displaying a catalog of all available Web Parts to add to a page. All of these features are enabled by changing the display mode of the Web Part manager; the only thing you have to do as the developer is to give users the ability to transition among the various modes. Table 6-1 shows the values the DisplayMode property of the Web-PartManager class can take on, and what effect it has on the portal page.

One common approach to exposing the display mode to the client is to add one or more LinkButton controls to your portal page that indicate the customization modes. In the handler for each button, set the Web Part manager's DisplayMode property as appropriate. Of course, the interface is entirely up to you; all that matters is that you give users some way of transitioning among the modes you want to make available. It is also wise to disable links to modes that are not currently available, as the available

TABLE 6-1: Display modes

Display Mode	Purpose
BrowseDisplayMode	Standard view mode. No personalization or editing.
DesignDisplayMode	Permits drag-and-drop layout personalization/customization.
EditDisplayMode	Permits personalization/customization of Web Part properties to change appearance and behavior. Also permits users to delete Web Parts that have been added to the page dynamically.
ConnectDisplayMode	Permits users to connect Web Parts together at runtime.
CatalogDisplayMode	Permits users to add Web Parts into Web Part Zones at runtime.

modes may change based on whether a user is authenticated, whether there are Web Parts on the page that support links, and whether specific zone types are defined on the page.

You can query the Web Part manager to find out if a particular mode is supported by using the SupportedDisplayModes collection's Contains() method. This collection will always have the current set of modes that are supported based on client credentials and Web Part features. For our "minimal" portal site, we will provide just two LinkButtons for now. These let users select between Browse mode and Design mode, making sure to toggle the visibility of the Design mode button based on whether the mode is actually supported. Listings 6-5 and 6-6 show the additions to our page and codebehind file.

LISTING 6-5: LinkButtons added to portal page to change display mode

```
<asp:LinkButton runat="server" ID="_browseViewLinkButton"
     Text="Browse View" OnClick="_browseViewLinkButton_Click" />
     
<asp:LinkButton runat="server" ID="_designViewLinkButton"
     Text="Design View" OnClick="_designViewLinkButton_Click" />
```

LISTING 6-6: Codebehind logic for LinkButtons on portal page

```
public partial class MinimalPortalPage : System.Web.UI.Page
{
    protected void Page_Load(object sender, EventArgs e)
    {
        _designViewLinkButton.Visible =
            _webPartManager.SupportedDisplayModes.Contains(
                    WebPartManager.DesignDisplayMode);
    }
    protected void _browseViewLinkButton_Click(object src, EventArgs e)
    {
        _webPartManager.DisplayMode = WebPartManager.BrowseDisplayMode;
    }
    protected void _designViewLinkButton_Click(object src, EventArgs e)
    {
        _webPartManager.DisplayMode = WebPartManager.DesignDisplayMode;
    }
}
```

With our customization link in place, users can now click on the Design View link button and drag and drop the Web Parts on the page between zones,[1] as shown in Figure 6-5. Each time users move a Web Part from one

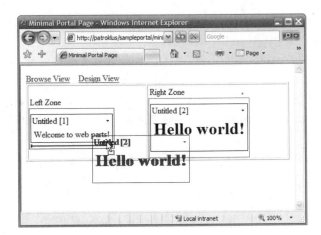

FIGURE 6-5: Customizing Web Parts in design view

---

1. The current release of ASP.NET 2.0 only supports visual drag and drop of Web Parts between zones using Internet Explorer 5.5 or higher. However, there is support in the Atlas framework (an add-on framework for ASP.NET 2.0) that provides drag and drop for the Mozilla Firefox browser as well.

zone to another, the customization data for that client is written to a data store, which we will describe in more detail shortly. Once a user has completed laying out the Web Parts on the page as she desires, she can then click the Browse View link button to transition back to normal viewing mode.

Catalog Parts and Zones

Currently the Web Parts available on our sample portal site are fixed—there is no way to add new Web Parts, and perhaps more importantly, there is no way to restore a Web Part a user closes using the Close item on the Web Part's menu. The solution to both of these problems is to include catalog parts on the page as well. Catalog parts provide the ability to select Web Parts for inclusion on the page, and they are contained in a catalog zone, much like Web Parts are contained in Web Part zones. Catalog parts become visible and active only when the page transitions into catalog display mode.

There are three types of catalog parts available: DeclarativeCatalogPart, PageCatalogPart, and ImportCatalogPart. The declarative catalog part contains a collection of Web Parts declared inside a WebPartsTemplate element, which will be made available to the user as available Web Parts when the page is in catalog display mode. The page catalog part is almost always one you want to include, as it will show all Web Parts that are no longer displayed (that is, have been closed) but are in the original page. This lets users recover parts that they have closed and want to reinstate in their page. Finally, the import catalog part provides the ability to import Web Part definitions complete with a set of property values and appearance attributes. We discuss the importing and exporting of Web Parts later in this section.

To add catalog parts to our sample portal site, we will begin by creating a new column in our table to house the catalog zone. Keep in mind that the catalog zone will not be visible until the user switches to the catalog display view, so it is common to place the catalog zone in a table's collapsible cell. Inside our catalog zone we will place an instance of the PageCatalogPart as well as a DeclarativeCatalogPart. Inside the WebPartsTemplate of the DeclarativeCatalogPart we add a Web Part declaration, in this case just our HelloWorldWebPart2 class. Finally, we need to add one more LinkButton to let users transition into catalog display mode. Listings 6-7 and 6-8 show the additions to our portal page and its codebehind file.

LISTING 6-7: Adding catalog support to a portal page (MinimalPortalpage.aspx)

```
<!-- This LinkButton is added immediately after the browse and design
     view buttons -->
<asp:LinkButton ID="_catalogViewLinkButton" runat="server"
        Text="Catalog View" OnClick="_catalogViewLinkButton_Click" />

<!-- This column is inserted immediately after the last
     WebPartZone column in our table -->
<td>
  <asp:CatalogZone runat="server" ID="_catalogZone">
    <ZoneTemplate>
      <asp:PageCatalogPart ID="_pageCatalogPart" runat="server"
                          Title="Local Page Catalog" />
      <asp:DeclarativeCatalogPart ID="_declarativeCatalogPart"
          runat="server" Title="Minimal Portal Web Parts">
        <WebPartsTemplate>
          <eadn2:HelloWorldWebPart2 runat="server"
                                    ID="_helloWorldWebPart2" />
        </WebPartsTemplate>
      </asp:DeclarativeCatalogPart>
            </ZoneTemplate>
  </asp:CatalogZone>
</td>
```

LISTING 6-8: Adding catalog support to a portal page (MinimalPortalPage.aspx.cs)

```
    protected void Page_Load(object sender, EventArgs e)
    {
        //...
        _catalogViewLinkButton.Visible =
            _webPartManager.SupportedDisplayModes.Contains(
                    WebPartManager.CatalogDisplayMode);
    }
    protected void _catalogViewLinkButton_Click(object src, EventArgs e)
    {
        _webPartManager.DisplayMode = WebPartManager.CatalogDisplayMode;
    }
```

With our catalog parts in place and our new LinkButton wired up, the user can now switch the page into catalog view and select from among the various Web Parts stored in our declarative catalog. Also, if the user closes one of the existing Web Parts on the page, she can restore it by entering catalog view and adding it again from the local page catalog. Figure 6-6 shows what the page looks like in catalog display mode assuming that the user has previously closed the Web Part in the left zone and has selected the Local Page Catalog link in the catalog zone.

FIGURE 6-6: Adding Web Parts using a catalog

Properties

In addition to adding, removing, and changing the layout of Web Parts on a page, users can also modify an individual Web Part's properties by placing the page into edit mode and using any edit parts available. By default, all Web Parts have a number of behavioral and appearance properties defined, which changes the features available for a given Web Part as well as how it looks on the page. Table 6-2 lists the set of behavioral and appearance properties available. In addition to all of these properties, the WebPart class inherits from WebControl, so all of the appearance properties defined there (like BackColor, BorderWidth, etc.) are also available to Web Parts.

TABLE 6-2: WebPart properties

Behavioral Properties	Description	Default
AllowClose	Whether the client can close the Web Part.	True
AllowConnect	Whether the client can connect a Web Part to another (if supported).	True

Behavioral Properties	Description	Default
AllowEdit	Whether the client can edit attributes of the Web Part.	True
AllowHide	Whether the client can hide a Web Part on a page.	True
AllowMinimize	Whether the client can minimize a Web Part on a page.	True
AllowZoneChange	Whether the client can move a Web Part from one zone to another.	True
AuthorizationFilter	String that can be used as a filter to determine whether a control can be added to a page.	—
ExportMode	Which properties (none, all, nonsensitive data) should be exported.	None
Appearance Properties		
CatalogIconImageUrl	URL of image to use as icon in catalog.	—
ChromeState	Get or set whether a Web Part is in a minimized state.	Normal
ChromeType	Type of border framing a Web Part.	Default of zone (typically title and border)
Description	Text description for a Web Part shown in tooltips and catalog.	—
Height	Height of a control.	—
HelpUrl	URL to a help file for a control.	—
Hidden	Whether a Web Part is hidden or visible.	False
Title	Title text of a Web Part.	Untitled
TitleIconImageUrl	URL of image to use as icon in title bar of Web Part.	—
Width	Width of Web Part.	—

When you create Web Parts, it is common to initialize several of these inherited properties to customize your Web Part. At the very least, you should make the effort to set the Title and Description properties so that the control doesn't show up on the page as "Untitled." Listing 6-9 shows the HelloWorldWebPart control presented earlier with the addition of a constructor that initializes the Title, TitleIconImageUrl, BackColor, and BorderWidth properties to some meaningful defaults.

LISTING 6-9: Initializing Web Part properties

```
namespace EssentialAspDotNet2.WebParts
{
    public class HelloWorldWebPart : WebPart
    {
        public HelloWorldWebPart()
        {
            this.Title = "Hello World Web Part";
            this.TitleIconImageUrl = "~/images/star.gif";
            this.BackColor = Color.Beige;
            this.BorderWidth = 3;
        }
        //...
    }
}
```

Like all custom controls, Web Parts can expose their own properties as well. Unlike other controls, however, Web Parts have a built-in interface for letting clients modify their properties and the ability to store property values for a client between login sessions. In order to enable client-editing of properties, you must annotate your properties with the WebBrowsable and Personalizable attributes, indicating to the PropertyGridEditorPart that it is okay to let users modify and persist these properties respectively. Typically you set both of these attributes together, since if you don't enable the Personalizable attribute but do enable WebBrowsable, the client will be able to modify the property, but its value will not be persisted between sessions. There are two additional attributes that you will typically want to include as well on any exposed properties, WebDisplayName and WebDescription, which provide user-friendly strings describing the property.

Listing 6-10 shows our HelloWorldWebPart control with two new custom properties, each annotated with the four attributes to enable friendly editing, and an updated RenderContents method to reflect the value of

those properties. Note that as with all control properties, the state is maintained in ViewState so that it persists across post-back requests.

LISTING 6-10: User-editable WebPart properties

```
namespace EssentialAspDotNet2.WebParts
{
  public class HelloWorldWebPart : WebPart
  {
    //...
    [WebBrowsable, Personalizable]
    [WebDisplayName("ShowTime")]
    [WebDescription("Display the current time")]
    public bool ShowTime
    {
      get { return (bool)(ViewState["showtime"] ?? false); }
      set { ViewState["showtime"] = value; }
    }

    public enum GreetingStyleEnum
            { Cordial, Informal, Friendly, Distant };

    [WebBrowsable, Personalizable]
    [WebDisplayName("GreetingStyle")]
    [WebDescription("Style for the greeting")]
    public GreetingStyleEnum GreetingStyle
    {
      get { return (GreetingStyleEnum)(ViewState["greetingstyle"] ??
                                  GreetingStyleEnum.Cordial); }
      set { ViewState["greetingstyle"] = value; }
    }

    protected override void RenderContents(HtmlTextWriter writer)
    {
      switch (GreetingStyle)
      {
        case GreetingStyleEnum.Cordial:
          writer.Write("Hello there, world.");
          break;
        case GreetingStyleEnum.Distant:
          writer.Write("hi");
          break;
        case GreetingStyleEnum.Friendly:
          writer.Write("Well hello there, world!");
          break;
        case GreetingStyleEnum.Informal:
          writer.Write("Whassup world??");
          break;
      }
```

continues

```
      if (ShowTime)
        writer.Write("<br />{0}", DateTime.Now.ToShortTimeString());

      base.RenderContents(writer);
    }
  }
}
```

Editor Parts and Zones

Now that our Web Part has custom properties to expose, we need to give the user the ability to modify those properties using the EditorZone and one or more editor parts. Much like the catalog zone, the editor zone is displayed only when the page is transitioned into edit view mode. Also, the editor zone will never be displayed at the same time as the catalog mode, so it is common practice to place the catalog and editor zones at the same location on the page. Once you have the editor zone in place, there are four different editor parts available that can be placed into the zone, as described in Table 6-3. Listings 6-11 and 6-12 show our minimal portal page augmented with an EditorZone containing an instance of each of the three core editor parts (we will discuss the BehaviorEditorPart shortly), along with a new LinkButton giving the user the ability to enter edit mode.

TABLE 6-3: Editor parts available for placement in an EditorZone

Editor Parts	Description
AppearanceEditorPart	Editor for inherited properties of WebParts including Title, ChromeType, Direction, Height, Width, and Hidden.
BehaviorEditorPart	Editor for inherited properties of WebParts including Description, TitleUrl, TitleIconImageUrl, CatalogIconImage-Url, HelpUrl, HelpMode, ImportErrorMessage, Export-Mode, AuthorizationFilter, AllowClose, AllowConnect, AllowEdit, AllowHide, AllowMinimize, AllowZoneChange. This part is only visible in shared scope.
LayoutEditorPart	Editor for inherited properties of WebParts including ChromeState, Zone, and ZoneIndex.
PropertyGridEditorPart	Editor for custom properties exposed by a WebPart that are annotated with the WebBrowsable attribute.

LISTING 6-11: Adding editing support to a portal page (MinimalPortalPage.aspx)

```
<asp:LinkButton ID="_editViewLinkButton" runat="server"
               Text="Edit View" OnClick="_editViewLinkButton_Click" />
<!--... -->

<asp:EditorZone ID="_editorZone" runat="server">
  <ZoneTemplate>
    <asp:AppearanceEditorPart ID="_appEditorPart" runat="server" />
    <asp:PropertyGridEditorPart ID="_propEditorPart" runat="server" />
    <asp:LayoutEditorPart ID="_layoutEditorPart" runat="server" />
  </ZoneTemplate>
</asp:EditorZone>
```

LISTING 6-12: Adding editing support to a portal page (MinimalPortalPage.aspx.cs)

```
protected void _editViewLinkButton_Click(object sender, EventArgs e)
{
    _webPartManager.DisplayMode = WebPartManager.EditDisplayMode;
}
```

With these additions in place, the user can now click on the Edit View link to enable the edit zone and its parts. Once in edit view, the Edit verb will appear on each Web Part's individual menu, which when selected will display the editor parts in the editor zone for that Web Part. All changes made to properties of Web Parts on the page are persisted to the client's repository and will be restored the next time he visits the portal site. Figure 6-7 shows what the portal page looks like when in EditDisplayMode with all three core edit parts available. Note that the PropertyGridEditorPart is smart enough to render CheckBox controls to edit Boolean values and DropDownList controls to edit enumerations even for custom properties.

Verbs

In addition to adding custom properties to your Web Parts, you can also define custom "verbs." A **Web Part verb** is an action that a client can perform on the Web Part by selecting a menu item on the individual Web Part's drop-down verbs menu in its title bar. There are four standard verbs—open, close, minimize, and edit—that show up on the menu in various modes of operation. To augment this standard set of verbs, you need to override the Verbs property collection and return a new WebPartVerb-Collection class populated with the additional verbs you would like displayed. Each verb can have an associated string and image, and must be

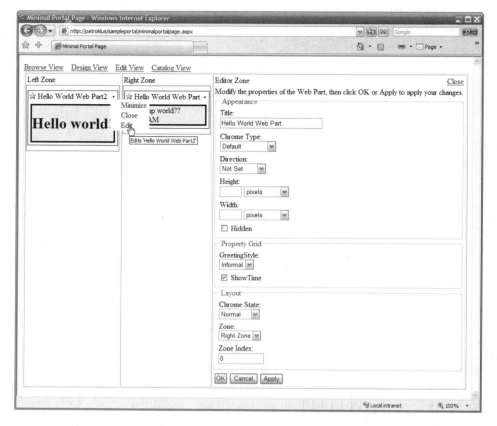

FIGURE 6-7: Editing Web Part properties using the editor zone

initialized with a delegate pointing to a method which will be invoked when the verb is selected from the menu. By default, all custom verbs that you add to your control are visible in all modes of editing. Listing 6-13 shows an example of implementing a custom verb in our HelloWorldWeb-Part for sending an e-mail, and Figure 6-8 shows our new Web Part with its mail verb in place on our portal page.

LISTING 6-13: Adding a custom verb to a Web Part

```
namespace EssentialAspDotNet2.WebParts
{
  public class HelloWorldWebPart : WebPart
  {
    //...
    public override WebPartVerbCollection Verbs
```

```
  {
    get
    {
      WebPartVerb verbMail =
              new WebPartVerb("verbMail", MailVerbHandler);
      verbMail.Text = "Email message";
      verbMail.Description = "Send message as email";
      verbMail.ImageUrl = "~/images/mail.gif";

      WebPartVerbCollection ret =
        new WebPartVerbCollection( new WebPartVerb[] {verbMail});
      return ret;
    }
  }

  public void MailVerbHandler(object src, WebPartEventArgs e)
  {
    // TODO - send hello world email message
  }
 }
}
```

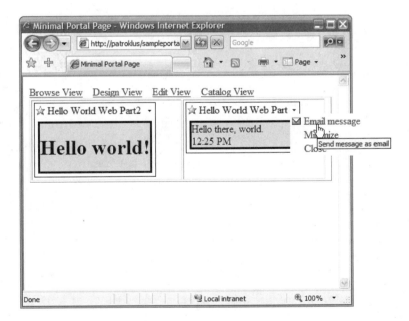

FIGURE 6-8: Custom verb in a Web Part

Connections

Web Parts also support the concept of **connections**, which define a way of sharing information through a common interface between two or more Web Parts. There are several potential applications for defining connections between Web Parts, including the ability to share preference data among many controls, as well as creating master-detail relationships between Web Parts. Consider a portal page where one Web Part collects a user's zip code as one of its properties, for example. Other Web Parts on the page, like a weather forecaster, could tap into the first Web Part's data to have one central location to retrieve (and perhaps update) the information.

To create a connection between two Web Parts, you must first define a common interface that will determine what properties can be shared. For example, if we wanted to share a string message, we could define a simple interface IMessage with a single string property, as shown in Listing 6-14.

LISTING 6-14: IMessage interface for sharing a string through connections

```
namespace EssentialAspDotNet2.WebParts
{
    public interface IMessage
    {
        string Message { get; }
    }
}
```

Next, you add support to a Web Part for being a provider of data using this interface by adding a method to the Web Part that returns a reference to an object implementing the interface. This method must then be annotated with the ConnectionProvider attribute with a friendly name describing the provider. It is usually reasonable to implement the interface on the Web Part itself, and then just return the Web Part reference in the method implementation. You also must decide where the data for the connection comes from. For our example, we will create a TextBox as a child control to let the user input the message. Listing 6-15 shows a sample provider Web Part that implements IMessage and then exposes it as a connection using the ConnectionProvider attribute. It also provides the user with a TextBox to enter the message and a Button to set it.

LISTING 6-15: Provider Web Part implementing IMessage

```
namespace EssentialAspDotNet2.WebParts
{
  public class MessageProvider : WebPart, IMessage
  {
    private TextBox _messageTextBox;

    // IMessage property implementation
    public string Message
    {
      get { return _messageTextBox.Text; }
    }

    [ConnectionProvider("MessageProvider")]
    public IMessage GetMessageProvider()
    {
      return this;
    }

    protected override void CreateChildControls()
    {
      _messageTextBox = new TextBox();

      Controls.Add(new LiteralControl("Enter text for message: "));
      Controls.Add(_messageTextBox);
      Button submitButton = new Button();
      submitButton.Text = "Submit message";
      Controls.Add(submitButton);

      base.CreateChildControls();
    }
    //...
  }
}
```

To make this provider Web Part useful, you must now define one or more Web Parts that are consumers of the IMessage interface. Consumers are a bit simpler, as they need only to define a single method that takes a reference to the interface that is annotated with the ConnectionConsumer attribute. Typically the Web Part will keep a reference to the interface so that it can pull data from the interface when the Web Part needs to for rendering. Listing 6-16 shows a sample consumer Web Part to the IMessage interface that displays the message sent by IMessage when it is connected to a producer, or a message indicating that it is not connected otherwise.

LISTING 6-16: Consumer Web Part consuming IMessage

```
namespace EssentialAspDotNet2.WebParts
{
  public class MessageConsumer : WebPart
  {
    private IMessage _provider;

    [ConnectionConsumer("MessageConsumer")]
    public void RegisterMessageProvider(IMessage provider)
    {
      _provider = provider;
    }

    protected override void RenderContents(HtmlTextWriter writer)
    {
      if (_provider != null)
        writer.Write("Message from provider: " +
                        _provider.Message);
      else
        writer.Write("No message provider attached");

      base.RenderContents(writer);
    }
  }
}
```

Now all that's left to do is to connect the two Web Parts. You can either connect the Web Parts dynamically using the connections zone or statically using the ProxyWebPartManager. Like the other modes of operation, connection mode is entered by setting the WebPartManager display mode and by defining a connection zone on the page. Like the catalog and editor zones, the connection zone only appears when activated, so it is often placed adjacent to these other two zones with the knowledge that only one will ever display at a time. Listings 6-17 and 6-18 show our Minimal-PortalPage updated to support connection mode with a new LinkButton and a ConnectionZone.

LISTING 6-17: Adding dynamic connection mode support to a portal page (MinimalPortalPage.aspx)

```
<asp:LinkButton ID="_connectViewLinkButton" runat="server"
      Text="Connect View" OnClick="_connectViewLinkButton_Click" />
<!-- … -->
<asp:ConnectionsZone ID="_connectionsZone" runat="server" />
```

LISTING 6-18: Adding dynamic connection mode support to a portal page
(MinimalPortalPage.aspx.cs)

```
protected void _connectViewLinkButton_Click(object src, EventArgs e)
{
    _webPartManager.DisplayMode = WebPartManager.ConnectDisplayMode;
}
```

When the user now enters connect display mode, the connect verb appears on all Web Parts that have connections available. By selecting the connect verb of the producer Web Part, the client is presented with an interface for creating consumer connections for the Web Part, as shown in Figure 6-9. Alternatively, if the client selects the connect verb of a consumer Web Part, she is presented with an interface for creating producer connections.

You can also set up connections between Web Parts declaratively using the ProxyWebPartManager control. This control has a StaticConnections subelement where you can list WebPartConnections to specify the association between Web Parts on your page. This is a top-level control, like the WebPartManager, and is typically placed near the top of the page. Listing 6-19 shows an example of specifying a connection between our consumer

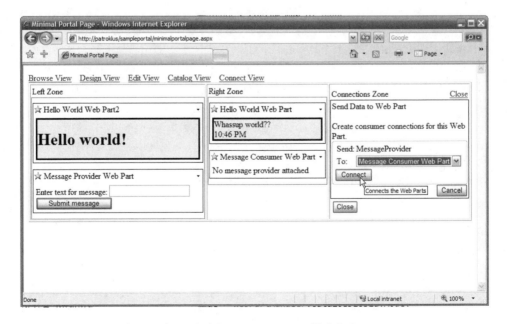

FIGURE 6-9: Connecting producer Web Parts to consumer Web Parts

and provider Web Parts so that as soon as the page is run, the connection exists without any intervention by the client.

LISTING 6-19: Declaratively specifying static connections between Web Parts

```
<asp:ProxyWebPartManager runat="server" ID="_proxyWPM">
  <StaticConnections>
    <asp:WebPartConnection  ID="_wpc"
        ConsumerID="_messageConsumer"
        ProviderID="_messageProvider" />
  </StaticConnections>
</asp:ProxyWebPartManager>
```

Personalization Scope

All of the personalization we have seen so far has been at the "user" scope, meaning property values and layout information was saved on behalf of individual users. Web Parts also support the concept of "shared" scope, where any changes made to property values or layout information of a page is saved on behalf of *all* users. When changes are made to shared scope, it changes the default values that all users have for a page. If a user already has her own custom settings that conflict with a setting in shared scope, her value will still be used.

The idea behind shared scope is for some designated users to be given the authority to modify settings on behalf of all users, so you cannot enter shared scope unless you have explicitly granted permission to a user or a group to which a user belongs. To grant permission, you must add an allow element under the authorization element for personalization that grants access to the *enterSharedScope* verb to your configuration file. Listing 6-20 shows an example of granting permissions to enter shared scope to users who belong to the *admin* role and to the user named *bob*.

LISTING 6-20: Granting permission for users to enter shared scope (web.config)

```
<configuration>
  <system.web>
    <!-- ... -->
    <webParts>
      <personalization>
        <authorization>
          <allow roles="admin" users="bob" verbs="enterSharedScope" />
        </authorization>
      </personalization>
    </webParts>
```

```
<system.web>
<configuration>
```

To actually enter shared scope, you call the ToggleScope() method on the Personalization property of the Web Part manager. You can also query to find out if the current user has the authority to enter shared scope by looking at the CanEnterSharedScope property of the Personalization property. Listings 6-21 and 6-22 show the addition of a LinkButton to our minimal portal page that allows the user to toggle the scope from *user* to *shared* if he has the permissions to do so. Note that if the user does not have permissions, we hide the button altogether.

LISTING 6-21: Adding support for toggling the scope (MinimalPortalPage.aspx)

```
<asp:LinkButton ID="_toggleScopeLinkButton" runat="server"
    Text="Toggle Scope" OnClick="_toggleScopeLinkButton_Click" /> 
<asp:Label runat="server" ID="_currentScopeLabel" Text="(scope=user)" />
```

LISTING 6-22: Adding support for toggling the scope (MinimalPortalPage.aspx.cs)

```
public partial class MinimalPortalPage : System.Web.UI.Page
{
    protected void Page_Load(object sender, EventArgs e)
    {
        _currentScopeLabel.Text = "(scope=" +
                _webPartManager.Personalization.Scope.ToString() + ")";

        if (!_webPartManager.Personalization.CanEnterSharedScope)
        {
            _currentScopeLabel.Visible = false;
            _toggleScopeLinkButton.Visible = false;
        }
    //...
}
```

When a page is running in shared scope, it also enables the Behavior-EditorPart if you have placed one in your editor zone. This allows an administrator to set not only the appearance and layout properties of Web Parts on the page, but also to set behavioral elements of each part, like whether it can be hidden, minimized, or closed. Figure 6-10 shows the BehaviorEditorPart as it is displayed in the editor zone when a user in shared scope is editing the properties of a Web Part.

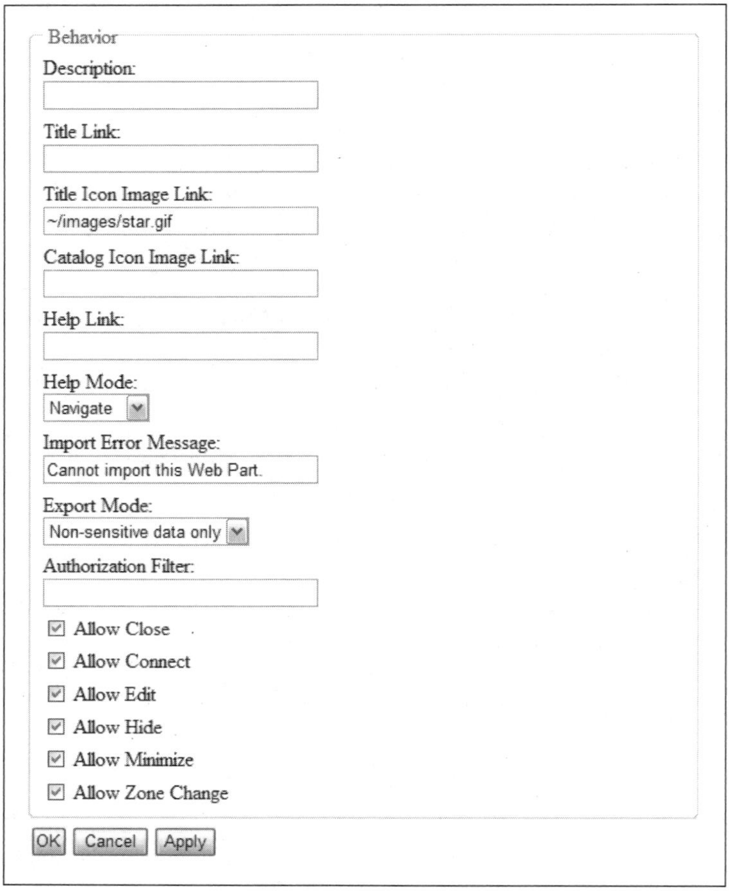

FIGURE 6-10: BehaviorEditorPart appearance for modifying behavioral properties of Web Parts when in shared scope

Exporting and Importing Web Parts

As clients interact with your portal site, they may find it useful to be able to export Web Parts that they have customized on your site for later importing. For example, a client may have customized a Web Part to her liking and want to share the customizations she has made with a colleague. By exporting the Web Part to a file, she could then share the customizations by handing the exported Web Part file to her colleague, who could then import the Web Part. The Web Part infrastructure in ASP.NET 2.0 supports the ability to export and import arbitrary Web Parts through an XML-formatted file with the extension .webpart. Note that for a Web Part to be imported, the Web Part definition must be available in the site—this is not a mechanism for sharing Web Part implementations between sites.

To enable the ability to export and import Web Parts, you first need to enable the capability in your web.config file by setting the enableExport attribute of webParts to true, as shown in Listing 6-23.

LISTING 6-23: Enabling Web Parts exporting and importing in web.config

```
<configuration>
  <system.web>
    <webParts enableExport="true" />
    <!-- ... -->
  </system.web>
</configuration>
```

Next, you need to explicitly allow the importing and exporting of each Web Part in your site by setting the ExportMode property to All or Non-SensitiveData (it defaults to None). This can be done programmatically or declaratively, but it typically will make sense for the builder of the Web Part to decide whether it should be exportable, and whether any of the data is sensitive so that it should never be exported. You indicate whether a particular property of your Web Part is sensitive by specifying a second parameter to the Personalizable attribute—true for sensitive and false for nonsensitive. The default is nonsensitive, so if your control uses the Non-SensitiveData setting, you want to be sure to go through your control's properties and mark those with potentially sensitive data as such. Listing 6-24 shows our HelloWorldWebPart initializing its ExportMode to Non-SensitiveData, and introducing a new property, EmailAddress, which is marked as sensitive. Note that our other properties are left with their default values, and so they will be assumed safe for export.

LISTING 6-24: Enabling exporting of Web Part properties

```
namespace EssentialAspDotNet2.WebParts
{
  public class HelloWorldWebPart : WebPart
  {
    public HelloWorldWebPart()
    {
      //...
      this.ExportMode = WebPartExportMode.NonSensitiveData;
    }
```

continues

```
[WebBrowsable, Personalizable(PersonalizationScope.User, true)]
[WebDisplayName("EmailAddress")]
[WebDescription("Email address to use for emailing message")]
public string EmailAddress
{
  get { return (string)(ViewState["emailaddress"] ?? ""); }
  set { ViewState["emailaddress"] = value; }
}
//...
  }
}
```

Once the Web Parts you want to be exportable are marked properly, and exporting is enabled in your web.config file, a new verb will appear on exportable Web Parts' menus—Export. When the user selects the verb, she will be prompted to save a file with an extension of .webpart that contains an XML description of all the properties for that Web Part. Figure 6-11 shows the interface presented to the user for exporting, and Listing 6-25 shows a sample .webpart file with exported Web Part property values.

LISTING 6-25: Sample .webpart file with exported Web Part property values

```
<?xml version="1.0" encoding="utf-8"?>
<webParts>
  <webPart xmlns="http://schemas.microsoft.com/WebPart/v3">
    <metaData>
      <type name="EssentialAspDotNet2.WebParts.HelloWorldWebPart" />
      <importErrorMessage>Cannot import this Web
                          Part.</importErrorMessage>
    </metaData>
    <data>
      <properties>
        <property name="AllowClose" type="bool">True</property>
        <property name="Width" type="unit" />
        <property name="AllowMinimize" type="bool">True</property>
        <property name="GreetingStyle" type="EssentialAspDotNet2.Web-
Parts.HelloWorldWebPart+GreetingStyleEnum, App_Code.11k7nmku, Ver-
sion=0.0.0.0, Culture=neutral, PublicKeyToken=null">Informal</property>
        <property name="AllowConnect" type="bool">True</property>
        <property name="ChromeType" type="chrometype">Default</property>
        <property name="TitleIconImageUrl"
                  type="string">~/images/star.gif</property>
        <property name="Description" type="string" />
        <property name="Hidden" type="bool">False</property>
        <property name="TitleUrl" type="string" />
        <property name="AllowEdit" type="bool">True</property>
        <property name="AllowZoneChange" type="bool">True</property>
```

```
        <property name="Height" type="unit" />
        <property name="HelpUrl" type="string" />
        <property name="Title" type="string">
                Hello World Web Part</property>
        <property name="CatalogIconImageUrl" type="string" />
        <property name="Direction" type="direction">NotSet</property>
        <property name="ChromeState"
                type="chromestate">Normal</property>
        <property name="ShowTime" type="bool">True</property>
        <property name="AllowHide" type="bool">True</property>
        <property name="HelpMode" type="helpmode">Navigate</property>
        <property name="ExportMode"
                type="exportmode">NonSensitiveData</property>
      </properties>
    </data>
  </webPart>
</webParts>
```

To enable the importing of Web Parts, you need to add an instance of the ImportCatalogPart to your catalog zone. This part provides a standard interface for uploading .webpart description files from the client's machine, and will take care of creating and initializing a new instance of the imported Web Part, setting all of the property values as specified in the import file. Listing 6-26 shows the CatalogZone on our minimal portal site augmented with an ImportCatalogPart. The user can access the import interface by switching the portal page into catalog view and selecting the import catalog link within the catalog zone, as shown in Figure 6-12.

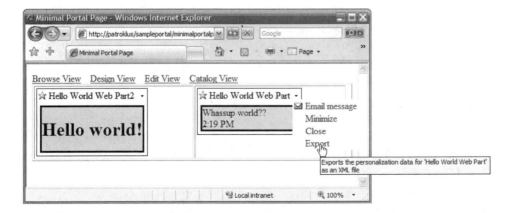

FIGURE 6-11: Exporting a Web Part

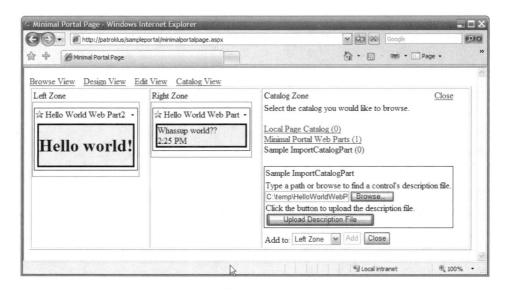

FIGURE 6-12: Interface for importing Web Parts from .webpart files

LISTING 6-26: Adding an import catalog to a portal page

```
<!-- ... -->
<asp:CatalogZone runat="server" ID="_catalogZone">
  <ZoneTemplate>
    <!-- ... -->
    <asp:ImportCatalogPart ID="_importCatalogPart"
        runat="server" Title="Sample ImportCatalogPart"
        BrowseHelpText="Type a path or browse to find a control's
description file."
        UploadButtonText="Upload Description File"
        UploadHelpText="Click the button to upload the description
file."
        ImportedPartLabelText="My User Information WebPart"
        PartImportErrorLabelText="An error occurred while trying to
import a description file."  />
  </ZoneTemplate>
</asp:CatalogZone>
```

If you want even more control over adding Web Parts to your site, you can always resort to adding Web Parts programmatically to a zone. The Web Part manager supplies a method called AddWebPart, which takes the zone into which the Web Part is to be placed, the instance of the WebPart-derived class, and the index in the zone (its order is relative to other Web

Parts). Listing 6-27 shows an example of adding an instance of our Hel-loWorldWebPart class to the top of the right zone in our portal page.

LISTING 6-27: Adding a Web Part programmatically

```
HelloWorldWebPart wp = new HelloWorldWebPart();
_webPartManager.AddWebPart(wp, _rightWebPartZone, 0);
```

Formatting Web Parts and Zones

All of the examples in this chapter have been intentionally devoid of styles in order to keep them short. It is important to be aware, however, that all of the Web Part components have a myriad of style attributes that can be altered to change the look and feel of your portal site. As an example, List-ing 6-28 shows a .skin file containing a WebPartZone definition populated with a number of styles, and Figure 6-13 shows the changes in appearance when this theme is applied. The .skin file and accompanying .css files are available in their entirety with the samples you can download with this book.

LISTING 6-28: Sample styles applied to a WebPartZone control in a .skin file

```
<asp:WebPartZone Runat="server" Height="100%" Width="100%"
                 PartChromeType="TitleAndBorder"
                 DragHighlightColor="255, 255, 128">
    <HeaderStyle CssClass="ZoneHeader" />
    <PartTitleStyle CssClass="WebPartTitle"  />
    <PartStyle CssClass="WebPart" CellSpacing=5  />
    <PartChromeStyle BorderWidth="1px" BackColor="#FFFFC0" />
    <EmptyZoneTextStyle CssClass="EmptyZone" />
    <MenuLabelHoverStyle BackColor="#EBFEFE" />
    <MenuLabelStyle BorderColor="Transparent" BackColor="#EBFEFE" />
    <MenuPopupStyle BackColor="#C4FAFB" BorderColor="#5072CB"
                    ShadowColor="#284286" BorderStyle="Solid"
                    BorderWidth="1px" GridLines="Horizontal"
                    Font-Names="Tahoma" Font-Size="9pt" />
    <MinimizeVerb ImageUrl="img/MinimizeVerb.gif"/>
    <RestoreVerb ImageUrl="img/RestoreVerb.GIF"/>
    <CloseVerb ImageUrl="img/PTCLOSE.GIF"/>
    <DeleteVerb ImageUrl="img/DELETE.GIF" />
    <EditVerb ImageUrl="img/EditVerb.gif"/>
</asp:WebPartZone>
```

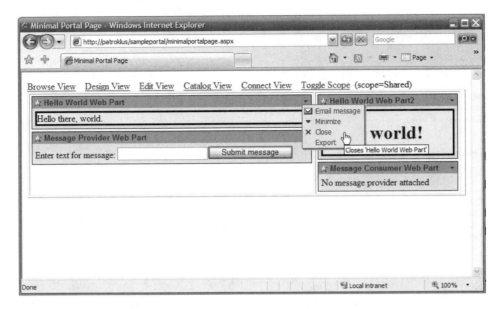

FIGURE 6-13: Portal appearance with WebPartZone styles applied

User Controls as Web Parts

So far we have looked at creating Web Parts only as custom classes, but there are actually several other options that may often be a better choice. In general, any control can be used directly as a Web Part, without requiring modifications or wrapping by the developer. This means that you could do something as simple as drag an instance of the TextBox control onto a Web Part zone in your page, and it would be treated as a separate Web Part. Single-control Web Parts aren't generally that useful, but where this feature shines is when you take a User Control and use it directly as a Web Part.

The way this works internally is if a standard control (non-Web Part) is added to a Web Part Zone, an implicit call to WebPartManager.CreateWeb-Part is made, which allocates an instance of the GenericWebPart class and initializes it with the control that was added. The GenericWebPart class derives from the WebPart base class, providing implementations of the core Web Part properties, and when it is constructed, it adds the control it was initialized with as a child control. During rendering, the GenericWebPart renders nothing to the response buffer itself, and simply delegates rendering to its child control, as do most composite controls. The end result is that you can add any control you like to a Web Part Zone on a page and it "just works." For example, the page in Listing 6-29 defines a WebPartZone with a User Control and a standard Calendar control, both of which will be implicitly wrapped by the GenericWebPart class at creation time.

LISTING 6-29: Using controls as Web Parts

```
<%@ Register Src="webparts/CustomerList.ascx"
    TagName="CustomerList" TagPrefix="eadn" %>

<asp:WebPartManager ID=" _webPartManager" runat="server" />

<asp:WebPartZone ID="_webPartZone" runat="server" HeaderText="Zone 1">
  <ZoneTemplate>
    <eadn:CustomerList runat="server" id="_customerList" />
    <asp:Calendar runat="server" id="_customerCalendar" />
  </ZoneTemplate>
</asp:WebPartZone>
```

As with standard Web Parts, it is possible to dynamically create controls wrapped by the GenericWebPart. If it is a User Control, you must first dynamically load and create the User Control instance with a call to Page.LoadControl. Second, you must explicitly assign a unique ID to the control. Third, you must call the WebPartManager object's CreateWebPart method to create an instance of the GenericWebPart class, which then acts as a wrapper around the User Control instance. Finally, you need to take the GenericWebPart reference returned from the call to CreateWebPart and pass it into a call to AddWebPart, specifying the Zone it should become a part of. These steps are shown in Listing 6-30.

LISTING 6-30: Adding a User Control-based Web Part programmatically

```
// create Web Part instance from User Control file
Control uc = this.LoadControl(@"webparts\CompanyNews.ascx");
uc.ID = "_wp2";
GenericWebPart wp2 = WebPartManager1.CreateWebPart(uc);
WebPartManager1.AddWebPart(wp2, WebPartZone1, 1);
```

The only disadvantage to this technique is that you lose the opportunity to control the Web Part-specific features of the control, because the GenericWebPart class is the one that inherits from WebPart, not your control. This will become obvious as soon as you run a page with controls wrapped by GenericWebPart, as they default to "Untitled" for their titles and have no icons or descriptions associated with them, which most Web Parts do.

One way to work around this problem is to add a handler for the Init event of your User Control, and if you are currently being wrapped by a GenericWebPart (which you can tell by querying the type of your Parent property), set the attributes of the GenericWebPart class, as shown in Listing 6-31.

LISTING 6-31: Setting attributes in the containing GenericWebPart of a UserControl

```
void Page_Init(object src, EventArgs e)
{
  GenericWebPart gwp = Parent as GenericWebPart;
  if (gwp != null)
  {
    gwp.Title = "My custom user control";
    gwp.TitleIconImageUrl = @"~\img\ALLUSR.GIF";
    gwp.CatalogIconImageUrl = @"~\img\ALLUSR.GIF";
  }
}
```

When you run the page again, as long as the User Control is being wrapped by GenericWebPart, the changes you made to the properties of the GenericWebPart parent will be reflected in the rendering of the Web Part containing your control.

There is one other solution that is even more compelling: to implement the IWebPart interface directly on your User Control class. This doesn't seem like it should help, since the User Control is never queried directly by the Web Part infrastructure for Web Part properties as those details are handled by the GenericWebPart class. Fortunately, the designers of the GenericWebPart class anticipated this need, and implemented the properties in the GenericWebPart class to automatically delegate to the wrapped control if that control implements the IWebPart interface.

So customizing the WebPart features of a User Control is just a matter of implementing the IWebPart interface and filling out the seven properties that it defines. Listing 6-32 shows an example of the codebehind class for a User Control that achieves the same results as we did before by dynamically altering the GenericWebPart properties.

LISTING 6-32: Implementing IWebPart

```
public partial class HelloWorld2 : UserControl, IWebPart
{
  protected string _title = "My custom user control";
  public string Title {
        get { return _title; }
        set { _title = value; }
  }

  private string _titleIconImageUrl = "~/img/ALLUSR.GIF";
  public string TitleIconImageUrl {
    get { return _titleIconImageUrl; }
    set { _titleIconImageUrl = value; }
  }

  private string _catalogIconImageUrl = "~/img/ALLUSR.GIF";
  public string CatalogIconImageUrl {
    get { return _catalogIconImageUrl; }
    set { _catalogIconImageUrl = value; }
  }

  // Remaining properties not shown...
}
```

You might even consider creating an alternative base class for your User Controls that implements IWebPart once and can then be inherited by all of the User Controls in your portal. With this solution, your User Controls can initialize the properties they care about in their constructors, and the rest takes care of itself. Listing 6-33 is a sample alternative base class for User Controls that implements IWebPart, and a corresponding codebehind class for a User Control that uses the class to set its title and icon properties.

LISTING 6-33: Creating a common UserControl base class that implements IWebPart

```
public class WebPartBase : UserControl, IWebPart
{

  protected string _title = "[Generic Title]";
  public string Title {
    get { return _title; }
    set { _title = value; }
  }

  private string _titleIconImageUrl = "~/img/star.GIF";
  public string TitleIconImageUrl {
    get { return _titleIconImageUrl; }
```

continues

```
      set { _titleIconImageUrl = value; }
    }

    private string _catalogIconImageUrl = "~/img/star.GIF";
    public string CatalogIconImageUrl {
      get { return _catalogIconImageUrl; }
      set { _catalogIconImageUrl = value; }
    }

    // Remaining properties not shown...
}

// Codebehind class for CustomerList.ascx User Control
public partial class CustomerList : WebPartBase {
  public CustomerList() {
    this.Title = "Sample Customer List";
    this.TitleIconImageUrl = @"~\img\ALLUSR.GIF";
    this.CatalogIconImageUrl = @"~\img\ALLUSR.GIF";
  }
}
```

If you want your User Control-based Web Part to expose custom verbs as well, you can implement another interface: IWebActionable. This simple interface has just one read-only property, Verbs, which you can implement to return custom verbs as shown earlier in this chapter.

Now that we have so much flexibility with User Controls, you may very well ask the question, "Why would I ever want to create a custom control when I can have designer support with User Controls and still customize the WebPart features?" There are several reasons, actually, starting with the fact that User Controls are intrinsically scoped to the application directory—that is, it isn't possible to share a User Control implementation across multiple Web applications without physically copying the .ascx file from one project to another. Custom Web Parts that derive from the WebPart class, on the other hand, can be compiled into a reusable DLL and deployed globally in the global assembly cache (GAC). Also, with a custom WebPart you have the option of writing a custom designer for your control to change its default appearance in Visual Studio, and you can create an icon to associate with the WebPart when it is dropped onto the toolbox. Table 6-4 shows a comparison of features for help when deciding between custom WebParts and UserControls for your WebPart components.

TABLE 6-4: Custom WebPart controls versus UserControls

Feature	WebPart-Inherited Class	User Control
Can be built in a separate DLL and installed in the GAC to reuse across applications	Yes	No
Can be added to Visual Studio toolbox with a fancy icon	Yes	No
Visual Designer support	No	Yes

Personalization Data and Providers

Like the Membership and Profile features of ASP.NET, the backend persistence mechanism for Web Parts is defined using a provider. By default, this provider maps onto a local SQL Server 2006 Express database in your /App_Data directory, but it can be changed to point to a completely different database, or even a completely different back-end medium with another provider.

The personalization provider is responsible for all of the data-related tasks dealing with Web Parts, including the following.

TABLE 6-5: Responsibilities of the personalization provider

For	The Personalization Provider
A particular page and a particular user	Saves the Web Part properties and layout
A particular page and a particular user	Loads the Web Part properties and layout
A particular page	Saves the general Web Part properties and layout (for general customization)
A particular page	Loads the general Web Part properties and layout (for general customization)
A particular page and a particular user	Resets the Web Part properties and layout to their defaults
A particular page	Resets the Web Part properties and layout to their defaults (for general customization)

There are some other ancillary features that are part of the personalization infrastructure that need persistence capabilities too, but it basically boils down to these six capabilities. If we assume that there is a class capable of performing these six actions and successfully saving and restoring the data, then the WebPartManager on each page can use that class to save and restore all personalization and customization data as the site runs. The abstract class that defines these methods is called PersonalizationProvider, and the one concrete derivative of this class that is used by default is the SqlPersonalizationProvider. Listing 6-34 shows the three methods that represent these six pieces of functionality. Note that each method is capable of working with either user personalization or general customization based on whether the incoming userName parameter is null or not.

LISTING 6-34: PersonalizationProvider class

```
public abstract class PersonalizationProvider : ProviderBase {
    protected abstract void LoadPersonalizationBlobs(
                            WebPartManager webPartManager,
                            string path, string userName,
                            ref byte[] sharedDataBlob,
                            ref byte[] userDataBlob);
    protected abstract void ResetPersonalizationBlob(
                            WebPartManager webPartManager,
                            string path, string userName);
    protected abstract void SavePersonalizationBlob(
                            WebPartManager webPartManager,
                            string path, string userName,
                            byte[] dataBlob);

    // remaining methods not shown
}
```

Note that all of the personalization data is stored as straight binary data (byte[]), which in the default SqlPersonalizationProvider is written to an image field in the database. Since ASP.NET 2.0 knows that there is a class that provides these methods, it can build much more logic into its base set of controls than would otherwise be possible. In our case, the WebPartManager in each page that uses WebParts is responsible for making the right calls to the current PersonalizationProvider class to serialize and restore the personalization settings for each page. Figure 6-14 shows the interaction between the EditorZone control and the default SqlPersonalizationProvider.

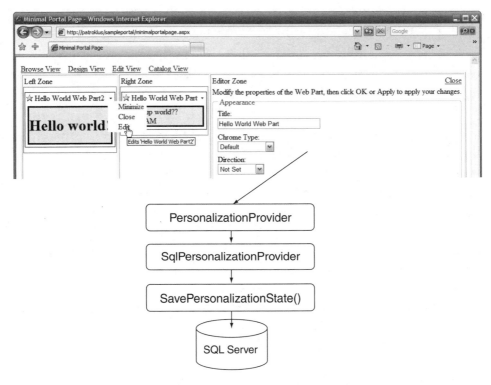

FIGURE 6-14: Interaction between the EditorZone control and the SqlPersonalizationProvider

Changing the Personalization Data Store

As with most of the providers in ASP.NET 2.0, the default provider for personalization is implemented to target a SQL backend. If you make no changes to the configuration files, the default SqlPersonalizationProvider uses a connection string for SQL Server 2005 Express, which supports a local file-based database. The connection string looks like this:

```
data source=.\SQLEXPRESS;Integrated Security=SSPI;
  AttachDBFilename=|DataDirectory|aspnetdb.mdf;
  User Instance=true
```

The advantage to using a SQL Server 2005 Express file-based database is that it can be created on the fly without any additional setup by the user. This means that you can create a brand new site, start using the personalization features without setting up any database, and it just works! When you first interact with the site, it will generate a new aspnetdb.mdf file in your site's App_Data directory, and initialize it with the tables and stored procedures necessary to support all of the default providers.

This is great for small sites that don't need to scale or support many concurrent users, but for enterprise systems it will be necessary to store the data in a fully administered, dedicated database server. Fortunately, changing the database used by the SqlPersonalizationProvider is quite straightforward. The SqlPersonalizationProvider configuration initializes the connection string to LocalSqlServer, which means that it looks for an entry in the <connectionStrings> section of the configuration file with that name, and uses the associated connection string to open a connection to the database. By default, this string is the connection string just shown, meaning that it will write to a local SQL Server 2005 express .mdf file. To change this, you must first clear the LocalSqlServer connection string collection and then reassign a new connection string value in your web.config file (alternatively, you could change this in your machine-wide machine.config file to affect all sites on that machine). Listing 6-35 shows a sample web.config file that will change the provider database to point to a local SQL Server 2000 instance.

LISTING 6-35: Changing the provider database

```
<configuration xmlns="http://schemas.microsoft.com/.NetConfiguration/v2.0">
  <connectionStrings>
    <remove name="LocalSqlServer" />
    <add name="LocalSqlServer"
      connectionString="server=.;integrated security=sspi;database=asp-
netdb"/>
  </connectionStrings>
  <!-- ... -->
</configuration>
```

Before this change will work, there of course must be a database named ASPNETDB on the local server with the necessary tables and stored procedures required by the SqlPersonalizationProvider. To create this database, there is a utility that ships with ASP.NET 2.0 called aspnet_regsql.exe. When run with the default settings, it will create a database locally called ASPNETDB with the necessary tables for all of the providers. Alternatively, you can choose to install the tables and stored procedures into an existing database. The table and stored procedure names are all prefixed with *aspnet*, so it is unlikely that they will clash with any existing tables.

As with all providers in ASP.NET 2.0, this level of indirection creates a very flexible architecture where the back-end data store can be completely changed without any modification to the pages or Web Parts contained within.

Creating Your Own Personalization Provider

The ability to change the connection string for the personalization provider gives you a certain amount of flexibility, but under the covers the SqlPersonalizationProvider uses the System.Data.Sql.Client namespace to perform its data retrieval. This means that it is limited to a SQL Server database. If you need to store your personalization in a different database, or perhaps in a completely different data store altogether, you'll have to take the next step and build your own custom personalization provider. Fortunately most of the hard work is already done for you and is easily leveraged. As an example of writing personalization data to a different data store, the samples available for this book have a custom personalization provider called FileBasedPersonalizationProvider that persists all personalization and customization data to local binary files in the application's App_Data directory. The binary file names are generated uniquely for each user and path, and there is one file per unique path for general user settings.

To build a custom personalization provider, you must first create a new class that inherits from the PersonalizationProvider base class and then override all of the abstract methods inherited from the base class. The class declaration in Listing 6-36 demonstrates how to do this.

LISTING 6-36: FileBasedPersonalizationProvider

```
namespace EssentialAspDotNet2.Providers {
  public class FileBasedPersonalizationProvider : PersonalizationProvider
  {
      public override string ApplicationName
      {
        get { /* todo */ }
        set { /* todo */ }
      }
      public override void Initialize(string name, NameValueCollection
configSettings)
      { /* todo */ }
```

continues

```
public override int GetCountOfState(PersonalizationScope scope,
                PersonalizationStateQuery query)
{ /* todo */ }
public override int ResetUserState(string path,
                DateTime userInactiveSinceDate)
{ /* todo */ }
protected override void LoadPersonalizationBlobs(
            WebPartManager webPartManager, string path,
            string userName, ref byte[] sharedDataBlob,
            ref byte[] userDataBlob)
{ /* todo */ }
protected override void ResetPersonalizationBlob(
            WebPartManager webPartManager, string path,
            string userName)
{ /* todo */ }
public override int ResetState(PersonalizationScope scope,
            string[] paths, string[] usernames)
{ /* todo */ }
protected override void SavePersonalizationBlob(
            WebPartManager webPartManager, string path,
            string userName, byte[] dataBlob)
{ /* todo */ }

public override PersonalizationStateInfoCollection FindState(
        PersonalizationScope scope,
        PersonalizationStateQuery query, int pageIndex,
        int pageSize, out int totalRecords)
{ /* todo */ }
    }
}
```

There are really only two significant methods that must be implemented for your personalization provider to begin working—LoadPersonalization-Blobs and SavePersonalizationBlob. These two methods represent the binary serialization of personalization data and are called by the personalization infrastructure to retrieve data when a page is loading, and to write the data back out (typically on behalf of a particular user) when data is changed in edit, catalog, or design view on a page with Web Parts. In the sample you can download that is associated with this book, the implementation of SavePersonalizationBlob writes the dataBlob parameter to a uniquely named file based on the userName and path that are passed in. Similarly, the LoadPersonalizationBlobs implementation looks for the file (using the same naming scheme) and returns either a user data blob or a shared data blob. Both of these two methods default to saving or loading shared data if the incoming userName parameter is null; otherwise, they save or load user data. The implementation of each of these methods in the sample FileBasedPersonalizationProvider is shown in Listing 6-37, along with a pair of helper methods to generate unique filenames based on user names and path information.

LISTING 6-37: Implementation of LoadPersonalizationBlobs and SavePersonalizationBlob

```
protected override void LoadPersonalizationBlobs(
                WebPartManager webPartManager,
                string path, string userName,
                ref byte[] sharedDataBlob, ref byte[] userDataBlob)
{
  string fileName;
  if (string.IsNullOrEmpty(userName))
    fileName = HttpContext.Current.Server.MapPath(ConstructAllUsersData-
FileName(path));
  else
    fileName = HttpContext.Current.Server.MapPath(
                        ConstructUserDataFileName(userName, path));

  if (!File.Exists(fileName))
    return;

  try
  {
    // lock on the filename in case two clients try accessing the
    // same file concurrently - note we lock on the interned filename
    // string, which will always return the same objref for identical
    // strings
    //
    if (Monitor.TryEnter(fileName, 5000))
    {
      if (string.IsNullOrEmpty(userName))
        sharedDataBlob = File.ReadAllBytes(string.Intern(fileName));
      else
        userDataBlob = File.ReadAllBytes(string.Intern(fileName));
    }
    else
      throw new ApplicationException("Monitor timed out");
  }
  finally
  {
    Monitor.Exit(string.Intern(fileName));
  }
}
```

continues

```
protected override void SavePersonalizationBlob(WebPartManager webPart-
Manager,
                string path, string userName, byte[] dataBlob)
{
  string fileName;
  if (string.IsNullOrEmpty(userName))
    fileName = ConstructAllUsersDataFileName(path);
  else
    fileName = ConstructUserDataFileName(userName, path);

  // lock on the filename in case two clients try accessing the same
  // file concurrently
  //
  try
  {
    if (Monitor.TryEnter(fileName, 5000))
      File.WriteAllBytes(HttpContext.Current.Server.MapPath(fileName),
dataBlob);
    else
      throw new ApplicationException("Failed to acquire lock on file to
write data");
  }
  finally
  {
    Monitor.Exit(fileName);
  }
}


// Helper function for creating a unique filename for all users based on
// a path
private string ConstructAllUsersDataFileName(string path)
{
  string pathConvertedToFileName = path.Replace('/', '_');
  pathConvertedToFileName = pathConvertedToFileName.Replace('~', '_');
  pathConvertedToFileName = pathConvertedToFileName.Replace('.', '_');

  return "~/App_Data/allusers" + pathConvertedToFileName + ".bin";
}


// Helper function for creating a unique filename for a particular user
// based on a path
private string ConstructUserDataFileName(string user, string path)
{
  string pathConvertedToFileName = path.Replace('/', '_');
  pathConvertedToFileName = pathConvertedToFileName.Replace('~', '_');
  pathConvertedToFileName = pathConvertedToFileName.Replace('.', '_');

  return "~/App_Data/" + user + pathConvertedToFileName + ".bin";
}
```

Once the provider is fully implemented, you use the providers section of the personalization configuration section to add it as a registered personalization provider. To actually begin using it, you must specify it as the default provider for personalization in your web.config file. Listing 6-38 shows an example of wiring up our custom file-based provider to be the default provider in our application.

LISTING 6-38: Configuration file wiring up of custom file-based provider

```
<webParts>
  <personalization defaultProvider="FileBasedPersonalizationProvider">
    <providers>
      <add name="FileBasedPersonalizationProvider"
           type="EssentialAspDotNet2.Providers.FileBasedPersonalization-
Provider" />
    </providers>
  </personalization>
</webParts>
```

If we run our site again, all personalization data will now be stored in local binary files. Obviously this isn't the most scalable solution, but the sample should give you an idea of how to implement your own personalization provider on whatever backend you like.

SUMMARY

ASP.NET 2.0 and its new Web Part infrastructure make it possible and relatively painless to create rich portal applications that support customization and personalization. Probably the most significant feature of this infrastructure is its plug-ability. Instead of being tied to a particular serialization implementation and data store, the provider architecture makes it relatively easy to write the personalization data to any back-end data store that makes sense for your site.

■7■
Diagnostics

M ANY PRODUCT TEAMS AT MICROSOFT have shifted focus in recent
years. Instead of just focusing entirely on whiz-bang features like
calendar controls and wizards, much of the team resources have been dedicated to shoring up important security and management features on the
platform. This has resulted in many new management features in
ASP.NET 2.0 (a quick look at the System.Web.Management namespace
will give you an idea of the scope of the effort).

One of the biggest improvements is the new health monitoring feature
in ASP.NET 2.0, which we'll explore in depth in this chapter. We'll also take
a look at the advances in ASP.NET tracing, and you'll see how easy it has
become to integrate ASP.NET's trace data with the existing System.Diag-
nostics tracing system, as well as how to programmatically access
ASP.NET trace data. Plus, at the end of the chapter we'll introduce you to a
powerful feature in Windows that you may never have heard of before:
Event Tracing for Windows (ETW). We'll show you how to use ETW to
"debug without a debugger," diagnosing problems as they occur in production servers without taking them down or attaching a debugger.

Health Monitoring and Web Events

ASP.NET 2.0 includes a new feature called **health monitoring** that allows
system administrators to monitor the status of running Web applications.
The goal of the health monitoring subsystem is to help keep applications

running smoothly, and when problems do occur, to make diagnosing those problems much easier.

To support this feature, the ASP.NET team built a sophisticated provider model for recording events as they occur in an application. The key abstraction here is something called a **Web event**. Each Web event is represented by a class, and several built-in Web event classes ship with ASP.NET out of the box. You can create your own custom events as well, as we'll show later in this chapter.

The ASP.NET infrastructure raises Web events when interesting things happen, and your application can raise custom Web events programmatically. By default, the health monitoring system is disabled and so these events are ignored. But once you enable health monitoring via configuration, you get to choose one or more providers that will record Web events as they occur. For example, you might choose to record certain events in the Windows event log while recording other events into a SQL database.

The idea behind this type of infrastructure isn't new. In ASP.NET 1.x, people used tools like the Logging Application Block, Enterprise Library, and log4net to build configurable event logging systems.[1] Now with Web events, you aren't forced to use add-ons like this.

Web Event Hierarchy

Web event classes are organized by inheritance, and all ultimately derive from WebBaseEvent, as shown in Figure 7-1. This base class defines some properties that all events have in common, including the date and time the event was raised, a unique ID for the event, two integers representing an event code and a detail code, and among other things, a human-readable message describing the event.

- WebManagementEvent adds information about the worker process, including process id and name, as well as the account name the process is using.

---

1. You can find the patterns & practices Enterprise Library at http://msdn.microsoft.com/ library/en-us/dnpag2/html/entlib.asp, and the open source log4net project at http://logging.apache.org/log4net/.

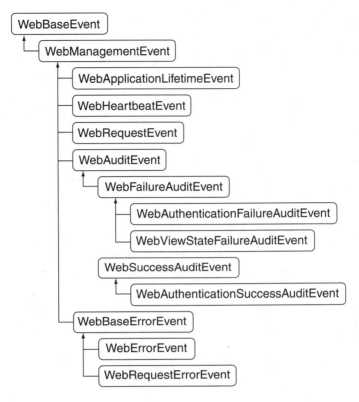

FIGURE 7-1: Web event hierarchy

- WebApplicationLifetimeEvent is raised whenever an application is compiled, started, or shut down.
- WebHeartbeatEvent is not normally raised unless you specifically configure a heartbeat interval via web.config. This event allows an administrator to be notified that the application is still running, and it provides some basic statistics about the Web server process, including how many requests are currently executing, how many are queued, how many bytes the managed heap occupies, and so on. To enable this special event, you need to set the heartbeatInterval attribute to something other than its default value of zero on the <healthMonitoring> element in web.config.
- WebRequestEvent is a base class that you can use for custom events. It is convenient for capturing details about a Web request. We'll talk more about custom events later in this chapter.

- WebAuditEvent is the base class for all security audits. It adds details about the Web request, including the path, the URL, and the name of the security account being used by the current thread, which can be different than the process' account if you're using impersonation.

- WebFailureAuditEvent is the base class for all security auditing failures, such as when a user tries to access a page to which she is not authorized.

- WebAuthenticationFailureAuditEvent is a specific failure audit raised by systems like Membership and Forms authentication when a user fails to authenticate. This class adds the submitted user name to the details being logged.

- WebViewStateFailureAuditEvent is raised when a user submits a Web form that contains invalid view state. This could indicate that an attacker is attempting to tamper with view state, and adds details about the exception collected when the view state was found to be invalid.

- WebSuccessAuditEvent and its derived classes can help you audit successful access to sensitive resources. This is one way to provide an audit trail as a user browses your Web site, but keep in mind that it generates a lot of events.

- WebBaseErrorEvent is the base class for all Web events that represent exceptions raised in the worker process. This class adds details about the exception that occurred.

- WebErrorEvent is raised when a configuration or compilation problem occurs with your application. This class adds details about the current request, as well as information about the thread executing the request including thread id, whether the thread is impersonating, and the user account the thread is running under, which could be different from the process' identity if you're using impersonation.

- WebRequestErrorEvent is raised when an error results from a particular request, for example, unhandled exceptions in ASPX pages or posted data that is too large. It includes the same details as WebErrorEvent.

Event classes are generally designed to represent a category of events. For the details of any given event, look at the EventCode and Message, and in many cases the DetailCode. For a comprehensive list of event codes, look at the documentation for the WebEventCodes enumeration.

Which Events Should I Monitor?

Every application is different, but design documents such as threat models[2] and performance models[3] can help you determine what to monitor. If you don't have the time to build these types of models, then at least take the time to identify key scenarios and determine which events should be logged on a normal basis. Do your best to ensure your application is configured by default to log these events.

Don't just consider the built-in Web events. You should also determine what data *must be available for monitoring*, even if ASP.NET doesn't provide built-in support for monitoring that data. Build custom Web events to cover these cases. When something goes wrong, the first thing a good administrator is going to do is crank up the level of monitoring in order to diagnose the problem. Verbose data need not be logged on a regular basis, but if it helps rapidly diagnose problems when your application is running, it could save lots of money over time.

One last thing to consider is that administrators often use monitoring tools to help determine when an application needs to be scaled up in some way. Consider instrumentation that assists in this planning process, including custom performance counters.

Built-in Providers

Now that you've seen the types of built-in events that you can monitor, we'll show how you can record them to various logs using the built-in providers that come with ASP.NET 2.0. Figure 7-2 shows the class hierarchy of the built-in providers, which all ultimately derive from WebEventProvider.

---

2. The Microsoft patterns & practices Web site has some excellent guidance on threat modeling at http://msdn.microsoft.com/library/en-us/dnpag2/html/tmwa.asp, or you can search for "Threat Modeling Web Applications."

3. See http://msdn.microsoft.com/library/default.asp?url=/library/en-us/dnpag/html/scalenetchapt02.asp to learn more about performance modeling. This is actually Chapter 2 of a book called, *Improving .NET Application Performance and Scalability* by Microsoft Press.

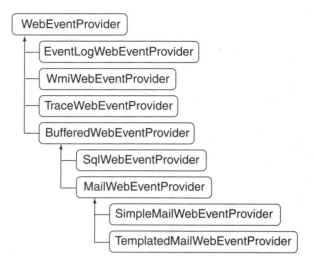

FIGURE 7-2: Built-in Web event providers

In order to use any of these providers, you need to refer to them in configuration. By default, three providers are already configured for you in the machine-wide web.config file, as shown in Listing 7-1 (I've removed the assembly strong names from many config snippets in this chapter for brevity).

LISTING 7-1: Default Web event providers in the root web.config file

```
<!-- excerpt from root web.config file that ships with ASP.NET 2.0 -->
<healthMonitoring>
  <providers>
    <add name="EventLogProvider"
         type="System.Web.Management.EventLogWebEventProvider" />

    <add name="SqlWebEventProvider"
         type="System.Web.Management.SqlWebEventProvider"
         connectionStringName="LocalSqlServer"
         maxEventDetailsLength="1073741823"
         buffer="false"
         bufferMode="Notification" />

    <add name="WmiWebEventProvider"
         type="System.Web.Management.WmiWebEventProvider" />
  </providers>
  <!-- ... -->
</healthMonitoring>
```

Notice that the "enabled" attribute on <healthMonitoring> isn't set here, which means the entire Web event system is disabled by default. As you'll see in the following listings, you'll need to enable this yourself in your web.config file if you want to record any Web events.

The event log provider is a simple example to start with. It doesn't need any configuration: its job is to synchronously write each event it receives to the Windows application event log. System administrators like a high signal-to-noise ratio in their event logs, so it's wise to limit the amount of data you log using this provider to higher priority events. Listing 7-2 is an example of what a Web event recorded by this provider looks like, as copied from the event log.

LISTING 7-2: A Web event sent to the event log

```
Event Type: Information
Event Source:     ASP.NET 2.0.50727.0
Event Category:   Web Event
Event ID:   1305
Date:       7/5/2006
Time:       4:06:35 PM
User:       N/A
Computer:   GROMIT
Description:
Event code: 1001
Event message: Application is starting.
Event time: 7/5/2006 4:06:35 PM
Event time (UTC): 7/5/2006 10:06:35 PM
Event ID: 4bd8b3da2b6142fcae0b6f4d150f9e5a
Event sequence: 1
Event occurrence: 1
Event detail code: 0

Application information:
    Application domain: a444bacb-10-127966107943906250
    Trust level: Full
    Application Virtual Path: /sample
    Application Path: C:\essentialasp.net\sample
    Machine name: GROMIT

Process information:
    Process ID: 2948
    Process name: WebDev.WebServer.EXE
    Account name: GROMIT\Alice
```

Windows Management Instrumentation (WMI) is a well-known interface for management tools such as IBM Tivoli, Microsoft Operations Manager, and so on. Using the WmiWebEventProvider, you can turn Web events into WMI events that will light up these management tools when events occur. WMI aficionados will be happy to know that ASP.NET ships with a Managed Object Format (MOF) file that describes the shape of all of the built-in Web events generated by ASP.NET.[4] To use this provider, you can simply refer to it (see Listing 7-1).

The TraceWebEventProvider is a special adapter that funnels each Web event it receives into the System.Diagnostics tracing engine. You'll see how to use this provider later in this chapter.

The E-Mail Providers

Two providers send SMTP (e-mail) messages for each Web event. Both of these providers can be configured with a common set of attributes that determine e-mail headers (from, to, cc, bcc), how many events should be buffered before sending an e-mail (maxEventsPerMessage), the maximum number of events you want in any given e-mail (maxMessagesPerNotification), as well as a subject prefix for the e-mail. These providers both use the services of System.Net.Mail, which relies on the system.net/mailSettings/ smtp section in web.config (see Listing 7-3). You won't see any exceptions if the e-mail provider fails to send e-mail, but you will see errors in the application event log that can help you diagnose problems about these e-mails. One thing that might confuse you when you first try to use either of these e-mail providers is that unless buffering is enabled, by default they will send a unique e-mail for each Web event. We'll talk about how buffering works shortly.

The SimpleMailWebEventProvider creates text e-mail messages and lets you control formatting at a very basic level through a set of additional string-valued attributes on the provider: bodyHeader, bodyFooter, and separator. The maxEventLength attribute allows you to throttle the length of text allotted to any single event description in case the notification e-mails get too large.

---

4. The ASPNET.MOF file can be found in the %SystemRoot%\Microsoft.NET\Framework\ <version> directory. For more information on MOF files and WMI, see *Developing WMI Solutions: A Guide to Windows Management Instrumentation* by Craig Tunstall and Gwyn Cole (Addison-Wesley, 2003).

If you need something fancier, TemplatedMailWebEventProvider lets you create an ASPX page that will be used to format these e-mail messages as HTML. Along with the common attributes listed above, you'll need to add one more attribute named "template" that specifies which ASPX page is to be used for formatting. The provider communicates the current set of events that need logging to your page via a static property on Templated-MailWebEventProvider called CurrentNotification, which is of type Mail-EventNotificationInfo. This gives you all the information you need to build an HTML page, which the provider will then use as the body of the e-mail message.

Listing 7-3 is a sample configuration you can use to get started with templated Web event e-mails. We've used the convenient "pickup directory" configuration for System.Net.Mail so that each e-mail will be represented by a file on the hard drive, which is great for quick testing (if you double-click one of the resulting .EML files, it will open up in Outlook Express so that you can view it). We've also set detailedTemplateErrors="true", so any errors that occur while compiling or processing the template will be output into the e-mail message as text, which is very helpful when you're developing a template.

LISTING 7-3: Configuring the TemplatedMailWebEventProvider

```
<!-- web.config -->
<configuration>
  <system.web>
    <healthMonitoring enabled="true" heartbeatInterval="30">
      <providers>
        <add name="MyMailProvider"
             type="System.Web.Management.TemplatedMailWebEventProvider"
             buffer="true"
             bufferMode="Critical Notification"
             from="webserver@fabrikam.com"
             to="sysadmins@fabrikam.com"
             template="~/formatter.aspx"
             detailedTemplateErrors="true"
          />
      </providers>
      <!-- we'll explain rules and profiles shortly -->
      <rules>
        <add name="Email These Events"
             eventName="All Events"
             provider="MyMailProvider"
             profile="Critical" />
```

continues

```
        </rules>
      </healthMonitoring>
    </system.web>

    <!-- specify that each e-mail should be placed in an .EML file -->
    <system.net>
      <mailSettings>
        <smtp deliveryMethod="SpecifiedPickupDirectory">
          <specifiedPickupDirectory pickupDirectoryLocation="c:\mail"/>
        </smtp>
      </mailSettings>
    </system.net>
</configuration>
```

Listing 7-4 contains the code for formatter.aspx. This page uses data binding to output a few details from the collection of Web events into a GridView. Figure 7-3 shows what one of these formatted e-mails looks like in Outlook Express.

LISTING 7-4: Formatter.aspx

```
<!-- formatter.aspx -->
<body>
    <form id="form1" runat="server">
    <div>
     <asp:GridView ID="gridView" runat="server"
                   AutoGenerateColumns="false"
                   EnableViewState="false">
        <Columns>
            <asp:BoundField DataField="EventCode" HeaderText="Code" />
            <asp:BoundField DataField="EventTime" HeaderText="Time" />
            <asp:BoundField DataField="Message"  HeaderText="Message" />
        </Columns>
     </asp:GridView>
    </div>
    </form>
</body>

// codebehind file formatter.aspx.cs
using System;
using System.Web;
using System.Web.UI;
using System.Web.Management;

public partial class WebEventMailFormatter : System.Web.UI.Page
{
    protected void Page_Load(object sender, EventArgs e)
    {
```

```
            gridView.DataSource = TemplatedMailWebEventProvider.
                CurrentNotification.Events;
            gridView.DataBind();
        }
    }
```

The SQL Provider

When you run aspnet_regsql, the resulting database includes a table called aspnet_WebEvent_Events, which includes columns for each property of WebBaseEvent. The SqlWebEventProvider writes each Web event it receives into this table, which you can then query using any tool you like. This is an excellent choice for detailed, noisy error messages, because you can write tools to view and manage the logged data however you like. Web events that you wouldn't want to e-mail to an administrator or put in the event log can be recorded in the database for later tracking. Nothing stops you from using a DELETE query to get rid of noise later on, once it's been analyzed. Also, nothing stops you from using more than one database. You might use one database for doing statistical data mining (this one might get pretty noisy, but that's what it's for). You could set up a separate database for critical security audit events and grant security personnel permission to use it. Listing 7-5 (in the next section) shows an example that uses two instances of the SQL provider simultaneously.

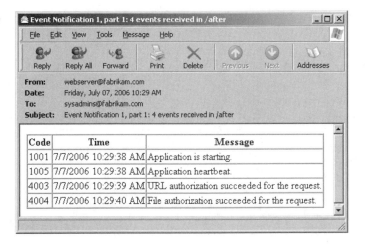

FIGURE 7-3: E-mail notification

Note that SqlWebEventProvider always obtains its database connection using the worker process' security identity (even if you've turned on impersonation), so be sure to add this user account to the database role called aspnet_WebEvent_FullAccess, granting it permission to log Web events in the database.

Buffering

Recording Web events takes time, and you might not like the impact this can have on the response time of your Web pages. Providers that derive from BufferedWebEventProvider support **buffering** (refer back to Figure 7-2), which in essence lets providers record Web events asynchronously by queuing the Web events in memory as they occur and then letting a background thread do the actual recording.

Buffered providers implicitly support two extra attributes in their configuration. The first is "buffer," which specifies whether or not you want to use buffering at all. Note that this attribute is "true" by default on all buffered providers, so you'll need to explicitly add this attribute and set it to "false" if you don't want buffering with, for example, the SQL provider. The second, which must be present if buffering is enabled, is bufferMode. This attribute allows you to choose how big the buffer will be, how often it will be flushed, and so on, by referring to a predefined buffer "mode."

Each buffer mode has six attributes that you can adjust, and as of this writing they aren't documented very clearly. Table 7-1 outlines what we've been able to learn about them by studying the code in BufferedWebEventProvider.

TABLE 7-1:　Buffer mode attributes

Attribute	Description
maxBufferSize	This is the maximum size of the queue. If an event is added and the queue is already at its maximum size, the oldest event in the queue will be discarded to make room for the new event, and a counter of lost events will be incremented.
maxFlushSize	This is the maximum number of events that will be flushed at one time.

Attribute	Description
regularFlushInterval	This is the amount of time (in milliseconds) that should normally occur between flushes. If set to "Infinite," flushes will only occur based on the size of the queue using "urgent" flushes.
urgentFlushThreshold	When the number of events in the queue reaches this number, the regular flush interval will be temporarily reduced to the urgentFlushInterval value. That is, the queue will be flushed more often when above this threshold. This must be a smaller value than maxBufferSize.
urgentFlushInterval	This is the number of milliseconds between scheduled flushes when the queue reaches the urgentFlushThreshold. This must be a smaller value than regularFlushInterval.
maxBufferThreads	This is the maximum number of background threads allowed to simultaneously flush. This is set to 1 for all default buffer modes, which makes us wonder if any of the built-in providers actually support multithreaded flushes.

There are several of these modes defined in the root web.config file, and you can define others by adding a <bufferModes> section to your application's web.config file. Table 7-2 will help you learn the built-in modes and how they differ.

TABLE 7-2:   Built-in buffer modes

Name	maxBufferSize	Comments
Critical Notification	100	Flushed every minute.
Notification	300	Flushed every minute.
Analysis	1,000	Normally flushed every 5 minutes, unless there are 100 or more queued events, in which case the flush interval reduces to 1 minute.
Logging	1,000	Normally flushed every 30 minutes, unless there are 800 or more queued events, in which case the flush interval reduces to 5 minutes.

While it might be tempting to use a more aggressive buffering scheme (such as Logging), you need to consider that when your worker process crashes, you'll lose any buffered messages that haven't yet been flushed to a persistent media. So even if you're only planning on using SqlWebEvent-Provider, you might actually create two entries in the <providers> element under the <healthMonitoring> section in web.config and choose different buffering strategies, as shown in Listing 7-5 (this example also shows how to log to different databases). You could then register the nonbuffered provider for important events that you can't afford to lose, and the buffered provider for events you're just tracking for statistical analysis.

LISTING 7-5: Configuring buffering for the SQL provider

```
<!-- web.config -->
<healthMonitoring enabled="true">
  <providers>
    <add name="SecuritySqlProvider"
         type="System.Web.Management.SqlWebEventProvider"
         connectionStringName="securityDatabase"
         buffer="false"/>

    <add name="StatisticsSqlProvider"
         type="System.Web.Management.SqlWebEventProvider"
         connectionStringName="statisticsDatabase"
         buffer="true"
         bufferMode="Logging"/>
  </providers>
  <!-- ... -->
</healthMonitoring>
```

Registering for Events

Once you've configured the providers you plan on using, you need to decide which events you want to funnel to each provider. You do this using the <eventMappings> and <rules> elements under the <healthMonitoring> section in web.config.

Event mappings define groups of events based on a class and/or range of event codes. Remember how every Web event is represented by a class? Since those classes form a hierarchy, it makes it easy to select an entire group of events through a base class. For example, Listing 7-6 illustrates a very useful event mapping defined in the root web.config file.

LISTING 7-6: A default event mapping

```
<!-- excerpt from root web.config file that ships with ASP.NET 2.0 -->
<healthMonitoring>
  <eventMappings>
    <add name="All Events"
        type="System.Web.Management.WebBaseEvent"
        startEventCode="0"
        endEventCode="2147483647" />
  </eventMappings>
</healthMonitoring>
```

This event mapping matches any Web event that is of (or derives from) the type WebBaseEvent and has an event code between 0 and Int32.MaxValue. In other words, this matches *all* events, even custom events that you might create for your application. The root web.config file defines several generic event mappings like this that you can use. These don't have any limit on the event code and are matched purely based on type. Table 7-3 lists the names of these default mappings, including the Web event type

TABLE 7-3: Built-in event mappings

Event Mapping Name	Matching Web Event Type
All Events	WebBaseEvent
Heartbeats	WebHeartbeatEvent
Application Lifetime Events	WebApplicationLifetimeEvent
Request Processing Events	WebRequestEvent
All Errors	WebBaseErrorEvent
Infrastructure Errors	WebErrorEvent
Request Processing Errors	WebRequestErrorEvent
All Audits	WebAuditEvent
Failure Audits	WebFailureAuditEvent
Success Audits	WebSuccessAuditEvent

they match. These predefined mappings may satisfy your needs, but you can add your own more specific groups by including an <eventMappings> section in your web.config file.

Once you have a set of event mappings that's granular enough for what you're doing, you can start funneling those events onto providers using rules. A **rule** is how you register a provider to listen for a group of events. The order of rules isn't important, and it's completely possible for any given event to be matched by two different rules and therefore sent to two different providers. The root web.config file doesn't include any rules, so if you want any Web events actually recorded, you'll need to add at least one rule to your web.config file.

Listing 7-7 is an example of a set of rules that sends all security audits to a security database, while sending *all* events to a statistical database (these providers were defined earlier in this chapter).

LISTING 7-7: Defining health monitoring rules in web.config

```
<!-- web.config -->
<healthMonitoring enabled="true">
  <!-- ... -->
  <rules>
    <add name="Log all security audits to the security database"
         eventName="All Audits"
         provider="SecuritySqlProvider" />

    <add name="Send a copy of all events to the statistics database"
         eventName="All Events"
         provider="StatisticsSqlProvider" />
  </rules>
</healthMonitoring>
```

Throttling and Profiles

While buffering can help flatten out the load from Web events generated in bursts, not all providers support buffering, and those that do have finite limits on the size of their buffers. To help control noise and mitigate potential attacks against the health monitoring system, you can turn on throttling and coalesce or discard events that are occurring too often. Throttling is controlled via the three optional attributes on a rule shown in Table 7-4.

TABLE 7-4: Throttling attributes

Attribute	Description
minInstances	A given event will only be sent to the provider if the same event has occurred this many times. This feature allows you to coalesce noisy events so that they don't show up so often in the log. The default value is 1, which effectively turns off this feature.
minInterval	A given event will only be sent to the provider if the same event has not already been sent within this time interval. Similar in spirit to minInstances, this is a time-based solution for coalescing noise. The default is 0, which effectively turns off this feature.
maxLimit	Only records the first *N* instances of a given event. The default is "Infinite," which turns off this feature.

To make it easy to reuse a set of throttling parameters on many different rules, you can factor these three attributes into a health monitoring *profile*[5] and then refer to that profile from your rules. The root web.config already defines two profiles (shown in Listing 7-8) or you can define your own.

LISTING 7-8: Using health monitoring profiles

```
<!-- excerpt from root web.config file that ships with ASP.NET 2.0 -->
<healthMonitoring>
  <!-- ... -->
  <profiles>
      <add name="Default"
          minInstances="1"
          maxLimit="Infinite"
          minInterval="00:01:00"
          custom="" />
      <add name="Critical"
          minInstances="1"
          maxLimit="Infinite"
          minInterval="00:00:00"
          custom="" />
  </profiles>
</healthMonitoring>
```

continues

---

5. Don't confuse this with the state management profiles discussed in Chapter 4. They are different animals altogether.

```
<!-- web.config file that enables throttling
     using the "Default" profile -->
<healthMonitoring enabled="true">
  <!-- ... -->
  <rules>
    <add name="Send a copy of all events to the statistics database"
         eventName="All Events"
         provider="StatisticsSqlProvider"
         profile="Default"/>
  </rules>
</healthMonitoring>
```

While you might not turn on throttling to begin with, it's good to know that it's there and that an administrator can turn it on in case of an attack or to eliminate excess noise.

Mapping the Health Monitoring Configuration Section

The five sections in the <healthMonitoring> configuration can be a little daunting at first, so we've summarized how they all fit together in Figure 7-4 (in the diagram, we've indicated cardinality with 1, ?, and n, as you might see in a class diagram). Here you can see that each rule couples a single event mapping onto a single provider and can optionally refer to a throttling profile. And with a buffered provider, if you turn on buffering, you'll need to refer to a buffer mode.

Custom Web Events

It's really trivial to add custom data that you'd like to be logged through the Web event system. Just derive a class from one of the existing Web-

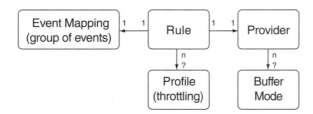

FIGURE 7-4: Health monitoring configuration

BaseEvent-derived classes or from WebBaseEvent itself, and use constructor arguments to specify the message and event code you want to log. Listing 7-9 illustrates a simple example.

LISTING 7-9: A custom Web event

```
using System;
using System.Web.Management;

public enum MyEventCodes {
    LowInventory = 0,
    InvalidInput = 1,
    // ...
}

public class CustomEvent : WebBaseEvent
{
    public CustomEvent(string message,
                       object eventSource,
                       MyEventCodes myEventCode)
        : base(message, eventSource,
               WebEventCodes.WebExtendedBase + (int)myEventCode)
    {}
}
```

To come up with unique event codes that won't step on ones that ASP.NET provides, note how this example starts at the integer value defined by WebEventCodes.WebExtendedBase and goes up from there. Listing 7-10 shows some code that fires this Web event to indicate that inventory is getting low.

LISTING 7-10: Firing a custom Web event

```
CustomEvent e =
    new CustomEvent("Low Inventory", this, MyEventCodes.LowInventory);
e.Raise();
```

By default, the only <eventMapping> that will match this custom event is All Events, because it matches the base class WebBaseEvent. So when you start using custom events, you'll likely want to create your own event mappings to match your custom events more specifically. Remember how event mappings can match events based on type, so if you're going to make extensive use of custom events, you should consider building a hierarchy of event classes that will simplify event mapping, as the ASP.NET team did with the default event classes (see Figure 7-1). Be sure to choose the base class for any given custom Web event carefully, and wherever possible derive from the existing Web event classes; this way, your events will naturally fit into the default event mappings and be an intuitive addition to the built-in events. As you'll see later on, some of the ASP.NET infrastructure reasons about Web events by looking at their base class (for example, a Web event is considered an "error" event if it derives from Web-BaseErrorEvent).

Some custom events might need to carry along extra information in addition to the message string. This is easy to do, but you'll need to override the FormatCustomEventDetails method to serialize this other data to the provider. If your event is being recorded by a buffered provider, this method will be called by a worker thread, and you won't have access to HttpContext.Current, so if you need to scrape out the request's details or any other thread-sensitive resources, be sure to do that during the initialization of your event. By the time FormatCustomEventDetails is called, it may be too late to get that extra data you need.

Listing 7-11 is a custom event that includes the name of the client making the request. Note how the class gathers all the data it needs in its constructor.

LISTING 7-11: Managing custom data in a custom Web event

```
public class CustomEvent : WebBaseEvent
{
    public CustomEvent(string message,
                        object eventSource,
                        MyEventCodes myEventCode)
        : base(message, eventSource,
               WebEventCodes.WebExtendedBase + (int)myEventCode)
    {
        userName = HttpContext.Current.User.Identity.Name;
    }
    public override void FormatCustomEventDetails(
            WebEventFormatter formatter) {
        base.FormatCustomEventDetails(formatter);
        formatter.AppendLine("Client name: " + userName);
    }
    readonly string userName;
}
```

Custom Providers

If the suite of built-in providers doesn't meet your needs, you can build your own provider. It can be as sophisticated as you like, supporting buffering (by deriving from BufferedWebEventProvider) if desired.

If you require any initialization parameters from web.config, you'll need to override the Initialize method and retrieve and then remove any configuration attributes specific to your class before calling your base class' Initialize method.

The interesting method you'll be overriding is ProcessEvent, where you'll be given the event that needs to be recorded. Listing 7-12 shows how to implement a custom provider that logs events to a text file.

LISTING 7-12: Implementing a simple custom Web event provider

```csharp
using System;
using System.IO;
using System.Collections.Specialized;
using System.Web.Management;

public class LogFileWebEventProvider : WebEventProvider {
   object fileLock = new object();
   string fileName;

   public override void Initialize(string name,
                                   NameValueCollection config)
   {
     fileName = config.Get("fileName");
     config.Remove("fileName");
     base.Initialize(name, config);
   }

   public override void Flush()      {}
   public override void Shutdown()   {}

   public override void ProcessEvent(WebBaseEvent raisedEvent)
   {
     lock (fileLock) {
       using (StreamWriter w = File.AppendText(fileName)) {
         w.WriteLine("{0} - {1} - {2}",
           raisedEvent.EventTime, raisedEvent.GetType(),
           raisedEvent.Message);
       }
     }
   }
}
```

Since this class doesn't implement buffering, we need to override the abstract method Flush() and do nothing. And since this class doesn't hold any resources like file handles open, there's nothing to do in Shutdown, but we must override it since it's an abstract method in the base class.

To add support for buffering, you'll need to derive from BufferedWebEventProvider instead, and implement ProcessEventFlush to handle batched events as they are being flushed. You'll also need to tweak your ProcessEvent implementation to check if buffering is enabled and let the base class handle the method if so, allowing it to add the message to its buffer. The example in Listing 7-13 adds buffering support to the text file provider.

LISTING 7-13: Implementing a buffered custom Web event provider

```
using System;
using System.IO;
using System.Collections.Specialized;
using System.Web.Management;

public class BufferedLogFileWebEventProvider : BufferedWebEventProvider
{
    object fileLock = new object();
    string fileName;

    public override void Initialize(string name,
                                    NameValueCollection config)
    {
        fileName = config.Get("fileName");
        config.Remove("fileName");
        base.Initialize(name, config);
    }

    public override void ProcessEvent(WebBaseEvent raisedEvent)
    {
        if (this.UseBuffering)
        {
            // let BufferedWebEventProvider buffer the event for us
            base.ProcessEvent(raisedEvent);
        }
        else
        {
            // do the normal synchronous thing
            lock (fileLock)
            {
                using (StreamWriter w = File.AppendText(fileName))
                {
```

```
                        writeEvent(w, raisedEvent);
                }
            }
        }
    }

    public override void ProcessEventFlush(
                        WebEventBufferFlushInfo info)
    {
        lock (fileLock)
        {
            using (StreamWriter w = File.AppendText(fileName))
            {
                w.WriteLine("--- Buffered Event Flush ---");
                w.WriteLine("Events in buffer: {0}",
                        info.EventsInBuffer);
                w.WriteLine("Events lost since last notification: {0}",
                    info.EventsDiscardedSinceLastNotification);
                foreach (WebBaseEvent e in info.Events)
                    writeEvent(w, e);
            }
        }
    }

    private void writeEvent(TextWriter w, WebBaseEvent raisedEvent)
    {
        w.WriteLine("{0} - {1} - {2}",
            raisedEvent.EventTime, raisedEvent.GetType(),
            raisedEvent.Message);
    }
}
```

Back in the description of how buffering works (refer to Table 7-1), we discussed a counter that tracks lost messages. In Listing 7-13 you can see how that counter is communicated to the provider via the WebEvent-BufferFlushInfo class. The buffered example logs this information to the text file along with the events themselves.

If you run both of these providers simultaneously, you'll see that the buffered provider ends up writing out several events at a time in bursts, with the interval dependent on the bufferMode you choose. The synchronous provider, on the other hand, writes each event as it occurs.

To use a custom provider, you need to refer to it in web.config, just like the built-in providers. The example in Listing 7-14 assumes that the provider has been built into a class library assembly called CustomProviders.dll, which is deployed in the bin directory of the Web application.

LISTING 7-14: Referring to a custom provider in web.config

```
<!-- web.config -->
<providers>
  <add name="BufferedLogFileProvider"
       type="BufferedLogFileWebEventProvider,CustomProviders"
       fileName="c:\temp\buffered_log.txt"
       buffer="true"
       bufferMode="Notification"/>
</providers>
```

While many people will likely need custom events, fewer will need to write a custom provider, but it's good to know this extensibility point exists in case you need it.

Tracing in ASP.NET 2.0

Essential ASP.NET explained the basics of tracing in ASP.NET. Here we'll show the new features that have been added in version 2.0.

In the original tracing implementation, the requestLimit attribute on the <trace> element limited the number of requests that would generate tracing data. By default this value is set to 10, which means that only the first 10 requests will be traced; requests after that will be ignored by the tracing system. In version 2.0, you can set the new mostRecent attribute to true to indicate you'd like to continue tracing indefinitely, using requestLimit to control the number of requests that you want to see in the output. With this setting in place, you'll now see the 10 most recent requests traced at all times, instead of the 10 first trace messages (which seems a lot more useful!).

Programmatic Access to Trace Output

In the past, there wasn't a clean way to hook into the tracing infrastructure to control formatting or perhaps even redirect the trace output to another logging system. Version 2.0 adds a tracing event to which you can wire up code to intercept ASP.NET trace messages as they are generated. You can use this to format the trace output however you like, or to redirect the trace output to a persistent medium (although you might find the next section on System.Diagnostics integration more useful if this is your goal).

The TraceContext object, which is exposed via HttpContext.Trace and Page.Trace, now exposes an event called TraceFinished, which fires once all trace messages for a request have been gathered. When this event fires, the associated TraceContextEventArgs includes a property called Trace-Records that you can enumerate to programmatically walk through each TraceContextRecord for the current request. The example in Listing 7-15 writes trace data to a text file.

LISTING 7-15: Writing trace output to a file

```
<!-- web.config to turn on tracing and supply trace filename -->
<configuration>
  <appSettings>
    <add key="traceFile" value="c:\temp\trace_log.txt"/>
  </appSettings>

  <system.web>
    <compilation debug="true"/>
    <trace enabled="true" pageOutput="false" localOnly="true" />
  </system.web>
</configuration>

// codebehind for a generic Tracing.aspx file that
// wires up to TraceFinished and writes a text file
using System;
using System.IO;
using System.Web;
using System.Configuration;

public partial class Tracing : System.Web.UI.Page
{
    protected void Page_Load(object sender, EventArgs e)
    {
        Trace.TraceFinished += Trace_Finished;
        Trace.Write("Using Page Trace",
                    "Subscribed to TraceFinished event");
    }

    void Trace_Finished(Object sender, TraceContextEventArgs e)
    {
        string traceFile =
            ConfigurationManager.AppSettings["traceFile"];
        using (StreamWriter w = File.AppendText(traceFile))
        {
            int i = 0;
            foreach (TraceContextRecord r in e.TraceRecords)
                w.WriteLine("{0}) {1}:{2}", ++i,
                            r.Category, r.Message);
        }
    }
}
```

While the example in Listing 7-15 will only record trace data for this one page, you could easily move this code into global.asax or an HttpModule where you'd watch for an event such as PreRequestHandlerExecute and use that to wire a handler onto HttpContext.Current.TraceContext.TraceFinished, enabling you to record traces for all pages in an application.

Integration with System.Diagnostics Tracing

ASP.NET 2.0 introduces a couple of adapters that make it easy to funnel trace messages back and forth between ASP.NET tracing and System.Diagnostics tracing. This is really helpful if you have existing components that use the Trace object in System.Diagnostics, or if you'd like to use the System.Diagnostics trace listeners to collect all trace data for your Web application.

To instruct ASP.NET to send trace output directly to the System.Diagnostics trace listeners you've configured in the <system.diagnostics> section of your web.config file, set the new writeToDiagnosticsTrace attribute of the <trace> element to true, as shown in Listing 7-16.

LISTING 7-16: Sending trace output to System.Diagnostics trace listeners

```
<!-- web.config -->
<configuration>
  <system.web>
    <trace enabled="true"
           pageOutput="false"
           writeToDiagnosticsTrace="true"/>
  </system.web>

  <system.diagnostics>
    <trace>
      <listeners>
        <add name="console"
             type="System.Diagnostics.ConsoleTraceListener"/>
      </listeners>
    </trace>
  </system.diagnostics>
</configuration>
```

With this configuration, if you run a Web page in the debugger, you'll be able to see the trace records for any Web page in the debugger's output window. With this feature it's even easier to dump ASP.NET trace information to a persistent medium by simply wiring up one of the built-in trace listeners from System.Diagnostics.

If you want to go the other way, the ASP.NET team has also included a new trace listener that writes its output to the ASP.NET TraceContext. It's called, appropriately enough, System.Web.WebPageTraceListener, and if you wire it up under the <system.diagnostics> section of your web.config file, it'll funnel all System.Diagnostics trace messages back into the ASP.NET tracing system. This can be helpful if you're accustomed to using ASP.NET tracing and would like to include System.Diagnostics trace messages from non-ASP.NET components in your output.

The example in Listing 7-17 calls into a Calculator class which is instrumented with System.Diagnostics.Trace calls.

LISTING 7-17: Funneling System.Diagnostics trace records into the ASP.NET tracing system

```
<!-- web.config that uses the WebPageTraceListener -->
<configuration>
  <system.web>
    <trace enabled="true" pageOutput="false" localOnly="true" />
  </system.web>

  <system.diagnostics>
    <trace>
      <listeners>
        <add name="aspnet" type="System.Web.WebPageTraceListener,
System.Web, Version=2.0.0.0, Culture=neutral, PublicKeyToken=
b03f5f7f11d50a3a" />
      </listeners>
    </trace>
  </system.diagnostics>
</configuration>


// Tracing.aspx.cs
// here's the codebehind that calls the Calculator
using System;

public partial class Tracing : System.Web.UI.Page
{
    protected double AddNumbers()
    {
        Trace.Write("Calling Calculator.Add");
        return Calculator.Add(2, 2);
    }
}

// here's the calculator code
using System;
using System.Diagnostics;
```

continues

```
public static class Calculator
{
    public static double Add(double a, double b)
    {
        double result = a + b;
        Trace.TraceInformation("Calculator.Add({0} + {1}) = {2}",
                               a, b, result);
        return result;
    }
}
```

Figure 7-5 shows the resulting output from trace.axd. Note how the Calculator's calls to Trace are included in line with the ASP.NET tracing data. This integration is sure to come in handy for a lot of people!

Funneling Web Events to System.Diagnostics Trace Listeners

ASP.NET 2.0 comes with a third adapter that lets you funnel Web events to the System.Diagnostics trace listeners. Simply wire up the TraceWeb-EventProvider as a normal Web event provider in the <providers> section of web.config to enable this feature. This provider doesn't require any configuration; it just forwards all Web events to the System.Diagnostics.Trace class. This is by far the simplest built-in Web event provider. Listing 7-18 shows the entire implementation of its ProcessEvent method.

LISTING 7-18: TraceWebEventProvider.ProcesEvent

```
public override void ProcessEvent(WebBaseEvent eventRaised)
{
    if (eventRaised is WebBaseErrorEvent)
    {
        Trace.TraceError(eventRaised.ToString());
    }
    else
    {
        Trace.TraceInformation(eventRaised.ToString());
    }
}
```

Note how this code checks to see if the incoming Web event derives from WebBaseErrorEvent to determine whether the event represents an error or not. This should help emphasize that when you create your own custom Web events, you should think carefully about the base class from which you derive. Don't just derive from WebBaseEvent blindly—pick the most appropriate base class for each of your custom event classes.

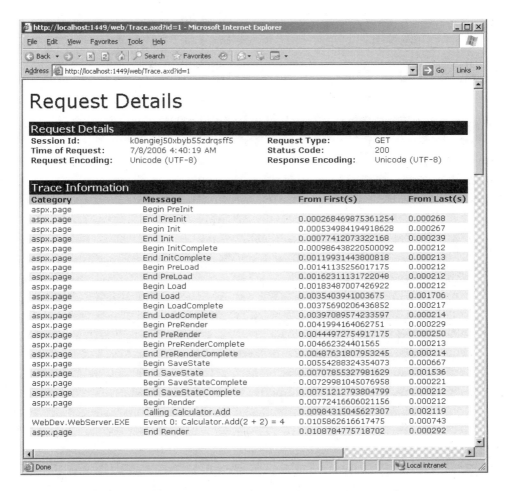

FIGURE 7-5: Funneling System.Diagnostics trace records into ASP.NET tracing

Event Tracing for Windows: Debugging Without a Debugger

While performance counters are great for discovering aggregate statistics about a Web application for planning or other purposes, they won't typically give you the detail you need to diagnose, say, a request that is taking longer than expected to complete. But there is a system called Event Tracing for Windows (ETW) that is designed to do exactly that.

ETW is a high-performance tracing system implemented in the Windows kernel. It was introduced way back in Windows 2000 to help add diagnostic support to the kernel and other subsystems such as IIS and Active Directory. In recent years, the teams working on IIS, ASP.NET, Windows Communication Foundation, and other infrastructures have been working hard to instrument their code with ETW.

Think for a moment about how ASP.NET tracing works. Imagine instrumenting your entire Web application using Trace statements, and then turning on tracing in a high-volume scenario where thousands of requests are being processed per minute. That's an awful lot of trace data, and it's probably going to put quite a load on your server. ETW was designed specifically to address this sort of scenario. By focusing on tight, binary trace data cached in locked pages of memory managed by the kernel, ETW tracing lets you capture high volumes of detailed data from a production server without killing that server's performance. On a production server, you can't afford to wire up a debugger to see what's wrong. ETW gives you the next best thing: it's like debugging without a debugger, as Chris St. Amand says in his webcast (you should watch this if you want to learn more about ETW).[6]

Figure 7-6 shows the output of an ETW command on Windows Server 2003 with the .NET Framework version 2.0 installed. This command lists the ETW providers that are installed by default.

Given all of these providers, you can literally trace a Web request as it flows through IIS (using the IIS: WWW Server provider) into ASP.NET (using the ASP.NET Events provider) down into the CLR (using the .NET Common Language Runtime provider) into the kernel (using the Windows Kernel Trace provider). You can even follow the request into SQL Server using the MSSQLSERVER Trace provider.

That's enough description; let's see ETW in action. The first step toward getting an ETW trace is to list the providers you want to participate in a text file (if you're only using a single provider, you can skip this step). Listing 7-19 shows an example of a provider file that includes IIS and ASP.NET. Each line in the file (besides the comment) includes a provider GUID, an integer which is really a set of provider-specific flags that turn on various tracing features for that particular provider, a second integer that

---

6. TechNet Webcast: Microsoft.com Operations Introduces Real World Debugging: Debugging Without the Debugger in IIS and ASP.NET (Level 300). In this video, you'll watch Chris log onto one of the production Web servers at microsoft.com and gather ETW trace data.

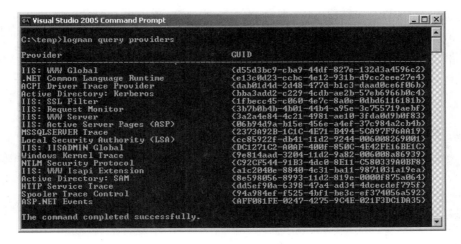

FIGURE 7-6: ETW providers on Windows Server 2003

indicates verbosity level, and lastly, a human-readable provider name (this name isn't strictly necessary, but it makes the file more readable).

LISTING 7-19: A sample provider text file

```
# providers.txt
{3a2a4e84-4c21-4981-ae10-3fda0d9b0f83} 0 5 IIS: WWW Server
{AFF081FE-0247-4275-9C4E-021F3DC1DA35} 0 5 ASP.NET Events
```

With this text file in hand, we can now start an ETW trace using the log manager (logman.exe):

```
C:\>logman start trace mytrace -o out.etl -pf providers.txt -ct perf -ets
```

The name "mytrace" is an arbitrary string that we'll use later to turn the trace off when we've finished gathering data. The output of the trace will go into a binary file called out.etl. The –ct switch with the "perf" argument[7] tells ETW that we want to use the multimedia clock for timestamping each log record. The normal clock doesn't have a high enough resolution to be useful for ETW tracing (logman can also be used to record performance monitoring data, and it doesn't require such a high resolution

---

7. The –ct switch isn't available on the version of logman that ships with Windows XP. Also note that if you run "logman query providers" on Windows XP, you won't see nearly as many providers as you do on Windows Server 2003.

clock). The –ets switch is one you'll almost always want to use, as it indicates that the trace should start immediately.

Now that the trace is running, we'll surf to an ASP.NET Web page on the server, which should generate some trace data. Then we'll stop the trace:

```
C:\>logman stop mytrace -ets
```

At this point we should have some output, shown in Listing 7-20.

LISTING 7-20: Output from an ETW trace

```
Directory of C:\temp

07/08/2006  06:46 AM    <DIR>          .
07/08/2006  06:46 AM    <DIR>          ..
07/08/2006  06:59 AM           131,072 out.etl
07/08/2006  06:57 AM               103 providers.txt
               2 File(s)        131,175 bytes
```

Keep in mind that the output is binary and you'll need a tool to view it. You can use the built-in TRACERPT.EXE tool to convert it into a comma-delimited file if you like. Get this: in a distributed system, you could even be running traces on multiple machines, and you could use TRACERPT.EXE to merge the trace files into one report! This is another benefit of using ETW, but it's one we'll leave you to explore on your own (be sure that the clocks on the machines from which you're collecting data are synchronized).

There's another tool called Log Parser[8] that can process these comma-delimited log files, and as of this writing, the latest version (2.2) also processes binary ETW files directly. We'll use that to select some output from the ETW trace.

The first command you'll probably want to run if you were following along on your own computer would be this:

```
C:\>logparser -i:ETW "select * from out.etl"
```

---

8. You can download Log Parser from the Microsoft Web site (www.microsoft.com/technet/scriptcenter/tools/logparser/default.mspx), and there's an unofficial support site at www.logparser.com that you might find helpful.

Unfortunately, the output from this is so wide that there's no way to show it to you in the book in any meaningful way. But suffice it to say that it includes an event number, name, type, timestamp, and a very long User-Data field. For the purposes of this demonstration, we'll limit the selection to just a few fields, and do some serious abbreviation of the UserData, which can be quite long. Listing 7-21 shows a more reasonable query that generates output that can actually fit on the page:

```
C:\>logparser -i:ETW "select EventName, EventTypeName, UserData from
out.etl"
```

LISTING 7-21: Viewing ETW trace records

```
EventName   EventTypeName              UserData
----------  -------------------------  -----------------------------------
IISGeneral  GENERAL_REQUEST_START      ...AppPoolId=DefaultAppPool...
IISGeneral  GENERAL_GET_URL_METADATA   ...PhysicalPath=C:\work...
IISISAPI    ISAPI_START                ContextId={00000000-0000-0000-...}
IISGeneral  GENERAL_ISAPI_HANDLER      ContextId={00000000-0000-0000-...}
AspNetReq   Start                      ...Method=GET|Path=...|QueryString=
IISGeneral  GENERAL_GET_URL_METADATA   ...PhysicalPath=C:\work\...
AspNetReq   End                        ConnID=13744592|ContextId={...}
IISISAPI    ISAPI_END                  ContextId={00000000-0000-0000-...}
IISGeneral  GENERAL_REQUEST_END        ...BytesSent=903|HttpStatus=200...

Statistics:
-----------
Elements processed: 9
Elements output:    9
Execution time:     1.33 seconds
```

Here you can see two providers at work: the IIS provider and the ASP.NET provider. Written by two entirely separate teams, they nonetheless are cooperating to provide a single trace output that shows the call stack for a request as it flows from IIS into ASP.NET and back again.

There's not a lot of detail in this request, so let's tweak the providers.txt file a bit to ask for more detail from the ASP.NET provider (see Listing 7-22).

LISTING 7-22: Asking for more detail

```
# providers.txt (with more detail)
{3a2a4e84-4c21-4981-ae10-3fda0d9b0f83} 0            5 IIS: WWW Server
{AFF081FE-0247-4275-9C4E-021F3DC1DA35} 0x0000000F 5 ASP.NET Events
```

This turns on all four flags that the ASP.NET provider defines (you can find this in the aspnet.mof file mentioned earlier in this chapter):

- 0x0001 = Infrastructure events
- 0x0002 = Pipeline module events
- 0x0004 = Page events
- 0x0008 = Application services events (provider-based services like Membership)

Listing 7-23 shows the more detailed output after running a trace with these new provider settings. Note how you can track the request as it flows through the ASP.NET pipeline, including all HttpModules that were invoked. You can also see every Web event that was generated, and the sequence in which it occurred on the stack. If you have a wider screen than this page, you can include other fields in your query as well, such as the timestamp, which will help you spot processing bottlenecks. If a problem occurs, this type of diagnostic output can often help you locate it very quickly.

LISTING 7-23: A more detailed ETW trace

```
EventName    EventTypeName              UserData
----------   ------------------------   ------------------------------------
IISGeneral   GENERAL_REQUEST_START      ...AppPoolId=DefaultAppPool...
IISGeneral   GENERAL_GET_URL_METADATA   PhysicalPath=...|AccessPerms=Read…
IISISAPI     ISAPI_START
IISGeneral   GENERAL_ISAPI_HANDLER
AspNetReq    Start                      Method=GET|Path=...|QueryString=
AspNetReq    RequestQueued
AspNetReq    RequestDequeued
AspNetReq    GetAppDomainEnter
IISGeneral   GENERAL_GET_URL_METADATA   PhysicalPath=C:\...|AccessPerms=…
AspNetReq    GetAppDomainLeave
AspNetReq    AppDomainEnter             DomainId=/LM/W3SVC/1/Root/...
IISGeneral   GENERAL_GET_URL_METADATA   PhysicalPath=C:\...|AccessPerms=…
AspNetReq    WebEventRaiseStart         EventClassName=...|EventCode=...
AspNetReq    WebEventDeliverStart       ProviderName=...|RuleName=myrule...
AspNetReq    WebEventDeliverEnd
AspNetReq    WebEventRaiseEnd
AspNetReq    StartHandler          HandlerName=HttpApplication…
AspNetReq    PipelineModuleEnter   ModuleName=WindowsAuthenticationModule
AspNetReq    PipelineModuleLeave   ModuleName=WindowsAuthenticationModule
AspNetReq    PipelineModuleEnter   ModuleName=FormsAuthenticationModule
```

```
AspNetReq PipelineModuleLeave ModuleName=FormsAuthenticationModule
AspNetReq PipelineModuleEnter ModuleName=PassportAuthenticationModule
AspNetReq PipelineModuleLeave ModuleName=PassportAuthenticationModule
AspNetReq PipelineModuleEnter ModuleName=DefaultAuthenticationModule
AspNetReq PipelineModuleLeave ModuleName=DefaultAuthenticationModule
AspNetReq PipelineModuleEnter ModuleName=RoleManagerModule
AspNetReq PipelineModuleLeave ModuleName=RoleManagerModule
AspNetReq PipelineModuleEnter ModuleName=AnonymousIdentificationModule
AspNetReq PipelineModuleLeave ModuleName=AnonymousIdentificationModule
AspNetReq PipelineModuleEnter ModuleName=UrlAuthorizationModule
AspNetReq WebEventRaiseStart    EventClassName=...|EventCode=4003...
AspNetReq WebEventDeliverStart ProviderName=...|RuleName=myrule...
AspNetReq WebEventDeliverEnd
AspNetReq WebEventRaiseEnd
AspNetReq PipelineModuleLeave  ModuleName=UrlAuthorizationModule
AspNetReq PipelineModuleEnter  ModuleName=FileAuthorizationModule
AspNetReq WebEventRaiseStart    EventClassName=WebSuccessAuditEvent...
AspNetReq WebEventDeliverStart ProviderName=SqlWebEventProvider...
AspNetReq WebEventDeliverEnd
AspNetReq WebEventRaiseEnd
AspNetReq PipelineModuleLeave ModuleName=FileAuthorizationModule
AspNetReq PipelineModuleEnter ModuleName=OutputCacheModule
AspNetReq PipelineModuleLeave ModuleName=OutputCacheModule
AspNetReq MapHandlerEnter
AspNetReq MapHandlerLeave
AspNetReq PipelineModuleEnter ModuleName=SessionStateModule
AspNetReq SessionDataBegin
AspNetReq SessionDataEnd
AspNetReq PipelineModuleLeave ModuleName=SessionStateModule
AspNetReq PipelineModuleEnter ModuleName=ProfileModule
AspNetReq PipelineModuleLeave ModuleName=ProfileModule
AspNetReq HttpHandlerEnter
AspNetReq PagePreInitEnter
AspNetReq PagePreInitLeave
AspNetReq PageInitEnter
AspNetReq PageInitLeave
AspNetReq PageLoadEnter
AspNetReq PageLoadLeave
AspNetReq PagePreRenderEnter
AspNetReq PagePreRenderLeave
AspNetReq PageSaveViewstateEnter
AspNetReq PageSaveViewstateLeave
AspNetReq PageRenderEnter
AspNetReq PageRenderLeave
AspNetReq HttpHandlerLeave
AspNetReq PipelineModuleEnter ModuleName=SessionStateModule
AspNetReq PipelineModuleLeave ModuleName=SessionStateModule
AspNetReq PipelineModuleEnter ModuleName=OutputCacheModule
AspNetReq PipelineModuleLeave ModuleName=OutputCacheModule
```

continues

```
AspNetReq PipelineModuleEnter ModuleName=SessionStateModule
AspNetReq PipelineModuleLeave ModuleName=SessionStateModule
AspNetReq PipelineModuleEnter ModuleName=FormsAuthenticationModule
AspNetReq PipelineModuleLeave ModuleName=FormsAuthenticationModule
AspNetReq PipelineModuleEnter ModuleName=PassportAuthenticationModule
AspNetReq PipelineModuleLeave ModuleName=PassportAuthenticationModule
AspNetReq PipelineModuleEnter ModuleName=RoleManagerModule
AspNetReq PipelineModuleLeave ModuleName=RoleManagerModule
AspNetReq PipelineModuleEnter ModuleName=ProfileModule
AspNetReq PipelineModuleLeave ModuleName=ProfileModule
AspNetReq EndHandler
AspNetReq End
IISISAPI   ISAPI_END
IISGeneral GENERAL_REQUEST_END BytesSent=903...HttpStatus=200…

Statistics:
-----------
Elements processed: 83
Elements output:    83
Execution time:     2.31 seconds
```

There's one last thing you should keep in mind. For this example, we're running a trace on a standalone machine where we're the only users. On a production box, these output files can grow large *very quickly*. For example, when Chris turned on ETW logging on the microsoft.com production Web server in his webcast, he traced using five different providers for one minute. The output file was roughly 120MB in size! So be careful not to start a trace and walk away from the machine, unless you use either logman to schedule a stop time or a maximum logfile size.

In case you are wondering, here's a brief explanation of how ETW works under the hood. A system that is instrumented with ETW registers itself as an ETW provider by calling a native Win32 function called Register-TraceGuids. This function requires that the caller pass in a pointer to a callback function. This is how ETW pings the various providers and tells them to turn on their trace logs or turn them off at runtime. When a provider receives a callback indicating that tracing should be turned on, it will typically flip on a global Boolean variable that turns on all sorts of tracing code deep in its innards. This tracing code calls another Win32 function, Trace-Event, to add records to the trace log.

ETW records the time of each trace record and writes the data to a locked memory page in the kernel. The goal here is to ensure that when you turn on tracing, you don't start thrashing the swap file and seriously impact the performance that you may be trying to measure. Behind the scenes, a daemon thread is busy writing out the contents of those kernel memory pages to disk in the form of the ETL trace log. When you run logman to start or stop a trace, under the covers it's using the Win32 functions StartTrace and StopTrace to instruct ETW to signal providers to start or stop tracing. There's really not a lot to ETW, but its ubiquity on the Windows platform makes it very powerful indeed.

SUMMARY

In this chapter we explored the new health monitoring system based on Web events. We've shown how easy it is to record the myriad of built-in Web events to the event log, SQL Server, WMI, or even to an administrator's e-mail inbox by doing nothing more than updating your web.config file. With a little bit of coding you can add application-level instrumentation using custom Web events. This is so easy to do that there's really no excuse not to do it—the more instrumentation you make available, the easier it is to diagnose problems quickly and save money once you're in production.

We explored the improved ASP.NET tracing facility, and how you can program against it or wire it up to the System.Diagnostics trace engine. And last but certainly not least, we provided you with a glimpse into the future of realtime tracing on this platform: ETW.

Think about management earlier rather than later, and take just a little bit of time to add diagnostic support to your applications. It's a great way to make your life easier when it comes time to debug a live application, and as a side benefit, you may just turn a system administrator into a friend rather than a foe.

■8■
Performance

O NE OF THE OVERARCHING GOALS of this release of ASP.NET was to improve the performance and scalability of applications. The ASP.NET team accomplished this in two ways: by optimizing code paths and improving resource utilization, and by making performance-enhancing features like caching and client callbacks easier to use and manage. This chapter looks in detail at the many new caching features, including declarative data source caching, SQL cache invalidation, and post-cache substitution. We will also cover general performance enhancements and the new client-callback architecture.

Caching

While much of ASP.NET was enhanced for performance with the 2.0 release, the caching-related features are the most visible and are likely to have the most impact on your applications. The most visible new caching feature, **data source caching**, provides a simple model for adding caching to data sources, making it much easier to add caching to Web applications. Next, **SQL cache dependencies** give you the ability to tie a cache entry to a database result, effectively eliminating cache coherency problems. Then, **post-cache substitution** solves the unique problem of needing to cache everything *except* a few small pieces. Finally, the **output caching** feature introduced in the first release is now enhanced with new configuration settings for making global cache policy changes easy to accomplish. Each of these features is a welcome addition and should make adding and managing caching in your Web applications much easier and more effective.

Data Source Caching

One of the big advantages of using declarative data sources in ASP.NET 2.0 is the ease with which you can enable caching. By setting the Enable-Caching property to true on a data source control, logic is in place to store data retrieved with the first call to the SelectCommand property in the application-wide cache. Subsequent calls to the select command for that data source will pull the data directly from the cache instead of going back to the data source. When you enable caching on a data source control, you can also specify settings for the cache entry by using the CacheDuration, CacheExpirationPolicy (whether it's sliding or absolute), and CacheKey-Dependency properties. Listing 8-1 shows a sample SqlDataSource control with its EnableCaching property set to true and its CacheDuration set to one hour (3,600 seconds). The GridView bound to this data source will load its data from the cache after the first request, avoiding a round trip to the database server for each subsequent request.

LISTING 8-1: Enabling caching on a SqlDataSource control

```
<asp:GridView ID="_authorsGrid" runat="server"
            AutoGenerateColumns="True" DataKeyNames="au_id"
            DataSourceID="_authorsDataSource" EnableViewState="false" />

<asp:SqlDataSource ID="_authorsDataSource" runat="server"
    EnableCaching="true" CacheDuration="3600"
    ConnectionString="<%$ ConnectionStrings:pubs %>"
    SelectCommand="SELECT au_id, au_lname, au_fname FROM authors" />
```

The behavior of a cached data source is exactly what you would see if you populated a DataSet and inserted it into the Page.Cache object your-self, using the cached instance to manually bind data to a control on subse-quent access. The caching feature of the SqlDataSource class only works when the data source has its DataSourceMode set to DataSet (the default), since it makes no sense to cache a DataReader that is a streaming data access mechanism only.

An important question to ask is how the cache key is generated for a cached data source, since that is no longer in your hands with data source control caching. For example, if you have two data source controls on separate pages returning the same result set, should they index into the same cache entry? What if you have parameters to your select command—should each unique parameter value point to a different entry in the cache? The data source controls answer both of these questions in the affirmative—data sources returning the exact same result sets will index into the same cache entry, and any variation in parameters for the select command will result in a new cache entry. The cache key itself is generated internally, taking into account all of these factors. For example, the cache key for the data retrieved by the data source in Listing 8-1 is:

```
u914027403600:0::server=.;integrated security=SSPI;database=pubs:SELECT
au_id, au_lname, au_fname FROM authors:0:-1
```

Note that as Table 8-1 shows, any variation in the cache settings, connection string, or text of the select command will result in a unique cache key and corresponding cache entry. This is important to know if you want

TABLE 8-1: Elements of the cache key generated by the SqlDataSource control with sample values

Cache Key Element	Sample Value
Marker character "u"	u
Hash code of the data source control's Type object	91402740
Value of CacheDuration	3600
Value of CacheExpirationPolicy	0
Value of SqlCacheDependency	
Value of ConnectionString	server=.;integrated security . . .
Value of SelectCommand	SELECT au_id, au_lname, . . .
Parameter values in xx=vv format separated by an "&"	

to try and share cached data across pages, since all of the attributes of the data sources must be essentially identical for sharing to occur. As with all caching, you want to be sure that you are using the cache entries effectively and not just wasting space in the cache with entries that are never hit. For example, if you are passing in a userid or some other value that may change on a per-request or per-user basis as a parameter to a data source's select command, your cache will quickly be polluted with entries that are rarely used and take up unnecessary space in the cache.

ObjectDataSource Caching

If you are working with a data access layer using the ObjectDataSource instead of SqlDataSource, you still have complete support for caching. All of the same attributes are available in the ObjectDataSource class, and as long as your data classes don't return IDataReader results, the enumerable collections will be saved in the cache whenever caching is enabled. The only difference is that the cache key no longer contains a connection string or a select command, but instead uses the TypeName and SelectMethod properties to ensure unique cache entries for each data request. Listing 8-2 shows a sample data class with a GetPeople method that returns a collection of Person objects (in this case artificially generated), and Listing 8-3 shows a sample page with a GridView being fed data from an ObjectData-Source mapped onto the sample data class' GetPeople method.

LISTING 8-2: Sample data class with Person entity class

```
public class Person
{
    private int _age;
    private string _name;
    private bool _isMarried;
    private DateTime _birthDay;

    public int Age
    {
        get { return _age; }
        set { _age = value; }
    }

    public string Name
    {
        get { return _name; }
        set { _name = value; }
    }
```

```
    public bool IsMarried
    {
        get { return _isMarried; }
        set { _isMarried = value; }
    }

    public DateTime BirthDay
    {
        get { return _birthDay; }
        set { _birthDay = value; }
    }

    public Person() { }
    public Person(int age, string name, bool isMarried, DateTime birthDay)
    {
        _age = age;
        _name = name;
        _isMarried = isMarried;
        _birthDay = birthDay;
    }
}

public static class SampleData
{
    public static ICollection<Person> GetPeople()
    {
        List<Person> ret = new List<Person>();

        for (int i = 0; i < 10; i++)
            ret.Add(new Person(i + 20, "Person " + i.ToString(),
                               (i % 2) == 0,
                               DateTime.Now.AddYears(i-40)));

        return ret;
    }
}
```

LISTING 8-3: Caching an object data source

```
<asp:GridView ID="_peopleGridView" runat="server"
            DataSourceID="_peopleObjectDataSource"
            EnableViewState="False" />

<asp:ObjectDataSource ID="_peopleObjectDataSource" runat="server"
                    CacheDuration="120"
                    EnableCaching="True" SelectMethod="GetPeople"
                    DataObjectTypeName="Person"
                    TypeName="SampleData" />
```

Data Source Caching and ViewState

In both Listings 8-2 and 8-3, the EnableViewState flag was set to false in the GridView, which should be done in almost all scenarios where declarative data source caching is enabled. The combination of using a cached data source with a control whose ViewState has been disabled is a "sweet spot" for building fast, scalable, data-driven pages. As covered in Chapter 3, the new suite of data-bound controls continue to function properly even when ViewState is disabled (through a separate state transfer mechanism called ControlState), so disabling ViewState only has the effect of not propagating the data for the control to the client and back using the hidden __VIEWSTATE field. This combined with data source caching provides an extremely efficient, low-bandwidth page-serving dynamic content. The only remaining issue is dealing with stale data, which we will address next with SQL cache dependencies.

Cache Dependencies

One of the most requested features for this release of ASP.NET was to add the ability to invalidate a cache entry when results from a SQL query changed. It was added in the form of the SqlCacheDependency class. This class (and its associated infrastructure) lets you flush a cache entry whenever the table (or result set) on which it depends changes in the underlying database. It is implemented in SQL Server 7 and 2000 using a custom "change" table, a database trigger, and a polling mechanism from the ASP.NET worker process. In SQL Server 2005, it is implemented using the service broker feature, which does not have to resort to polling and does not need any instrumentation (since it is supported natively by the database engine). This new dependency system is also completely pluggable so that if you needed to have cache entries flushed when some other external event occurs, you can write your own custom class that can be associated with any cache entry, as we will explore shortly.

SQL cache dependencies can be used in three different caching contexts. First, you can associate a SQL cache dependency with a cached declarative data source by populating the SqlCacheDependency property with the name of the dependency. You can also use SQL cache dependencies to flush output-cached pages from the cache whenever associated data changes with the OutputCache directive's SqlDependency property.

Finally, you can directly specify a SqlCacheDependency class in the call to the Cache object's Insert method by specifying the dependence in the constructor. All three of these mechanisms work with both the SQL Server 2000 polling mechanism as well as the SQL Server 2005 callback mechanism; only the names of the dependencies change.

SQL Server 7 and 2000 Cache Dependencies

To set up a SQL cache dependency in SQL Server 7 or 2000, you must first populate the database to be used with a change notification table so that records of table changes can be recorded and detected. To do this, use the aspnet_regsql.exe command-line utility with -ed as an option. The database to instrument is specified with the -d option if it is a local database, or with -C to provide the full connection string. To use integrated authentication, use –E; otherwise, specify the SQL credentials in the connection string. For example, the following command will instrument the "pubs" database to work with notifications:

```
aspnet_regsql.exe -d pubs -ed -E
```

Once you have instrumented the target database with the change notification table, you must next enable change detection on the table (or tables) from which data is being retrieved. Use the aspnet_regsql.exe utility again, this time with the -et option to enable table change notification, and use the -t option to specify the table name. This will add a trigger that is invoked any time the table in question is modified. It will also add a row to the change notification table with the table name and an associated changeid field. Whenever the trigger is invoked, it will increment the value in the changeid field. For example, the following command will enable the authors table in the pubs database for change detection:

```
aspnet_regsql.exe -d pubs -et -t authors -E
```

The last steps are to register your SQL cache dependency in your configuration file, and then reference the configured dependency wherever you would like it to take effect. Listing 8-4 shows an example of registering a sqlCacheDependency with an existing connection string, and Listings 8-5, 8-6, and 8-7 show examples of using this dependency referencing the authors table in a declarative data source, an output cache directive, and a manual cache insertion, respectively. You can also specify multiple cache dependencies by listing them with a comma delimiter (*pubs:authors, pubs:publishers*).

LISTING 8-4: Configuring a SQL cache dependency for SQL Server 7/2000

```
<system.web>
  <!-- ... -->
  <caching>
    <sqlCacheDependency enabled="true" pollTime="3000">
      <databases>
        <add name="pubs" connectionStringName="pubs" />
      </databases>
    </sqlCacheDependency>
  </caching>
</system.web>
```

LISTING 8-5: Specifying a SQL Server 7/2000 cache dependency in a declarative data source

```
<asp:GridView ID="_authorsGrid" runat="server"
              AutoGenerateColumns="True" DataKeyNames="au_id"
              DataSourceID="_authorsDataSource" EnableViewState="false" />

<asp:SqlDataSource ID="_authorsDataSource" runat="server"
    EnableCaching="true" CacheDuration="3600"
    SqlCacheDependency="pubs:authors"
    ConnectionString="<%$ ConnectionStrings:pubsConnectionString %>"
    SelectCommand="SELECT au_id, au_lname, au_fname FROM authors" />
```

LISTING 8-6: Specifying a SQL Server 7/2000 cache dependency in an OutputCache directive

```
<%@ OutputCache Duration="3600" SqlDependency="pubs:authors"
        VaryByParam="none" %>
```

LISTING 8-7: Specifying a SQL Server 7/2000 cache dependency in a manual cache insertion

```
string sql, dsn;
dsn = ConfigurationManager.ConnectionStrings["pubs"].ConnectionString;
sql = "SELECT au_id, au_lname, au_fname FROM Authors";
SqlDataAdapter da = new SqlDataAdapter(sql, dsn);
DataSet authorsDs = new DataSet();
da.Fill(authorsDs);

Cache.Insert("authors", authorsDs,
        new SqlCacheDependency("pubs", "authors"));
```

Once the SqlCacheDependency is set up in ASP.NET, it will poll the database and invoke a stored procedure every *n* milliseconds (as specified

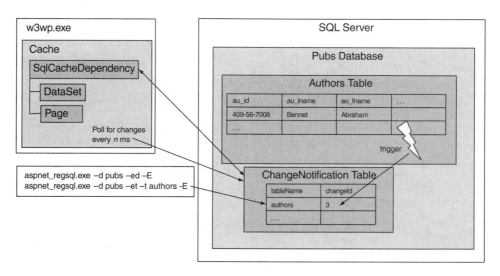

FIGURE 8-1: SQL cache dependencies in SQL Server 7/2000

in the configuration file entry). This is performed on a dedicated worker thread inside of the ASP.NET worker process and is not executed from a request thread. If the stored procedure detects that the changeid column for a particular table has changed, ASP.NET will flush the associated entries for that SQL dependency. Figure 8-1 shows all of the elements of SQL cache dependencies interacting when using SQL Server 7 or 2000.

SQL Server 2005 Cache Dependencies

SQL Server 2005 uses a completely different implementation of the Sql-CacheDependency class (although it technically is the same class, it operates in two distinct states). The SQL Server 2005 implementation uses the query notifications feature of SQL Server 2005 to mark a particular command as generating a notification when it changes. When a command is issued with a request for change notification, the database creates an indexed view (which is essentially a physical copy of the results of the command) and monitors anything that happens in the database that may affect the results (inserts, updates, deletes). When it detects a change, a query notification event is triggered, at which point the database uses the Service Broker feature of SQL Server 2005 to send a message back to the ASP.NET worker process indicating that the cache entry associated with that command needs to be flushed. This callback mechanism is generally much more efficient and generates much less network traffic than the polling mechanism used for SQL 7 and 2000. Figure 8-2 shows the general architecture of SQL Server 2005 cache dependencies.

The setup involved with using SQL Server 2005 cache dependencies is also much less than the polling mechanism just described, primarily because the entire infrastructure to issue the notifications is already built into the database—all you have to do in your ASP.NET application is request the notification. Before you can receive notifications, however, you must signal that your application is going to be monitoring service broker notifications using the static Start method of the SqlDependency class for each database connection you intend to receive notifications from. This call sets up a connection to the database and issues an asynchronous command to wait for notifications (using WAITFOR and RECEIVE). You only need to call this method once before you issue any requests to the database that include notifications, so it is common practice to place the call in the Application_Start event of the global application class, usually defined in the application-wide global.asax file, as shown in Listing 8-8.

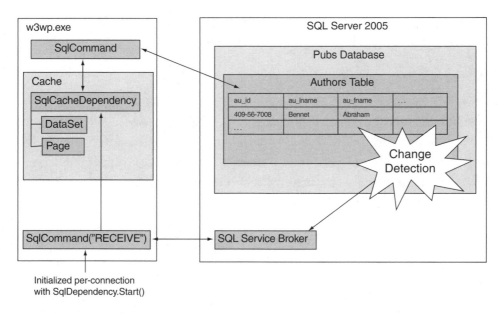

FIGURE 8-2: SQL cache dependencies in SQL Server 2005

LISTING 8-8: Calling SqlDependency.Start in Application_Start

```
<%--Global.asax--%>
<%@ Application Language="C#" %>
<%@ Import Namespace="System.Data.SqlClient" %>

<script runat="server">
  void Application_Start(object sender, EventArgs e)
  {
    string dsn =
        ConfigurationManager.ConnectionStrings["pubs"].ConnectionString;
    SqlDependency.Start(dsn);


  }
</script>
```

With the worker process ready to receive notifications, you can now use the SqlCacheDependency class to create dependencies on commands sent to the database. Unlike the polling mechanism described earlier, this dependency mechanism is enabled on a per-command basis, not a per-table basis. This means that you can associate the results of almost any command that returns results, including a stored procedure (there are limitations to the types of commands, however, which we will cover shortly). To create a dependency programmatically, you must first prepare the SqlCommand you would like to set up notifications for, and then pass the command object in as a parameter to the constructor of the SqlCacheDependency class. Listing 8-9 shows an example of programmatically inserting the results of a query into the cache with an associated SQL cache dependency.

LISTING 8-9: Programmatically specifying a cache dependency with SQL Server 2005

```
using (SqlConnection conn = new SqlConnection(dsn))
{
  SqlCommand cmd = new SqlCommand(
        "SELECT au_id, au_lname, au_fname FROM dbo.[Authors]", conn);
  SqlCacheDependency scd = new SqlCacheDependency(cmd);
  SqlDataAdapter da = new SqlDataAdapter(cmd);
  DataSet authorsDs = new DataSet();
  da.Fill(authorsDs, "authors");

  Cache.Insert("au", authorsDs, scd);
}
```

To set up cache dependencies declaratively that rely on SQL Server 2005 notifications, you use the same SqlCacheDependency property of the

SqlDataSource control as we did with the SQL 7/2000 dependencies, but instead of specifying a list of table names, you just use the *CommandNotification* string. This tells the data source to prepare a SqlCacheDependency initialized with the select command it uses to retrieve data, and to add that to the cache insertion, as shown in Listing 8-10.

LISTING 8-10: Specifying a SQL Server 2005 cache dependency in a declarative data source

```
<asp:GridView ID="_authorsGrid" runat="server"
            AutoGenerateColumns="True" DataKeyNames="au_id"
            DataSourceID="_authorsDataSource" EnableViewState="false" />

<asp:SqlDataSource ID="_authorsDataSource" runat="server"
    EnableCaching="true" CacheDuration="3600"
    SqlCacheDependency="CommandNotification"
    ConnectionString="<%$ ConnectionStrings:pubsConnectionString %>"
    SelectCommand="SELECT au_id, au_lname, au_fname FROM dbo.[authors]" />
```

Similarly, you can use the CommandNotification string in the Sql-Dependency attribute of the OutputCache directive of a page. It's not obvious how simply adding the CommandNotification string to your OutputCache directive would enable any dependencies, since the Output-Cache directive itself is not associated with any commands. What it will do is set a flag in the call context as the page executes, which the SqlCommand class checks internally as it is preparing a command. If the flag is set, it will implicitly associate a dependency with the command and associate it with the cache entry for the page itself. The end result is that if any of the queries are made on the page, the page will be flushed from the cache and reevaluated. This can have side effects that may not be obvious, for example, if one of the queries on the page doesn't adhere to the constraints for using SQL Server 2005 dependencies, that dependency will behave like it is always invalid, effectively invalidating the output caching for that page entirely. If you do decide to enable CommandNotification dependencies on an output cached page, take care that all of your queries work with SQL Server 2005 notifications.

Listing 8-11 shows an example of an output cached page with CommandNotification specified as the SqlDependency. This page has two data sources populating two separate GridViews, and because the queries used by each data source are compatible with notifications, the page will be cached until either of the results of the two queries changes.

LISTING 8-11: Specifying a SQL Server 2005 cache dependency in an OutputCache directive

```
<%@ Page Language="C#" %>
<%@ OutputCache Duration="120" SqlDependency="CommandNotification"
                VaryByParam="none" %>

<html xmlns="http://www.w3.org/1999/xhtml" >
<body>
  <form id="form1" runat="server">
  <div>
    <asp:GridView ID="_authorsGrid" runat="server"
        AutoGenerateColumns="True" DataKeyNames="au_id"
        DataSourceID="_authorsDataSource"
        EnableViewState="False" />

    <asp:SqlDataSource ID="_authorsDataSource" runat="server"
          ConnectionString="<%$ ConnectionStrings:pubs %>"
          SelectCommand="SELECT [au_id], [au_lname], [au_fname] FROM
dbo.[authors]"  />

    <asp:GridView ID="_publishersGrid" runat="server"
          AutoGenerateColumns="True" DataKeyNames="pub_id"
          DataSourceID="_publishersDataSource"
          EnableViewState="False" />

    <asp:SqlDataSource ID="_publishersDataSource" runat="server"
          ConnectionString="<%$ ConnectionStrings:pubs %>"
          SelectCommand="SELECT [pub_id], [pub_name], [city] FROM
dbo.[publishers]"  />

  </div>
</body>
</html>
```

As simple as it sounds to use SQL Server 2005 dependencies, in practice they can be somewhat tricky to get working because of all the pieces that have to be properly in place, and all of the queries used must adhere to the limitations of indexed views. The most common symptom you will see if a dependency isn't working is that the data associated with that dependency will be retrieved from the database every time and never drawn from the cache. After enabling a SQL Server 2005 cache dependency, it is usually wise to verify that it is indeed caching by watching a trace of the database as you access the page that references the cached data. Some problems will show themselves in the form of an exception, which will usually have good information on how to address the problem. If you find that a SQL cache dependency is not working, the following list of common issues and resolutions may help you diagnose why:

- Verify that you have called SqlDependency.Start with each connection string you are using dependencies for (just once over the lifetime of the application, typically in Application_Start).

- The database you are using in SQL Server 2005 must have the SQL service broker feature enabled. If it is not enabled, you should see an exception when you run a page that uses cached data, which indicates that the broker service is not enabled. To enable the service broker feature for a particular database, run the following command in the master database (replacing <dbname> with the name of your database):

```
ALTER DATABASE <dbname> SET ENABLE_BROKER
```

- The identity used to access the database must have permissions to register for notifications. If you are using integrated authentication and running under IIS 6.0, this identity will be the local Network Service account, unless you have changed the identity of the Application Pool in which the application runs. To grant notification permissions to a particular identity in the database, you can use the following T-SQL command (replacing <username> with the name of the identity):

```
GRANT SUBSCRIBE QUERY NOTIFICATIONS TO <username>
```

- The queries you use in the commands on which you want to receive notifications of change must be constrained in the following ways (these are the same set of restrictions in place when creating indexed views in SQL Server 2005).
  - Column names must be named explicitly (no "*" queries).
  - Table and user-defined function names must be referenced using their two-part names (schema.object), like dbo.Authors and Sales.SalesPerson.
  - Queries must not use any aggregation functions (like SUM, AVG, COUNT, and so on). One exception to this is the COUNT_BIG function, which is compatible (SUM is also allowed in some cases, but not always).

- CLR-based user-defined functions must not access SQL Server (they can't perform SELECT and may not have EXTERNAL_ACCESS).
- Queries must not use any windowing or ranking functions (which unfortunately includes the extremely useful ROW_NUMBER() function so commonly used in efficient paging queries).
- Queries must not reference any temporary tables or views (again unfortunate, as using temporary tables is a common alternative mechanism for implementing paging in a query).
- Queries can't include subqueries, outer joins, or self joins.
- Queries can't return fields of type *text*, *ntext*, or *image*.
- Queries can't use DISTINCT, HAVING, CONTAINS, or FREETEXT keywords.
- Stored procedures are restricted to all of these same rules, but in addition they may not use the SET NOCOUNT ON statement.

If you can work through these potential pitfalls when working with SQL Server 2005 cache dependencies, the results are definitely worth the effort. The ability to cache data that is frequently accessed for efficiency without having to worry about cache coherency ever being an issue is truly an impressive achievement, and taking advantage of it will increase the scalability and responsiveness of your application without compromising data integrity.

Custom Cache Dependencies

If none of the prebuilt cache dependency classes fits the bill for the type of caching you are doing, there is always the possibility of creating your own custom cache dependency. In this release of ASP.NET the cache dependency system is now completely pluggable, opening the door for third-party cache dependency classes (possibly for compatibility with other data stores) or completely custom dependencies that you write yourself. Any class that derives from the common CacheDependency base class can be used to tie flushing logic to any cache entry.

As an example, consider a site that uses a collection of Web services to supply data to its pages. It might make sense to build a custom cache dependency class that invoked a Web service periodically, to find out whether the results of other (more data-laden) Web service calls have changed since the last time they were called. The first step is to create a new class that inherits from CacheDependency (in the System.Web.Caching namespace). Your primary task when creating a custom cache dependency class is to identify when cache entries associated with your class should be expelled from the cache, and to fire the inherited NotifyDependency-Changed event when this happens.

Listing 8-12 shows a sample implementation of a custom cache dependency class called WSDataDependency. This example uses a timer to periodically poll a Web service (much like the SQL Server 2000 cache dependency class) to find out whether data has changed or not. This implementation assumes that the Web service contains a single method for checking the validity of the data with a signature of *bool IsValid()*. It also lets users of the class set the URL of the Web service, and thus this would work with any Web service that supported a method called IsValid with the correct signature. You can also customize the interval at which the polling timer will fire with the constructor's second parameter. Finally, in the timer handler implementation, it invokes the Web service's IsValid method to detect a change, and if it finds one it fires the NotifyDependencyChanged event inherited from the base CacheDependency class.

LISTING 8-12: Custom cache dependency class **WSDataDependency**

```
namespace EssentialAspDotNet2.Performance
{
  public class WSDataDependency : CacheDependency
  {
    private string _wsUrl;
    private int    _pollInterval;
    private Timer  _timer;

    public string WsUrl
    {
      get { return _wsUrl; }
      set { _wsUrl = value; }
    }

    public int PollInterval
    {
      get { return _pollInterval; }
      set { _pollInterval = value; }
    }
```

```
      public WSDataDependency()
            : this("http://localhost/DataService/DataValidService.asmx",
                3000)
      {
      }

      public WSDataDependency(string wsUrl, int pollInterval)
      {
        _wsUrl = wsUrl;
        _pollInterval = pollInterval;

        // Create timer and initiate poll
        _timer = new Timer(new TimerCallback(OnTimerCallback),
                        null, 0, _pollInterval);
      }

      public void OnTimerCallback(object state)
      {
          // Call IsValid method of Web service to check for data validity
          // Call this.NotifyDependencyChanged(this, EventArgs.Empty)
          // when change is detected
          localhost.DataValidService dvs =
                    new localhost.DataValidService();
          dvs.Url = _wsUrl;
          if (!dvs.IsValid())
              NotifyDependencyChanged(this, EventArgs.Empty);
      }
    }
}
```

With this class in place, you could then use it like any of the other cache dependency classes, by creating a new instance, initializing it, and passing it in as the third parameter to the Cache.Insert method. Listings 8-13 and 8-14 show a sample use of the class applied to a Web service call that returns a simple DateTime class as its response. Once inserted into the cache, the time shown in the rendered Label would only update whenever the IsValid Web method invoked by the WSDataDependency class returned false, or the hard-coded limit of 60 seconds was reached.

LISTING 8-13: Sample use of the custom WSDataDependency class

```
<%@ Page Language="C#" AutoEventWireup="true"
        CodeFile="CustomDependency.aspx.cs" Inherits="CustomDependency" %>
<html xmlns="http://www.w3.org/1999/xhtml" >
```

continues

```
<body>
   <form id="form1" runat="server">
   <div>
   <h2>Custom dependency sample</h2>
   The following timestamp is generated by a Web service call:
   <br />
   <asp:Label runat="server" ID="_dataLabel" EnableViewState="false" />
   </div>
   </form>
</body>
</html>
```

LISTING 8-14: Sample use of the custom WSDataDependency class (codebehind)

```
public partial class CustomDependency : Page
{
  protected void Page_Load(object sender, EventArgs e)
  {
    DateTime data;
    if (Cache["data"] == null)
    {
      localhost.DataService ds = new localhost.DataService();
      data = ds.GetData();

      WSDataDependency wsdd = new WSDataDependency(
        ConfigurationManager.AppSettings["localhost.DataValidService"],
          3000);

      Cache.Insert("data", data, wsdd,
                   DateTime.Now + new TimeSpan(0, 0, 60),
                   Cache.NoSlidingExpiration);
    }
    else
      data = (DateTime)Cache["data"];

    _dataLabel.Text = data.ToLongTimeString();
  }
}
```

Programmatic Fragment Caching

In ASP.NET 1.1 (and 2.0), it is possible to programmatically configure a page's output cache settings by using the Response.Cache property of the Page class, which references an instance of the HttpCachePolicy class. This means that you can make decisions about how long a page should stay in the cache, whether it has a sliding expiration, whether it has a dependency, and so on programmatically, which opens up many possibilities for controlling the output caching of your pages. On the other hand, while it has always been possible to cache user controls as well (often called **page fragment caching**), it was not possible in ASP.NET 1.1 to programmatically modify the cache control settings for an output cached control. This changes in 2.0, as the UserControl class has a new property, CachePolicy, that is an instance of the ControlCachePolicy class. You can now use this to manipulate the output caching behavior of a user control in your site. The ControlCachePolicy exposes all of the attributes of an output cached control, as shown in Listing 8-15.

LISTING 8-15: The ControlCachePolicy class

```
public sealed class ControlCachePolicy
  {
     public void SetExpires(DateTime expirationTime);
     public void SetSlidingExpiration(bool useSlidingExpiration);
     public void SetVaryByCustom(string varyByCustom);

     public bool Cached { get; set; }
     public CacheDependency Dependency { get; set; }
     public TimeSpan Duration { get; set; }
     public bool SupportsCaching { get; }
     public string VaryByControl { get; set; }
     public HttpCacheVaryByParams VaryByParams { get; }
  }
```

As an example, consider a user control that displays the results of a database query in a GridView control. If this user control is marked with an OutputCache directive, you could then modify any of the settings associated with the output cache entry through the CachePolicy property. The sample user control shown in Listings 8-16 and 8-17 programmatically alters the duration of the cache entry for this user control from 120 seconds (two minutes) to 60 (one minute).

LISTING 8-16: Output cached user control

```
<%@ Control Language="C#" AutoEventWireup="true"
    CodeFile="AuthorsControl.ascx.cs"  Inherits="AuthorsControl" %>

<%@ OutputCache VaryByParam="none" Shared="true" Duration="120" %>

<asp:Label runat="server" ID="_timestampLabel"
        EnableViewState="false" />
```

continues

```
<hr />
<asp:GridView ID="_authorsGrid" runat="server"
         AutoGenerateColumns="True" DataKeyNames="au_id"
         DataSourceID="_authorsDataSource" EnableViewState="False" />

<asp:SqlDataSource ID="_authorsDataSource" runat="server"
    ConnectionString="<%$ ConnectionStrings:pubs %>"
    SelectCommand="SELECT [au_id], [au_lname], [au_fname] FROM
dbo.[authors]" />
```

LISTING 8-17: Output cached user control (codebehind)

```
public partial class AuthorsControl : System.Web.UI.UserControl
{
    protected void Page_Load(object sender, EventArgs e)
    {
        // Enable output caching programmatically on this control,
        // setting the expiration for 1 minute from now
        //
        CachePolicy.Cached = true;
        CachePolicy.SetExpires(DateTime.Now + new TimeSpan(0, 1, 0));

        _timestampLabel.Text = "This control generated at " +
                              DateTime.Now.ToLongTimeString();
    }
}
```

Post-Cache Substitution

In ASP.NET 1.1, the only way to cache everything on a page except one small piece was to encapsulate the entire page into user controls marked with OutputCache directives. Post-cache substitution provides a cleaner way of accomplishing this by letting you mark a page as output cached, but placing a substitution control at the location you would like to keep dynamic. This substitution control is initialized with a static callback method that is called to return a string to populate that portion of the page when a request is made, and it then retrieves the rest of the page from the cache. Figure 8-3 shows the general architecture of post-cache substitution.

There are two ways to specify post-cache substitution. One way is to use the Response.WriteSubstitution method at the appropriate location in the response stream, which specifies a callback method that will be invoked whenever the page is requested (even when it is cached). Listing 8-18 shows an example of using WriteSubstitution to dynamically insert a

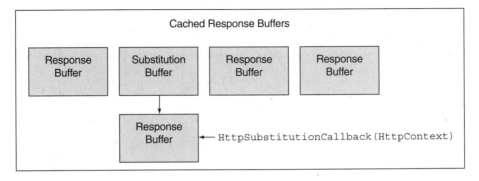

FIGURE 8-3: Post-cache substitution

substitution block into an output cached page. In this example, the entire page will be cached (in this case, the <h1> title and <h2> footer), but when a request comes in, it will invoke the GetServerTimeStamp method to populate the "substitution block" used as a placeholder in the cached page. Note that the Page class is never instantiated on subsequent requests when the page is cached, which is why the callback method must be static. It does have access to the HttpContext object, so it can use information from Request/Response/Session, and so on, but it cannot access elements of the Page itself.

LISTING 8-18: Using Response.WriteSubstitution

```
// within your page class
public static string GetServerTimeStamp(HttpContext ctx)
{
  return DateTime.Now.ToLongTimeString();
}

protected void Page_Load(object src, EventArgs e)
{
  Response.Write("<h1>title</h1>");
  Response.WriteSubstitution(
        new HttpResponseSubstitutionCallback(GetServerTimeStamp));
  Response.Write("<h2>footer</h2>");
}
```

The second way to use post-cache substitution is to use the Substitution control. This control gives you a declarative way of accomplishing the same thing that Response.WriteSubstitution does, and it has the advantage of integrating into a page's declarative control layout. To use the control, place it in the page where you want the substitution block, assign it the static callback method name, and mark the page as output cached. Listing 8-19 shows an example of using the Substitution control.

LISTING 8-19: Using the Substitution control

```
<%@ Page Language="C#" %>
<%@ OutputCache VaryByParam="none" Duration="120" %>

<script runat="server">
public static string GetServerTimeStamp(HttpContext ctx)
{
  return DateTime.Now.ToLongTimeString();
}

protected void Page_Load(object sender, EventArgs e)
{
  _timeStampLabel.Text = DateTime.Now.ToLongTimeString();
}
</script>

<html xmlns="http://www.w3.org/1999/xhtml" >
<head runat="server" />
<body>
    <form id="form1" runat="server">
    <div>
       Substitution: <asp:Substitution ID="_timeStampSubstitution"
               runat="server" MethodName="GetServerTimeStamp" />
        <br />
   Static label: <asp:Label runat="server" ID="_timeStampLabel" />

        <br />
    </div>
    </form>
</body>
</html>
```

Cache Profiles

Cache profiles give you a way to define output cache parameters for collections of pages. Instead of hard-coding values in each of your pages scattered throughout your site, you can create output cache profiles and have each page draw its settings from the profile in your configuration file. This consolidates your cache settings, making it much easier to try out different caching strategies with minimal effort. Listings 8-20 and 8-21 show an example of specifying three different output cache profiles and how to reference a profile with an output cache directive.

LISTING 8-20: Using output cache profiles

```
<configuration>
  <system.web>
    <caching>
      <outputCacheSettings>
        <outputCacheProfiles>
          <add name="Default" duration="60" varyByParam="user"/>
          <add name="Aggressive" duration="3600" varyByParam="user"/>
          <add name="Default" duration="60" varyByParam="user"/>
        </outputCacheProfiles>
      </outputCacheSettings>
    </caching>
  </system.web>
</configuration>
```

LISTING 8-21: Referencing an output cache profile

```
<%@ OutputCache CacheProfile="Aggressive" %>
...
```

In addition to controlling output cache settings from the configuration file, you can also control some global settings associated with both the output cache and the data cache. For the data cache, you can completely disable memory collection and/or expiration, and you can also put a limit on the total percentage of physical memory used by the data cache.

Output caching can be disabled or enabled at an application-wide scope, which is very useful for debugging purposes, as well as fixing a live server that has cache coherency problems. Listing 8-22 shows the various caching configuration file settings in use.

LISTING 8-22: Configuration file control over cache settings

```
<caching>
  <cache disableMemoryCollection="false"
         disableExpiration="false"
         percentagePhysicalMemoryUsedLimit="90" />

  <outputCache enabled="true"
               enableFragmentCache="true"
               sendCacheControlHeader="true"
               omitVaryStar="false" />
</caching>
```

General Performance Enhancements

In addition to the performance-specific features discussed earlier, a significant amount of work was put into optimizing the core of ASP.NET as well in this release. Significant performance gains on 8-CPU multiprocessor machines, specifically, will be noticed on sites with this type of hardware. In general, the efficiency of the pipeline and the interaction between ASP.NET and HTTP.SYS has been optimized, achieving up to 30% performance improvements over ASP.NET 1.1 alone. Also improved is the startup time, as all of the system assemblies are now precompiled (using NGen) and no longer have to be JIT-compiled on first access. Finally, many memory optimizations were made, so the overall working set of the worker process will be lower.

Client Callbacks

Many Web applications today are leveraging asynchronous JavaScript calls over HTTP in the client to provide a more interactive user interface experience. Instead of issuing a standard POST request with an HTML form, these applications leverage client-side events and the XMLHttpRequest object available in all modern-day browsers to issue HTTP requests back to the server without issuing a full postback. This type of request is much more innocuous to the user as there is no visible impact on the page except for the additional data displayed, and when done well, the Web application feels more like a responsive desktop application rather than a typical Web application. This technique has other advantages too, including the fact that the page will maintain its scroll and cursor positions without having to resort to server-side tricks to reset them as desired with each request.

Client Callback Framework

There is a lot of work involved with using asynchronous callbacks by hand, including setting up the XMLHttpRequest object, preparing and formatting the request, and building the handler for the response. If you want your client code to be browser independent as well, the work increases even more. ASP.NET 2.0 introduces a framework that relieves you of much of the grunt work for performing client callbacks, and has a collection of client-side JavaScript routines and a server-side interface for simple interaction, complete with browser independence. You are left to write some client-side JavaScript to issue the callback as well as a handler for processing the result, and then implementing a server-side callback method that returns the data you need. Typically in your client-side handler, you would then manipulate the client-side document object model (DOM) to display the results of your callback in some fashion.

Figure 8-4 shows a typical interaction between the client and server for a page that is using client callbacks to retrieve data instead of the typical HTML POST. Note that the initial request is a standard GET request to retrieve the initial page, and that the subsequent POST request is initiated by a client-side event (onclick on the lookup symbol input element). The call back to the server is handled by a fresh instance of the Page class, but the Page is only executed through the Load event, at which point the Callback event is raised and the server-side callback method is executed to return the requested data.

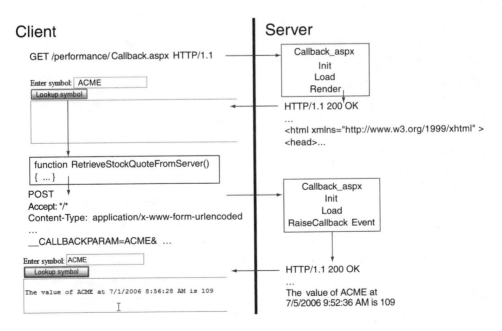

FIGURE 8-4: Client callback architecture

There are two core elements you need to put in place to use the callback architecture in ASP.NET 2.0: you need to implement the ICallback-EventHandler interface and call the ClientScript.GetCallbackEventReference from client-side JavaScript. The data passed from client to server and back again is always just a string, so it is up to you to decide what format that string should take and how much effort you want to put into formatting and parsing it. The ICallbackEventHandler interface, shown in Listing 8-23, defines two methods that your control (or page) must implement.

LISTING 8-23: The ICallbackEventHandler interface

```
public interface ICallbackEventHandler
{
  string GetCallbackResult();
  void RaiseCallbackEvent(string eventArgument);
}
```

The RaiseCallbackEvent method will be called first with the string parameter passed by the client callback method, and the GetCallbackResult method will be called next, which is where you return the string of data for your client-side script to process. This interface defines two methods instead of just one to perform the callback to support asynchronous processing scenarios. This interface can be implemented for an entire page, or if you are building a custom control or user control and would like to leverage client callbacks, you can implement it at the control level as well. Several of the built-in Web controls implement this interface to support on-demand population of data through client callbacks, including the TreeView, GridView, and DetailsView controls.

As an example of using client callbacks, Listings 8-24 and 8-25 show the implementation of a page that lets a user check a stock quote, and that maintains a list of each quote requested in a multiline text box on the page. The request to get a quote is performed using a client callback instead of a traditional HTML POST. In this page, the server-side callback method, GetCallbackResult, returns a simple string indicating the value of the requested stock symbol. The client-side work is done in a pair of methods registered using the ClientScript.RegisterClientScriptBlock method from within the Init event handler. The first JavaScript method, RetrieveStock-QuoteFromServer, retrieves the value from the input element where the user types the symbol to be requested and stores it in a local variable, symbolInput. Next, it invokes the callback method retrieved by calling Get-

CallbackEventReference of the ClientScript class, passing in the string value (the symbol) and the name of the callback method (StockQuote-FromServer). Finally, the method that processes the result of the callback, StockQuoteFromServer, takes a result string and adds it to the list of strings in the multiline text box.

LISTING 8-24: Callback.aspx—using client callbacks

```
<%@ Page Language="C#" AutoEventWireup="true"
                CodeFile="Callback.aspx.cs" Inherits="Callback" %>

<html xmlns="http://www.w3.org/1999/xhtml" >
<head runat="server" />
<body>
    <form id="form1" runat="server">
    <div>
    Enter symbol:
        <asp:TextBox ID="_symbolTextBox" runat="server" /><br />
        <input id="_lookupSymbolInput" name="_lookupSymbolInput"
            type="button" value="Lookup symbol"
            onclick="RetrieveStockQuoteFromServer()" /><br />
        <asp:TextBox ID="_resultTextBox" runat="server" Rows="4"
                TextMode="MultiLine" Width="75%" /><br />
    </div>
    </form>
</body>
</html>
```

LISTING 8-25: Callback.aspx.cs—using client callbacks

```
public partial class Callback : Page, ICallbackEventHandler
{
  public string GetCallbackResult()
  {
    return string.Format("The value of {0} at {1} is {2}", _arg,
                DateTime.Now.ToString(),
                new Random(Environment.TickCount).Next(0, 120));
  }

  private string _arg;
  public void RaiseCallbackEvent(string eventArgument)
  {
    _arg = eventArgument;
  }

  protected void Page_Init(object sender, EventArgs e)
  {
```

continues

```
string callbackEventRef =
    ClientScript.GetCallbackEventReference(this,
                "symbolInput.value", "StockQuoteFromServer", "");

string callbackMethod =
        "function RetrieveStockQuoteFromServer() { \r\n" +
        "var symbolInput = document.getElementById('"
                    + _symbolTextBox.ClientID +
            "');" + callbackEventRef +
        ";\r\n}\r\n";

string processResultMethod =
        "function StockQuoteFromServer(result, context) { \r\n"+
        "var resultTextBox = document.getElementById('" +
        _resultTextBox.ClientID + "');\r\n" +
"resultTextBox.value = resultTextBox.value + '--' + result;\r\n" +
        "}\r\n";

    ClientScript.RegisterClientScriptBlock(this.GetType(),
        "CallbackFunctions",
        callbackMethod + processResultMethod, true);
}

}
```

On-Demand TreeView Node Population

As mentioned earlier, several of the built-in Web controls support client callbacks for on-demand population of their data. For example, the Tree-View control lets you specify an attribute on individual nodes of the tree called PopulateOnDemand, which will cause the TreeView to issue a callback to retrieve the next child node when it is expanded. Once you mark one or more nodes in a TreeView to be populated on demand, you then must define a handler for the TreeNodePopulate event, which will be called every time an on-demand node is expanded. Listing 8-26 shows a simple example of creating a TreeView that populates its nodes on demand, in this case to enumerate the Fibonacci number sequence. Figure 8-5 shows what the TreeView looks like once it has been expanded several times.

LISTING 8-26: On-demand TreeView displaying Fibonacci numbers

```
<%@ Page Language="C#" Title="Fibonacci Tree On Demand" %>

<script runat="server">
protected void PopulateNode(Object source, TreeNodeEventArgs e)
{
```

```
  // The text of a node in this tree is the current Fibonacci number
  // The value of a node in this tree is the *next* Fibonacci number
  double nodeText = double.Parse(e.Node.Text);
  double nodeValue = double.Parse(e.Node.Value);

  // Create new tree node with new value and set to populate on demand
  TreeNode newNode = new TreeNode(nodeValue.ToString(),
                                   (nodeText + nodeValue).ToString());
  newNode.PopulateOnDemand = true;

  // Insert new node as child
  e.Node.ChildNodes.Add(newNode);
}

</script>

<html xmlns="http://www.w3.org/1999/xhtml" >
<head runat="server" />
<body>
  <form id="form1" runat="server">
  <div>
  <h3>Fibonacci Tree</h3>

    <asp:TreeView ID="_fibonacciTree"
                  OnTreeNodePopulate="PopulateNode"
                  runat="server" ExpandDepth="1">
      <Nodes>
        <asp:TreeNode Text="1" Value="1">
          <asp:TreeNode PopulateOnDemand="true" Text="1" Value="2" />
        </asp:TreeNode>
      </Nodes>
    </asp:TreeView>

    </div>
    </form>
</body>
</html>
```

Atlas

It turns out that client callbacks were just the tip of the iceberg for the supporting AJAX-style application development with ASP.NET 2.0. After the 2.0 framework was released, the ASP.NET team set to work on building **Atlas**, a rich framework for building AJAX-enabled Web applications with ASP.NET. This new Web development framework provides both client-side and server-side components for closing the gap between Web and desktop user interfaces. Atlas' browser-neutral client script library is easily

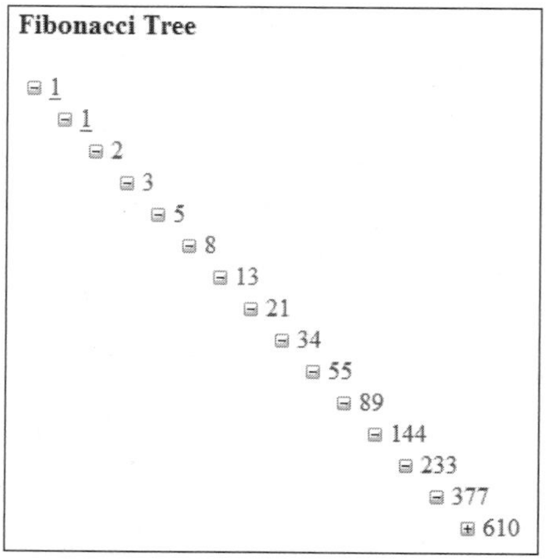

```
Fibonacci Tree

⊟ 1
  ⊟ 1
    ⊟ 2
      ⊟ 3
        ⊟ 5
          ⊟ 8
            ⊟ 13
              ⊟ 21
                ⊟ 34
                  ⊟ 55
                    ⊟ 89
                      ⊟ 144
                        ⊟ 233
                          ⊟ 377
                            ⊞ 610
```

FIGURE 8-5: On-demand TreeView displaying numbers from the Fibonacci sequence

integrated with existing Web applications (including ASP.NET 1.x and non-.NET sites), improving response times and enhancing UIs with DHTML and JavaScript features that in the past would have taken enormous development efforts and extensive client-side knowledge. ASP.NET 2.0 applications can take advantage of Atlas' server-side features to further enhance their UIs, often through simple markup, without having to resort to adding their own client-side JavaScript at all. The scope of Atlas is too large to do it justice in this book, and as of this writing, it is still under development. To get the latest information and resources on developing with Atlas, visit http://atlas.asp.net.

SUMMARY

With the addition of simplified caching using declarative data sources, SQL cache dependencies, and post-cache substitution, ASP.NET 2.0 makes it much easier to successfully incorporate caching into your Web applications to increase their overall performance and scalability. In addition, the client-callback framework opens the door to building much more responsive, sophisticated Web applications by wrapping the complexities of working with the XMLHttpRequest object.

9

Asynchrony

A T FIRST GLANCE, it almost seems unnecessary to discuss asynchrony in building Web applications with ASP.NET. One of the key advantages of building applications that execute in the context of a Web server is that the application is intrinsically asynchronous, without any extra effort on your part. For each page you write, you will undoubtedly have multiple concurrent users accessing that page once it is deployed. ASP.NET is built to handle as many concurrent requests as possible for any given application, and it manages the details of allocating and pooling threads for servicing requests. With each request, ASP.NET creates a fresh instance of the target page class, so unless you are dealing with globally or statically scoped data, you don't need to worry about the fact that client requests are fulfilled concurrently for your application.

While it is true that each page may be running on a separate thread, there are still occasions where introducing additional asynchrony into a request makes sense. The most obvious case is when a page is performing multiple time-consuming I/O-bound operations that could be made to run in parallel. By splitting tasks across multiple asynchronous I/O operations, the total response time of the page can be reduced. You can also introduce asynchrony into a request to relax contention for threads in the thread pool by launching one or more asynchronous requests and then returning the original request thread back to the pool, thereby completing the request only when all of the outstanding tasks have completed.

ASP.NET 2.0 provides support for introducing both of these types of asynchrony into your applications when needed. This chapter introduces the details of the asynchronous page model and three techniques for handling requests asynchronously: implicitly using the AsyncOperationManager, explicitly using asynchronous page tasks, and at a lower level using the AddOnPreRenderCompleteAsync method.

The Need for Asynchrony

A good rule of thumb to follow when you are considering introducing asynchrony in an application is that you should successfully convince at least four of your peers that it is a good idea before you actually take the step. Asynchronous operations generally make it much harder to understand application flow and can introduce subtle bugs that are difficult to track down. When used properly, however, they can also significantly increase performance and/or make the user interface much more responsive. This section outlines two of the most common reasons you might consider introducing asynchrony into your Web pages in ASP.NET: to exploit parallelism and to relax thread-pool contention.

Exploiting Parallelism

The first and most obvious case for introducing asynchrony is to parallelize tasks in a request. Instead of executing each task (like a database retrieval or a Web service invocation) sequentially, you can run all the tasks concurrently (as long as they are not interdependent) and reduce the overall time taken to respond to the client. Figure 9-1 shows a sample ASP.NET page that displays four different sets of data to the client—news headlines, a set of stock quotes, a collection of sales reports, and a weather forecast. Assuming each of these data sets come from separate sources, this page is an ideal candidate for introducing parallelism.

To make this example concrete, let's assume that the news headlines, stock quotes, and weather forecast are all retrieved from remote Web service calls, and that the sales report is generated from a SQL query to a database on the local network. Let's also assume that each data retrieval takes approximately the same (non-negligible) amount of time, which we achieve in our sample application by artificially sleeping for three seconds

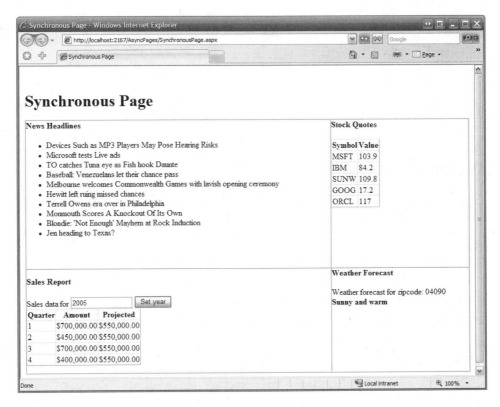

FIGURE 9-1: Synchronous page performing multiple independent tasks

in each Web method implementation and by adding a delay of three seconds in our SQL query. Listing 9-1 shows the sample .aspx page source, and Listing 9-2 shows the corresponding codebehind that populates the controls.

LISTING 9-1: SynchronousPage.aspx

```
<%@ Page Language="C#" AutoEventWireup="true"
        CodeFile="SynchronousPage.aspx.cs"
        Inherits="SynchronousPage" %>

<!DOCTYPE html PUBLIC "-//W3C//DTD XHTML 1.0 Transitional//EN" "http://
www.w3.org/TR/xhtml1/DTD/xhtml1-transitional.dtd">

<html xmlns="http://www.w3.org/1999/xhtml" >
<head runat="server">
    <title>Synchronous Page</title>
```

continues

```
</head>
<body>
    <form id="form1" runat="server">
    <div>
        <h1>Synchronous Page</h1>

        <table border="1" cellpadding="0" cellspacing="0"
                style="width:100%;height:500px" >
            <tr>
                <td valign="top">
                    <h4>News Headlines</h4>
                    <asp:BulletedList ID="_newsHeadlines"
                                        runat="server" />
                </td>
                <td valign="top">
                    <h4>Stock Quotes</h4>
                    <asp:GridView runat="server" ID="_stocksGrid" />
                </td>
            </tr>
            <tr>
                <td valign="top">
                    <h4>Sales Report</h4>
                    Sales data for
                    <asp:TextBox ID="_yearTextBox" runat="server"
                                Width="120px">2005</asp:TextBox>
                    <asp:Button ID="_setYearButton" runat="server"
                                Text="Set year" /><br />

                    <asp:GridView ID="_salesGrid" runat="server"
                                AutoGenerateColumns="False"
                                DataKeyNames="id">
                        <Columns>
                            <asp:BoundField DataField="id"
                                            HeaderText="id"
                                Visible="False" ReadOnly="True" />
                            <asp:BoundField DataField="quarter"
                                            HeaderText="Quarter" />
                            <asp:BoundField DataField="amount"
                                            HeaderText="Amount"
                                DataFormatString="{0:c}"
                                HtmlEncode="False" />
                            <asp:BoundField DataField="projected"
                                            HeaderText="Projected"
                                DataFormatString="{0:c}"
                                HtmlEncode="False" />
                        </Columns>
                    </asp:GridView>

                    <asp:Label runat="server" ID="_messageLabel"
                            ForeColor="red" EnableViewState="false" />
```

```
                    </td>
                    <td valign="top">
                        <h4>Weather Forecast</h4>
                        Weather forecast for zipcode: 04090 <br />
                        <asp:Label Font-Bold="true" runat="server"
                                ID="_weatherLabel" />
                    </td>
                </tr>
            </table>
        </div>
        </form>
</body>
</html>
```

LISTING 9-2: SynchronousPage.aspx.cs

```
public partial class SynchronousPage : Page
{
  protected void Page_Load(object sender, EventArgs e)
  {
    // Instantiate Web service proxy for retrieving data
    //
    using (PortalServices ps = new PortalServices())
    {
      // News headlines Web service call
      _newsHeadlines.DataSource = ps.GetNewsHeadlines();
      _newsHeadlines.DataBind();

      // Stock quote Web service call
      string[] stocks = new string[] { "MSFT", "IBM", "SUNW",
                                        "GOOG", "ORCL" };
      _stocksGrid.DataSource = ps.GetStockQuotes(stocks);
      _stocksGrid.DataBind();

      // Weather report Web service call
      _weatherLabel.Text = ps.GetWeatherReport("04090");
    }

    // Data access
    //
    string dsn = ConfigurationManager.ConnectionStrings["salesDsn"].
                                      ConnectionString;
    string sql = "WAITFOR DELAY '00:00:03' SELECT [id], [quarter]," +
        "[year], [amount], [projected] FROM [sales] WHERE year=@year";

    using (SqlConnection conn = new SqlConnection(dsn))
    using (SqlCommand cmd = new SqlCommand(sql, conn))
    {
      cmd.Parameters.AddWithValue("@year",
                int.Parse(_yearTextBox.Text));
```

continues

```
        conn.Open();
        _salesGrid.DataSource = cmd.ExecuteReader();
        _salesGrid.DataBind();
    }
  }
}
```

The total time required to retrieve the data and render this page will be the sum of the times taken to invoke the Web services and issue the query to the database (t_{1-4}), plus the time taken to do the normal page processing and data binding (t_{p1-2}), as shown in Figure 9-2. With our explicit delays of three seconds built into every call, this page will take more than 12 seconds to render. This is frustrating not just because it is a long time to wait for the page to display, but because each data retrieval is completely independent of the others and could feasibly be done in parallel, cutting the response time to potentially a quarter of what it is sequentially.

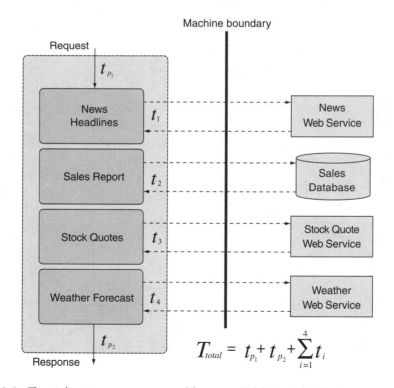

$$T_{total} = t_{p_1} + t_{p_2} + \sum_{i=1}^{4} t_i$$

FIGURE 9-2: Time taken to process a page with sequential data retrieval

Our goal for this type of page—one making several independent requests for data—is to parallelize all of the data retrieval calls. If each request is made asynchronously with respect to the primary request thread, the overall time to process requests for this page will no longer be the sum of the times, but instead the maximum of the four data retrieval times (t_{1-4}), plus the time taken to do the normal page processing and data binding (t_{p1-2}), as shown in Figure 9-3. In our sample application with built-in three second delays, we should see a response time closer to three seconds—a near four-fold improvement! In many pages, the speed improvements to be gained by introducing parallelism can be quite dramatic, and can often make the difference between an application with unacceptable response times and one that is quite responsive.

As you will see, .NET 2.0 has significant support for issuing remote Web service calls and data access calls asynchronously, and the Page class

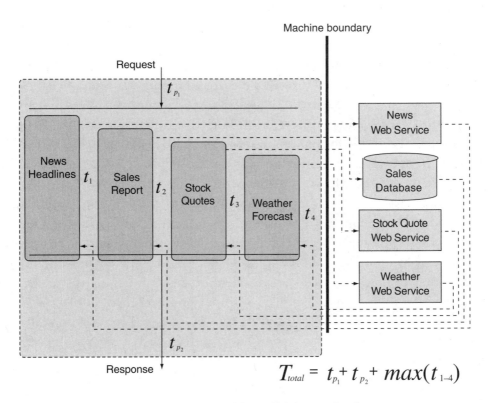

$$T_{total} = t_{p_1} + t_{p_2} + max(t_{1-4})$$

FIGURE 9-3: Time taken to process a page with parallel data retrieval

in ASP.NET 2.0 has been augmented to support the management of asynchronous tasks so that parallelizing pages as in our example is completely feasible.

Relaxing Thread-Pool Contention

The other reason to introduce asynchrony into a Web page in ASP.NET 2.0 is to make more efficient use of the thread pool threads. This reason is more esoteric than the straightforward rationale of introducing parallelism. Basically, if you have pages that perform I/O-bound tasks, it may be possible to perform those tasks asynchronously, and relinquish the primary request thread back to the thread pool so that it can be used to service other requests while your page awaits the completion of its tasks.

The purpose of the thread pool is to efficiently allocate CPU time for processing requests with an upper limit on the total number of threads allocated. This is an important restriction to have in place, as creating an unbounded number of threads can be extremely inefficient, and can grind a system to a halt when a large number of requests are made concurrently. While the thread pool is an important element to have in place to make sure the CPU is efficiently shared, it also comes with a cost of its own. The thread pool allocates new threads on demand based on a set of heuristics driven primarily by how many requests for work have been queued. It also monitors CPU utilization, and when things slow down, it takes threads out of the pool too. All of this takes time and resources to manage, so if you can do anything to relax the contention for threads in the thread pool, you will improve the overall efficiency of your application.

If you have pages in your site that spend most of their time waiting for I/O requests to complete (network calls to databases or Web services being the most common), these are ideal pages to consider making asynchronous. Our sample application with three Web service calls and one remote database call turns out to be an ideal candidate for relieving thread-pool contention too. By relinquishing the primary request thread after issuing all of the I/O-bound requests, and then completing the request once all of the I/O-bound requests have completed, it frees up the request thread to service other requests. Fortunately, ASP.NET 2.0 has added support for doing exactly this using a feature called **asynchronous pages**.

Techniques for Issuing Asynchronous Tasks

This section introduces the two standard techniques for issuing asynchronous tasks in an ASP.NET page: implicitly using the AsyncOperationManager and explicitly using the PageAsyncTask mechanism.

Asynchronous Web Access

In the sample application described in the previous section, three Web parts are using Web services to retrieve their data, and one is using ADO.NET to access a database. Let's start to introduce parallelism by making the Web service invocations asynchronous, since there is some nice support in the Web service proxy classes generated by WSDL.exe (or the Visual Studio 2005 Add Web Service Reference tool) for performing Web method invocation asynchronously.

When a Web service proxy class is created in ASP.NET 2.0, it actually generates three different ways of invoking any particular method—one synchronous and two asynchronous. For example, the Web service proxy that our Web parts are using has the following methods available for invoking the GetNewsHeadlines Web method:

```
public string[] GetNewsHeadlines()
public IAsyncResult BeginGetNewsHeadlines(
               AsyncCallback callback, object asyncState)
public string[] EndGetNewsHeadlines(
               IAsyncResult asyncResult)
public void GetNewsHeadlinesAsync()
public void GetNewsHeadlinesAsync(object userState)
public event GetNewsHeadlinesCompletedEventHandler
               GetNewsHeadlinesCompleted;
```

The first method, GetNewsHeadlines, is the standard synchronous method. The next two, BeginGetNewsHeadlines and EndGetNewsHeadlines, can be used to invoke the method asynchronously and can be tied into any number of asynchronous mechanisms in .NET because of the use of the standard IAsyncResult interface. But the most interesting method for our scenario is the last one—GetNewsHeadlinesAsync. To use this method, you must register a delegate with the proxy class' event that was specifically generated to perform asynchronous invocations (the GetNews-HeadlinesCompleted event in our example). The delegate signature is strongly typed to contain the method's return values so that you can easily extract the results in your method implementation. Here is the delegate declaration added to the proxy class for our GetNewsHeadlines method:

```
public delegate void GetNewsHeadlinesCompletedEventHandler(
        object sender, GetNewsHeadlinesCompletedEventArgs e);

public partial class GetNewsHeadlinesCompletedEventArgs :
                                    AsyncCompletedEventArgs
{
    private object[] results;

    internal GetNewsHeadlinesCompletedEventArgs(
            object[] results, Exception exception,
            bool cancelled, object userState) :
            base(exception, cancelled, userState)
    {
        this.results = results;
    }

    public string[] Result
    {
        get
        {
            this.RaiseExceptionIfNecessary();
            return ((string[])(this.results[0]));
        }
    }
}
```

Using this event-based asynchronous method, rewriting our Web method invocation that retrieves the headline news takes two steps. We first subscribe a delegate to the proxy class' GetNewsHeadlinesCompleted event and then call the GetNewsHeadlinesAsync method. In the implementation of the method subscribed to the completed event, we use the results—in this case by binding them to a BulletedList to display to the client, as shown in Listing 9-3. There's one last step before our Web request will actually launch asynchronously: we must mark the containing page with the Async="true" attribute, as shown in Listing 9-4. This attribute changes several things about the way the page processes requests, which we will explore in detail shortly. For now, just be aware that any time you make asynchronous Web service calls, this attribute must be set to true.

LISTING 9-3: Asynchronous Web service call

```
protected void Page_Load(object sender, EventArgs e)
{
  // Instantiate Web service proxy for retrieving data.
  //
  using (PortalServices ps = new PortalServices())
  {
    // Invoke Web service asynchronously
    // and harvest results in callback.
    //
    ps.GetNewsHeadlinesCompleted +=
            new GetNewsHeadlinesCompletedEventHandler(
                    ps_GetNewsHeadlinesCompleted);
    ps.GetNewsHeadlinesAsync();
  }


}

// This callback is invoked when the async Web service completes.
//
void ps_GetNewsHeadlinesCompleted(object sender,
                                  GetNewsHeadlinesCompletedEventArgs e)
{
    // Extract results and bind to BulletedList.
    //

    _newsHeadlines.DataSource = e.Result;
    _newsHeadlines.DataBind();
}
```

LISTING 9-4: Marking the page as asynchronous

```
<%@ Page Language="C#" AutoEventWireup="true"
        CodeFile="AsynchronousPage.aspx.cs"
        Inherits="AsynchronousPage"
        Async="true"
%>
```

Once we update the other two Web parts that use Web services to retrieve their data asynchronously like this one, our page is much more responsive. In fact, it renders to the client in just over three seconds, just as predicted. Even though our sales report data retrieval is still sequentially accessing the database, our three Web service calls are now invoked asynchronously, so our primary request thread is no longer waiting for their completion.[1] Of course, we ultimately want to have all of our I/O-bound work be asynchronous, so that we can relinquish our primary request thread back to the thread pool as well.

AsyncOperationManager and Asynchronous Web Service Calls

Before we look at how to make our database access asynchronous, it's worth spending a little time on exactly how the asynchronous Web method calls work. This model of asynchronous method invocation is new to .NET 2.0, and in general is simpler to work with than the standard Asynchronous Programming Model (APM) involving the IAsyncResult interface. Note that we didn't even have to touch an IAsyncResult interface, nor did we have to let the containing page know that we were performing asynchronous operations (by registering a task or some other technique), and yet it all seemed to work as we had hoped.

The secret lies in the Web service proxy class' implementation of the asynchronous method, along with a helper class introduced in .NET 2.0 called the AsyncOperationManager. When we called the GetNewsHeadlinesAsync method of our proxy class, it mapped the call onto an internal helper method of the SoapHttpClientProtocol base class from which the proxy class derives, called InvokeAsync. InvokeAsync does two important things: it registers the asynchronous operation with the AsyncOperationManager class by calling its static CreateOperation method, and it then launches the request asynchronously using the WebRequest class' BeginGetRequestStream method. At this point the call returns and the page goes on processing its lifecycle, but because the page has been marked with the Async="true" attribute, it will only continue processing the request up to the PreRender event and will then return the request thread to the thread pool.[2]

Once the asynchronous Web request completes, it will invoke the method we subscribed to the completed event of the proxy on a separate thread drawn from the I/O thread pool. If this is the last of the asynchro-

---

1. Note that if you are calling multiple Web service methods asynchronously, you must do so through separate instances of the Web proxy class because of the way it is built internally.

2. While the request thread *will* be returned to the thread pool in this example, keep in mind that it is still used to process the ADO.NET query in its entirety before being returned to the pool. Because of this, we are not really relieving pressure on the thread pool because the thread is not returned to the pool quickly enough to make it available to service other requests while our page is still awaiting I/O-bound tasks to complete.

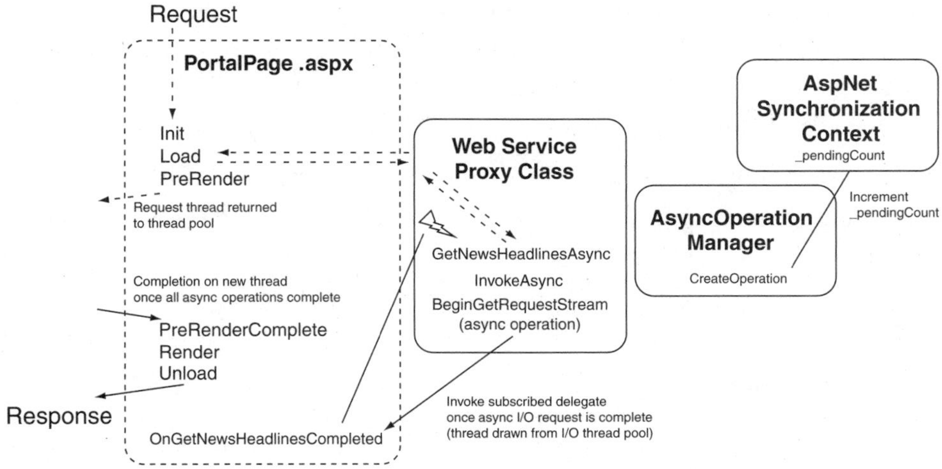

Request

PortalPage .aspx

Init
Load
PreRender

Request thread returned
to thread pool

Completion on new thread
once all async operations complete

PreRenderComplete
Render
Unload

Response

OnGetNewsHeadlinesCompleted

Web Service
Proxy Class

GetNewsHeadlinesAsync

InvokeAsync

BeginGetRequestStream
(async operation)

Invoke subscribed delegate
once async I/O request is complete
(thread drawn from I/O thread pool)

AspNet
Synchronization
Context

_pendingCount

Increment
_pendingCount

AsyncOperation
Manager

CreateOperation

FIGURE 9-4: Asynchronous Web requests in asynchronous pages

nous operations to complete (kept track of by the synchronization context of the AsyncOperationManager), the page will be called back and the request will complete its processing from where it left off, starting at the PreRenderComplete event. Figure 9-4 shows this entire lifecycle when you use asynchronous Web requests in the context of an asynchronous page.

The AsyncOperationManager is a class that is designed to be used in different environments to help in the management of asynchronous method invocations. For example, if you called a Web service asynchronously from a WinForms application, it would also tie into the AsyncOperationManager class. The difference between each environment is something called the **SynchronizationContext** associated with the AsyncOperationManager. When you are running in the context of an ASP.NET application, the Synchronization-Context will be set to an instance of the AspNetSynchronizationContext class, whose primary purpose is to keep track of how many outstanding asynchronous requests are pending so that when they are all complete, the page request processing can resume.

Asynchronous Tasks

Let's now get back to our problem of making our data access asynchronous, and the general issue of performing asynchronous data retrieval with ADO.NET. There is unfortunately no equivalent to the simple asynchronous mechanism exposed by Web service proxies for performing asynchronous data retrieval, so we're going to have to do a little more work to get our final I/O-bound operation to participate in our asynchronous shuffle. What we do have to work with are the new asynchronous methods on the SqlCommand class and the asynchronous task feature of ASP.NET. Using SqlCommand you can now invoke commands asynchronously using one of the following methods:

```
IAsyncResult BeginExecuteReader(AsyncCallback ac, object state)
IAsyncResult BeginExecuteNonQuery(AsyncCallback ac, object state)
IAsyncResult BeginExecuteXmlReader(AsyncCallback ac, object state)
```

and the corresponding completion methods once the data stream is ready to begin reading:

```
SqlDataReader EndExecuteReader(IAsyncResult ar)
int EndExecuteNonQuery(IAsyncResult ar)
XmlReader EndExecuteXmlReader(IAsyncResult ar)
```

To use any of these asynchronous retrieval methods, you must first add "async=true" to your connection string. For our scenario, we are interested in populating a GridView by binding it to a SqlDataReader, so we will use the BeginExecuteReader method to initiate the asynchronous call.

To tie this into our asynchronous page, ASP.NET 2.0 also supports the concept of registering asynchronous tasks you would like to have executed prior to the page completing its rendering. This is a more explicit model than the one we used with our Web service proxies, but it also gives us some more flexibility because of that. To register an asynchronous task, you create an instance of the PageAsyncTask class and initialize it with three delegates—a begin handler, an end handler, and a timeout handler. Your begin handler must return an IAsyncResult interface, so this is where we will launch our asynchronous data request using BeginExecuteReader. The end handler is called once the task is complete (when there is data ready to read in our example), at which point you can use the results. ASP.NET will take care of invoking the begin handler just before it relinquishes the request thread (immediately after the PreRender event completes). Listing 9-5 shows the updated implementation of our sales report data retrieval, which performs asynchronous data access using the asynchronous tasks and the SqlCommand class' asynchronous BeginExecuteReader method.

LISTING 9-5: Asynchronous data access using asynchronous tasks

```
public partial class AsyncPage : Page
{
  // Local variables to store connection and command for async
  // data retrieval
  //
  SqlConnection _conn;
  SqlCommand _cmd;

  protected void Page_Load(object sender, EventArgs e)
  {
    // ... Web service calls not shown ...

    string dsn = ConfigurationManager.
          ConnectionStrings["salesDsn"].ConnectionString;
    string sql = "WAITFOR DELAY '00:00:03' SELECT [id], [quarter], " +
        "[year], [amount], [projected] FROM [sales] WHERE year=@year";

    // Append async attribute to connection string
    //
    dsn += ";async=true";

    _conn = new SqlConnection(dsn);
    _cmd = new SqlCommand(sql, _conn);
    _conn.Open();
    _cmd.Parameters.AddWithValue("@year", int.Parse(_yearTextBox.Text));

    // Launch data request asynchronously using
    // page async task
    //
    PageAsyncTask salesDataTask = new PageAsyncTask(
                new BeginEventHandler(BeginGetSalesData),
                new EndEventHandler(EndGetSalesData),
                new EndEventHandler(GetSalesDataTimeout),
                null, true);
    Page.RegisterAsyncTask(salesDataTask);
  }

  IAsyncResult BeginGetSalesData(object src, EventArgs e,
                      AsyncCallback cb, object state)
  {
    return _cmd.BeginExecuteReader(cb, state);
  }

  void EndGetSalesData(IAsyncResult ar)
  {
    try
    {
      _salesGrid.DataSource = _cmd.EndExecuteReader(ar);
```

continues

```
      _salesGrid.DataBind();
    }
    finally
    {
      _conn.Close();
    }
  }

  void GetSalesDataTimeout(IAsyncResult ar)
  {
    // Operation timed out, so just clean up by
    // closing connection
    if (_conn.State == ConnectionState.Open)
        _conn.Close();

    _messageLabel.Text = "Query timed out...";
  }
}
```

Note that we could use this same technique with our Web service requests by using the alternate asynchronous methods provided on the proxy class (BeginGetNewsHeadlines, for example). One potential advantage to this technique over the simpler delegate-based technique is that you can also specify a timeout handler. If your remote invocations fail to return in time, the associated timeout handler will be invoked. This timeout is specified for the entire page in the @Page directive using the Async-Timeout attribute, and it defaults to 20 seconds (note that this timeout is for the entire time it takes to process all tasks, not one individually). One other potential advantage of working directly with asynchronous tasks is that they work on pages that are not marked with async="true" in addition to those that are. This gives you the option of performing your tasks in parallel for efficiency without relinquishing the request thread back to the thread pool, an option we will discuss further in the next section.

Dependent Asynchronous Tasks

The asynchronous task feature of ASP.NET also supports the concept of task ordering and setting up dependencies between tasks. For example, imagine that you had a page that had five I/O-bound tasks to perform, but that task 1 had to be completed before tasks 2, 3, and 4 could be started (most likely because they took data as input that was retrieved in task 1), and that task 5 could not be started until all of the other four tasks had completed. Figure 9-5 shows the dependence chain of our five tasks.

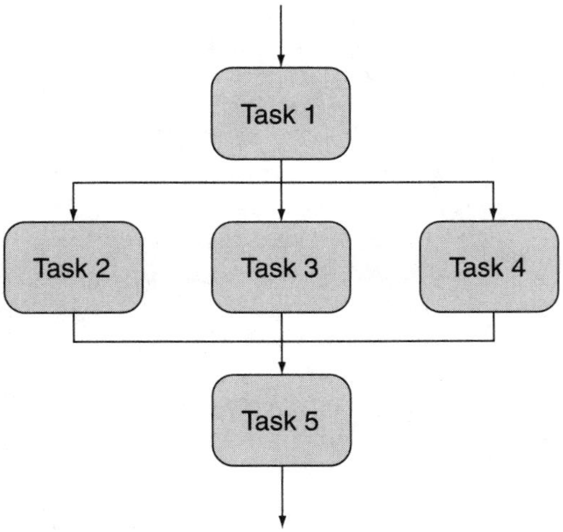

FIGURE 9-5: Interdependent asynchronous tasks

To set up dependencies like this, the constructor of the PageAsyncTask class has a final Boolean parameter that indicates whether the task is to be performed in parallel or not. If it is set to false, the task will be executed to completion before the next registered task is started. To achieve the set of dependencies outlined in Figure 9-5, we would mark tasks 1 and 5 as false for parallel execution, and tasks 2, 3, and 4 as true. By then registering the tasks with the page (by calling RegisterAsyncTask) in order from 1 to 5, we would achieve the desired ordering and dependency enforcement, as shown in Listing 9-6.

LISTING 9-6: Asynchronous dependent tasks

```
protected void Page_Load(object sender, EventArgs e)
{

  PageAsyncTask task1 = new PageAsyncTask(
                new BeginEventHandler(BeginTask1),
                new EndEventHandler(EndTask1),
                new EndEventHandler(Task1Timeout),
                null, false);
  PageAsyncTask task2 = new PageAsyncTask(
                new BeginEventHandler(BeginTask2),
                new EndEventHandler(EndTask2),
                new EndEventHandler(Task2Timeout),
                null, true);
```

continues

```
    PageAsyncTask task3 = new PageAsyncTask(
                new BeginEventHandler(BeginTask3),
                new EndEventHandler(EndTask3),
                new EndEventHandler(Task3Timeout),
                null, true);
    PageAsyncTask task4 = new PageAsyncTask(
                new BeginEventHandler(BeingTask4),
                new EndEventHandler(EndTask4),
                new EndEventHandler(Task4Timeout),
                null, true);
    PageAsyncTask task5 = new PageAsyncTask(
                new BeginEventHandler(BeginTask5),
                new EndEventHandler(EndTask5),
                new EndEventHandler(Task5Timeout),
                null, false);

  RegisterAsyncTask(task1);
  RegisterAsyncTask(task2);
  RegisterAsyncTask(task3);
  RegisterAsyncTask(task4);
  RegisterAsyncTask(task5);
}

// Individual begin/end task methods not shown
```

The combination of parallel execution and the ability to specify dependencies makes asynchronous tasks extremely flexible. You have the ability to define parallel tasks using the standard IAsyncResult interface, specify timeouts, set up dependencies between tasks, and execute these tasks in either a synchronous or an asynchronous page. There is a significant amount of threading and synchronization code backing up this feature, which takes the burden off your shoulders. Most ASP.NET pages that need to introduce asynchronous behavior should end up using asynchronous tasks.

Asynchronous Pages

This section covers the @Page directive's Async attribute, and looks at the changes it makes to the flow of a page and how it alters the page to integrate with the asynchronous task invocation models discussed earlier.

Async="true"

In order for our asynchronous tasks to work, we had to mark our @Page directive with the Async attribute. If you set this attribute to true on a page that does not register any tasks or invoke any asynchronous Web service proxies, it will actually not have much effect on the running of the page. The page will be processed on the same thread throughout its lifecycle, much like any other page in ASP.NET. If, however, you have registered one or more asynchronous tasks or have invoked one or more Web service proxies asynchronously, then the page will be executed asynchronously.

When you mark a page with Async="true", it does three important things. First, it explicitly implements the IHttpAsyncHandler interface on your generated Page-derived class. Next, it implements that interface's BeginProcessRequest/EndProcessRequest methods to map onto the Page class' AsyncPageBeginProcessRequest/AsyncPageEndProcessRequest helper methods respectively. Finally, it sets the AsyncMode property of the Page-derived class to true in its constructor. This last point is important if you are ever authoring controls or Web parts that may be deployed in both synchronous and asynchronous pages. It lets you check to see whether your containing page is in fact asynchronous or not and adjust your data retrieval as needed.

Once a page has been marked as asynchronous, the most important change to you (the developer) is the page's flow of control. The page will begin execution on the standard request thread, processing the page lifecycle all the way through the PreRender event, as shown in Figure 9-6.

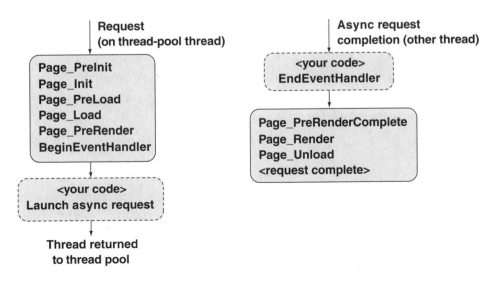

FIGURE 9-6: Asynchronous page flow of control

Relaxing Thread-Pool Pressure

When the page is marked as asynchronous and the bulk of the page's work has been pushed into asynchronous I/O-bound tasks, it means that the thread pool will be used much more efficiently. Instead of each request holding onto a thread waiting for data to return from I/O operations, the thread is relinquished back to the thread pool while the I/O operations execute asynchronously without any overhead of thread allocation. Once the final I/O operation completes, the I/O thread-pool thread that is used to harvest the results of the I/O request continues the execution of the page, including its rendering, and the result is sent back to the client.

You can observe the effect that introducing asynchronous pages into your application has by performing load tests on your system and observing the average response times of individual pages. Slow synchronous pages that are I/O-bound often occupy threads in the thread pool for long slices of time, preventing other requests that normally are very responsive from responding quickly. Relegating the slow I/O-bound pages to be serviced on alternative threads should ensure that all of your "fast" pages always return promptly.

Marking your pages as asynchronous and using asynchronous tasks is not the only way to change the way the thread pool behaves. You can also modify the settings of the thread pool through the machine.config file's processModel element (note that you cannot apply this configuration setting in local web.config files). By default, the thread pool defaults to a cap of 100 worker threads per CPU and 100 I/O threads per CPU (used to service asynchronous I/O calls when they complete). It is unlikely you would need to adjust these values, since 100 worker threads should be more than sufficient for any server. What you may want to consider adjusting, however, is the minimum number of worker threads. This tells the thread pool to allocate a fixed number of threads and to keep them running ready to process requests. In practice, the thread pool's heuristics for allocating new threads does not seem to kick in very quickly, so any time you receive a burst of a large number of concurrent requests, you often see requests queued even though the thread pool has not reached its maximum count. Listing 9-7 shows an example of setting the minimum thread-pool count for worker threads to 50 to alleviate the implicit constraints of the thread pool when responding to a burst of requests.

LISTING 9-7: Changing the minimum worker thread count in machine.config

```
<configuration>
  <system.web>
    <processModel minWorkerThreads="50" />
    <!-- ... -->
  </system.web>
</configuration>
```

To make the best decisions about asynchronous pages and thread-pool settings, it is always best to devise load tests for your applications that model their anticipated deployed use.

AddOnPreRenderCompleteAsync

Technically, it is also possible to build asynchronous processes directly into your asynchronous pages by calling the AddOnPreRenderCompleteAsync method with two event handlers—begin and end. The only constraint is that your begin event handler must return an IAsyncResult interface, adhering to the Asynchronous Programming Model found throughout .NET. If your begin event handler returns a valid IAsyncResult interface, it will register with the callback delegate exposed by the interface, and return the primary thread back to the thread pool to service subsequent requests. Once your asynchronous operation completes and signals the callback method, ASP.NET will resume execution of the Page class at the PreRenderComplete method, on whatever thread your asynchronous work called it back on. Listing 9-8 shows a sample asynchronous page implementation that uses this technique to map the begin and end event handlers onto an asynchronous Web service request.

LISTING 9-8: Using AddOnPreRenderCompleteAsync

```
<%@ Page Language="C#" Async="true" %>
<script runat="server">
   Slow slowWebService = new Slow();

   protected void Page_Load(object sender, EventArgs e)
   {
     BeginEventHandler bh = new BeginEventHandler(this.BeginGetAsyncData);
     EndEventHandler eh = new EndEventHandler(this.EndGetAsyncData);

     AddOnPreRenderCompleteAsync(bh, eh);
   }
```

continues

```
//...
</script>

IAsyncResult BeginGetAsyncData(Object src, EventArgs args,
                               AsyncCallback cb, Object state)
{
  // Note—-this is serviced on the same thread as Page_Load
  // but a different thread is used to service EndGetAsyncData
  //
  return slowWebservice.BeginHelloWorld(cb, state);
}

void EndGetAsyncData(IAsyncResult ar)
{
  string ret = slowWebservice.EndHelloWorld(ar);
  // Use ret here
}
```

Thread-Relative Resources

Each of the asynchronous mechanisms we have looked at in this chapter give you the ability to execute code on a different thread from the one that is initially allocated to process your page. One of the consequences of this is that thread-relative resources may not be propagated to these secondary threads, which may impact what you do in code that runs on these secondary threads. The primary thread-relative resources that concern ASP.NET developers include the culture, UI culture, HttpContext, and Windows identity. Fortunately, both the asynchronous task feature and the Async-OperationManager are implemented to propagate everything, including the Windows identity, to all secondary threads. This means that you can use HttpContext.Current (which retrieves the current context from the thread) and that you can be sure that the culture settings for your thread are the same as they were for the initial request thread. This is not true for the last technique we presented, using AddOnPreRenderCompleteAsync, which is yet another reason to prefer asynchronous tasks for this technique.

SUMMARY

It is always wise to think twice before introducing asynchrony into your applications, as it makes it much more difficult to predict how your application will behave and can easily introduce difficult-to-track-down bugs.

However, with ASP.NET 2.0's asynchronous task and page support, the details of managing secondary threads are mostly hidden from the developer, and the advantages of spawning work onto different threads are still gained.

The two primary reasons for using asynchronous tasks and pages in ASP.NET 2.0 are to leverage potential parallelism of concurrent I/O-bound calls in the context of a single page, and to relieve thread-pool pressure for long-running requests that are I/O-bound. If your Web application suffers from long-running pages and what seems like arbitrarily slow pages that should be very fast, you should feel comfortable introducing asynchronous operations using these asynchronous pages and tasks, without having to worry too much about managing all of the details usually encountered with multithreaded programming.

Index

Microsoft .NET Development Series

.NET Framework Standard Library Annotated Reference
Volume 1: Base Class Library and Extended Numerics Library

Brad Abrams
.NET Framework Team, Microsoft Corporation

0321154894

.NET Framework Standard Library Annotated Reference
Volume 2: Networking Library, Reflection Library and XML Library

Brad Abrams
Tamara Abrams

0321194454

.NET Web Services
Architecture and Implementation

Keith Ballinger

0321113594

A Developer's Guide to SQL Server 2005

Bob Beauchemin
Dan Sullivan

0321382188

The .NET Developer's Guide to Windows Security

Keith Brown

0321228359

Visual Studio Tools for Office
Using C# with Excel, Word, Outlook, and InfoPath

Eric Carter
Eric Lippert

0321334884

Visual Studio Tools for Office
Using Visual Basic 2005 with Excel, Word, Outlook, and InfoPath

Eric Carter
Eric Lippert

0321411757

GDI+ Programming with C#

Mahesh Chand

0321160770

The C# Programming Language
Second Edition

Anders Hejlsberg
Scott Wiltamuth
Peter Golde

0321334434

ADO.NET and System.Xml v. 2.0
The Beta Version

Alex Homer
Dave Sussman
Mark Fussell

0321247124

ASP.NET 2.0 Illustrated

Alex Homer
Dave Sussman

0321418344

ASP.NET v. 2.0–
The Beta Version

Alex Homer
Dave Sussman
Rob Howard

0321257278

Data Binding with Windows Forms 2.0
Programming Smart Client Data Applications with .NET

Brian Noyes

032126892X

Essential ASP.NET
with Examples in C#

Fritz Onion

0201760401

Essential ASP.NET
with Examples in Visual Basic .NET

Fritz Onion

0201760398

Windows Forms Programming in Visual Basic .NET

Chris Sells
Justin Gehtland

0321125193

The Visual Basic .NET Programming Language

Paul Vick

0321169514

A First Look at SQL Server 2005 for Developers

Bob Beauchemin
Niels Berglund
Dan Sullivan

0321180593

Essential .NET
Volume 1
The Common Language Runtime

Don Box
with Chris Sells

0201734117

Framework Design Guidelines
Conventions, Idioms, and Patterns for Reusable .NET Libraries

Krzysztof Cwalina
Brad Abrams

0321246756

Effective Use of Microsoft Enterprise Library
Building Blocks for Creating Enterprise Applications and Services

Len Fenster

0321334213

Software Engineering with Microsoft Visual Studio Team System

Sam Guckenheimer
with Juan J. Perez

0321278720

The .NET Developer's Guide to Directory Services Programming

Joe Kaplan
Ryan Dunn

0321350170

Essential C#

Mark Michaelis

0321150775

The Common Language Infrastructure Annotated Standard

Jim Miller
Susann Ragsdale

0321154932

Enterprise Services with the .NET Framework
Developing Distributed Business Solutions with .NET Enterprise Services

Christian Nagel

032124673X

Building Applications and Components with Visual Basic .NET

Ted Pattison
with Dr. Joe Hummel

0201734958

eXtreme .NET
Introducing eXtreme Programming Techniques to .NET Developers

Dr. Neil Roodyn

0321303636

Windows Forms 2.0 Programming

Chris Sells
Michael Weinhardt

0321267966

Windows Forms Programming in C#

Chris Sells

0321116208

Programming in the .NET Environment

Damien Watkins
Mark Hammond
Brad Abrams

0201770180

Pragmatic ADO.NET
Data Access for the Internet World

Shawn Wildermuth

0201745682

.NET Compact Framework Programming with C#

Paul Yao
David Durant

0321174038

.NET Compact Framework Programming with Visual Basic .NET

Paul Yao
David Durant

0321174046

Register
Your Book

at www.awprofessional.com/register

You may be eligible to receive:

- Advance notice of forthcoming editions of the book
- Related book recommendations
- Ch_____oming titles
- I_____notions
  th_____
- N_____nces,
  t_____ests

Con

If you a_____
manus_____

Editor
Addiso
75 Arli
Bostor
Email:

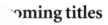

Visit u